BUILDING ACADEMIC LANGUAGE

BUILDING ACADEMIC LANGUAGE

Meeting Common Core
Standards Across Disciplines,
Grades 5–12

Second Edition

Jeff Zwiers

Published by Jossey-Bass
A Wiley Brand
One Montgomery Street, Suite 1200, San Francisco, CA 94104-4594—www.josseybass.com

Jossey-Bass books and products are available through most bookstores. To contact Jossey-Bass directly call our Customer Care Department within the U.S. at 800-956-7739, outside the U.S. at 317-572-3986, or fax 317-572-4002.

Wiley publishes in a variety of print and electronic formats and by print-on-demand. Some material included with standard print versions of this book may not be included in e-books or in print-on-demand. If this book refers to media such as a CD or DVD that is not included in the version you purchased, you may download this material at http://booksupport.wiley.com. For more information about Wiley products, visit www.wiley.com.

Library of Congress Cataloging-in-Publication Data
Zwiers, Jeff.
    Building academic language: meeting common core standards across disciplines, grades 5–12/Jeff Zwiers.—Second edition.
        pages cm
    Includes bibliographical references and index.
ISBN 978-1-118-74485-7 (pbk.)
ISBN 978-1-118-74481-9 (ebk.)
ISBN 978-1-118-74480-2 (ebk.)

    1.   Academic language—Study and teaching.   I. Title.
    P120.A24.Z85 2014
    407.1—dc23

                                                                            2013044987

Printed in the United States of America
SECOND EDITION
PB Printing   SKY10027552_062821

Contents

• • •

1   **Understanding How Students Use Language**

This chapter introduces foundational social and cultural perspectives of
complex uses of languages in and out of school. It explores ways in
which the Common Core State Standards provide new opportunities and
challenges with respect to building academic language. These standards
present new cognitive and literacy targets that can be reached only with
heightened cultivation of academic language, the language used to describe
complex ideas, abstract concepts, and critical thinking.

2   **Language Skills Required by the Common Core State Standards**

This chapter clarifies the functions and features of academic language
with direct references to the Common Core State Standards. This includes
academic grammar and discourse levels of language use. Science, math,
and history teachers must teach the use of language beyond vocabulary
knowledge, given that each discipline emphasizes different ways of
thinking and communicating in complex ways. When students learn these
ways of using language, they gain access to the codes and strategies that
accelerate their disciplinary abilities and knowledge.

3   **Cultivating Academic Language Acquisition**

This chapter provides an overview of how students acquire language, along
with key teacher habits and strategies for modeling and scaffolding its
development across content areas. This chapter also helps us improve our
own language use in classroom settings.

might do. It provides ideas for modeling, scaffolding, and analyzing texts that students will be asked to write.

9 Building Language Development into Lessons and Assessments   245

This chapter introduces ways to formatively and summatively assess ways of using academic language to show learning of Common Core State Standards, as well as hints for planning for instruction based on assessments. It emphasizes the importance of identifying the thinking and language that we want students to learn before we leap into instruction.

10 Concluding Thoughts   281

This book ends with some final thoughts and next steps for weaving the ideas presented in it into daily practice.

● ● ●

● ● ●

Preface to the Second Edition

The need to develop students' academic language abilities has become more urgent in light of the new standards. The Common Core State Standards (CCSS), in particular, require students to use language in more sophisticated ways: arguing, evaluating evidence, analyzing complex texts, and engaging in academic discussions. Many of these language demands are also found in the Next Generation Science Standards and various sets of English Language Development standards. So while this book emphasizes the Common Core, I often use the term *new standards* throughout the chapters. The first edition of this book provided a general overview of academic language development; this second edition zooms in on more specific standards and ways to build language for meeting them.

As students leave the primary grades, their academic success depends more and more on their abilities to use academic language—the language used to describe abstract concepts, complex ideas, and critical thinking. A common misconception of academic language is that it is just a long list of key content words, such as *covalent, meritocracy, reciprocal, hyperbole*, and *onomatopoeia*. Yet content vocabulary—knowing the big words—is just one dimension of academic language. Students must also develop skills with the many "smaller words" and grammatical conventions that make the big words stick together to make meaning. This book therefore emphasizes the terms and tactics that tend to slip under our content vocabulary radar but are vital for describing the abstract concepts, higher-order thinking processes, and complex relationships in each discipline.

Academic language is often cited as one of the key factors affecting the achievement gap that exists between high- and low-performing groups of students in our schools (Wong Fillmore, 2004). And whether performance is measured by large tests or informal observations, many students perform poorly because they cannot meet the linguistic demands of different disciplines. This is especially visible in upper-elementary and secondary classes. As students move out of the primary grades, they enter not only new classrooms but also new ways of knowing, thinking, and communicating.

Students who underperform often have backgrounds that have not primed them for mainstream schooling's ways of learning, speaking, reading, and thinking. You can probably picture several (perhaps several dozen) of these students right now. They are immigrants, great-grandchildren of immigrants, speakers of nonmainstream dialects, special education students, and others who have not been immersed in the academic thought and talk that is valued in school. As a result, their performances are not valued when they take tests, as they read and write, or as they participate in class discussions. These students need more than tutoring sessions, new software programs, special classes, extra visuals, and test preparation programs. They need rich classroom experiences that accelerate the language that supports their content knowledge, thinking skills, communication skills, and literacy skills. Students need curricula and teaching that connect to their cultural and cognitive roots, and they need accelerated learning because their high-performing peers do not linger around, waiting for them to catch up.

This book looks at general types of academic language used across subject areas, as well as the variations of language used specifically in science, math, history, and language arts. It also offers suggestions for making content classrooms more conducive to building students' language and thinking abilities to meet the Common Core and other new standards. The suggestions and activities are meant to be woven into and added to current teaching and assessment practices.

My own teaching experiences inspired me to write this book. In each of the elementary, middle school, high school, and even university courses that I have taught, my students have struggled with the language of academic reading, writing, and discussion. I realized that I was not doing enough to build their academic language abilities. I researched what other teachers were doing to apprentice students into different communities of practice (science, math, history, language arts) through language use. My ongoing work with elementary and secondary teachers has also influenced the content of this book. I work with a variety of content teachers to come up with effective support for their many diverse learners. I coach and engage in action research with many teachers who are focused on developing the language of the new standards. Most of the work centers on the literacy and discourse standards of the Common Core State Standards.

Academic language was also the focus of my doctoral research, a six-month case study in which I recorded and analyzed language use in middle school content-area classes three times a week. My main question was, *How do teachers develop the language that students need for success in different content classes?* I concluded that academic language is (1) intricately linked to higher-order thinking processes, (2) developed by extensive modeling and scaffolding of classroom talk, and (3) accelerated by weaving direct teaching of its features while teaching content concepts. I also concluded that academic language and its teaching are much more complex and important than most educators realize (Zwiers, 2005).

Many of the classroom dialogue excerpts in this book come from my study, conducted in classrooms in which more than half the students in each class came from diverse cultural and linguistic backgrounds. Many students spoke other languages at home (most often Spanish) and African American vernacular English. I have continued to observe similarly diverse upper-elementary, middle, and high school content classrooms. In every class, I see students struggle to use language in ways desired by teachers and the new standards, especially on assessments. But I also notice that as students enter upper grades and secondary school, their teachers typically focus less on language development and more on content learning. The results of my research aligned with the findings of other scholars who argue that teachers need more practical awareness of the language that is what I call the lifeblood of learning in all classes (Fillmore & Snow, 2002; Valdés, Bunch, Snow, Lee, & Matos, 2005).

In addition, teachers around the world tell me about the scores of minority-language speakers who fail in school because they lack the valued skills of school literacy and language use. For example, in Mexico students lack academic Spanish, in China they lack academic Mandarin, and in Egypt they lack academic Arabic.

A challenging set of questions has emerged in my ongoing work with teachers and in my own classroom teaching. These questions have helped shape and organize this book:

- What is academic language, and how can I build it as I teach content?
- How can I adapt my curriculum and assessment to build on my students' cultural and linguistic strengths?
- How can I get students to think together to coconstruct meaning rather than just study to memorize?
- How can I build language skills for complex reading and writing?
- How can I assess thinking skills and language proficiency in useful ways?
- How can I most effectively apprentice students into thinking and talking like experts in my discipline?

In my discussions with teachers about these questions, I realized that a practical guide might be useful, particularly for teachers in grades 5 through 12 who do not have time to sift through more theoretical (and, ironically, more academic) books on the topic. I drew from research in the areas of language development, language acquisition, and cognitive psychology. I looked closely at work by scholars of school language, such as Courtney Cazden, Alan Luke, Robin Scarcella, Susana Dutro, Deborah Short, Gordon Wells, Neil Mercer, Shirley Brice-Heath, James Gee, Lisa Delpit, Mary Schleppegrell, Victoria Purcell-Gates, Lev Vygotsky, Guadalupe Valdés, and Lily Wong Fillmore. I then included research-based teaching activities that would be of interest to preservice teachers, content-area teachers who work with diverse populations, English language development teachers, bilingual teachers, special education teachers, teacher trainers, and others who wish to improve the ways in which we help students add the languages valued in school.

To do this, I argue that all teachers should become what I call practical educational linguists. We must know about the basic inner workings of language in our discipline and put this knowledge into practice in our classrooms. Before looking at the surface features of academic language, we need to understand its roots. Chapter 1 therefore introduces foundational social and cultural perspectives of languages used in and out of school.

Chapter 2 clarifies the functions and features of academic language, including academic grammar, which is the set of rules and conventions that organize words and phrases in school. Science, math, and history teachers should also teach some grammar, given that each discipline emphasizes different ways of thinking that require different grammatical conventions. When students learn these conventions, they gain access to the codes (or blueprints) that accelerate their comprehension and writing abilities. And as an intentional bonus, students learn and understand more content in the process.

Chapter 3 provides an overview of language acquisition, along with key teacher habits and strategies for modeling and scaffolding academic language. And because we teachers are not perfect communicators, this chapter also helps us improve our own language use in classroom settings. Chapter 4 then describes variations of language that correspond to the main content areas taught in schools: math, language arts, history, and science.

The latter half of the book is about designing classroom experiences and assessments to help students reach sustainable and growing levels of academic language use. (Most classroom activities are marked with a symbol ⇒ for easy reference.) Chapter 5 offers strategies for developing students' academic speaking and listening in whole-class settings. Chapter 6 focuses on ways to adapt and fortify commonly used group and pair activities strategies for academic language development. Chapter 7 looks at the language of reading, emphasizing the development of language to help in comprehending difficult texts. It also includes a section on teaching content-area vocabulary. Chapter 8 provides ways to develop language for academic writing. Chapter 9 introduces ways to assess academic language and plan for instruction based on what we see in assessments. It emphasizes that before we leap into instruction, we must identify the thinking skills, concepts, and language that we want students to learn. Chapter 10 offers some final thoughts and next steps for weaving the ideas in this book into daily practice. The appendixes provide helpful references, examples of academic words, and suggestions for lesson design.

References

Fillmore, L., & Snow, C. (2002). What teachers need to know about language. In C. A. Adger, C. E. Snow, & D. Christian (Eds.), *What teachers need to know about language* (pp. 7–54). McHenry, IL, and Washington, DC: Delta Systems and Center for Applied Linguistics.

Valdés, G., Bunch, G., Snow, C., Lee, C., & Matos, L. (2005). Enhancing the development of students' language(s). In L. Darling-Hammond & J. Bransford (Eds.), *Preparing teachers for a changing world: What teachers should learn and be able to do* (pp. 126–168). San Francisco, CA: Jossey-Bass.

Wong Fillmore, L. (2004). *The role of language in academic development.* Keynote address given at Closing the Achievement Gap for EL Students conference, Sonoma, CA.

Zwiers, J. (2005). *Developing academic language in middle school English learners: Practices and perspectives in mainstream classrooms.* Unpublished doctoral dissertation, University of San Francisco.

BUILDING ACADEMIC LANGUAGE

Chapter 1

Understanding How Students Use Language

The words are just the tip of the iceberg.

We need language to do just about everything, especially school work. School language, often called academic language, may be the most complicated tool set in the world to learn how to use. Many students learn enough to get by, but too many don't. Millions of bright and capable students around the world struggle in school and even give up because they lack the abilities to use language in ways that are expected in academic settings.

Many of the students in the United States who perform poorly in school have been raised speaking, reading, and writing a non-English language or a variation of English that differs from the language that mainstream teachers and curricula use (Ovando & Collier, 1998). Most of these learners were not immersed from birth in the types of English that are valued by schools, teachers, texts, and tests.

Nonmainstream students have not had the same conversations or literacy experiences (including books and movies) that their mainstream middle-class peers have had. They have not been exposed to hundreds of books or play with as many educational toys, computer programs, and English-proficient older siblings. Moreover, most of the diverse students who do perform well have been immersed in academic literacy and school-like conversations in their home and community settings, which have primed them to transfer their skills into school English.

Unfortunately, most schools have made little progress in narrowing the overall academic gaps between speakers of nonmainstream versions of English and their peers who were raised speaking more school-aligned varieties of English (National Center for Education Statistics, 2011). Many middle and high school teachers have seen the gap continue to widen between students' communication skills and the language required for the many tasks that students encounter in school. These gaps might even increase in light of the robust language demands of the Common Core State Standards and other new standards.

To complicate matters, we might not identify large numbers of students with language-based academic issues: they have little or no accent, they turn in homework, they are well behaved, and they try hard. Yet they fall further behind each year, often just getting by, as they play the game of school. Contrary to what too many people consider to be common sense, simple equal treatment and basic immersion are not enough for many students who are significantly below grade level. They do not just naturally pick up academic language as easily as they pick up other types of social language (Scarcella, 2003).

In the United States, the narrow range of accents, vocabulary, and grammar typically valued by those in power (politicians, business leaders, media, and so on) is often called standard English (Gollnik & Chinn, 2002). Because this is also the type of language that most mainstream members of society speak, it is often called *mainstream English.* A *mainstream student* (in this book) is a student who has been raised speaking the dominant dialect (mainstream English, in the United States) by educated middle- or upper-class parents who have provided books, computers, academic support, and rich conversations. Mainstream students typically belong to dominant classes whose members control most of a society's economic and social institutions, including schools. By contrast, nonmainstream students in the United States, such as English learners, children of English learners, speakers of African American vernacular English (AAVE), and children from poor families, have often grown up with less academic support, fewer educational materials, and fewer school-like conversations.

THE ROLE OF HOME AND COMMUNITY

Students bring with them to school a wide range of social experiences, cultural practices, ways of thinking, and communication styles. These form powerful yet hard-to-see foundations for their learning. Diverse students are often raised learning and thinking in ways that tend to differ from the ways valued by mainstream teachers, school cultures, and test makers. Most teachers learn about these differences in preservice teacher training, but we often fail to consistently apply this knowledge when we teach and assess during full-time teaching. For this reason, this chapter briefly introduces (1) some of the significant mismatches between home and classroom, (2) how to help diverse students add on ways of thinking and communicating that will help them succeed academically, and (3) some major curricular and assessment changes that can more effectively educate diverse students.

For many diverse students, school is a large set of very new situations, with new things to learn and new ways to talk and think—and it can be overwhelming for them. As James Gee (1996) states, "It is just that only a narrow range of these culturally specific home-based skills are rewarded in school, namely those most often found in mainstream homes" (p. 24). For example, certain home-based language practices, such as storybook reading and parental questioning at the dinner table, correlate strongly with academic success (Cook-Gumperz, 1986; Wells, 1986).

When a student enters school, linguistic and conceptual mismatches can have a negative effect on learning. When a mismatch occurs, the student struggles to learn new rules of talk and literacy because these rules are implied—even invisible. That is, we teachers often take them for granted because we assume common knowledge and procedures among learners (Edwards & Mercer, 1993). It makes sense that the more school-like the tasks and communication are at home, the better students are likely to perform at school. Likewise, the more teacher-like the language of a student is, the more the student will meet our expectations and be considered successful.

In her famous ethnolinguistic study, Shirley Brice Heath (1983) found that the middle-class mainstream students had been socialized from a very young age to use many of the language patterns found in school, such as answering questions to which the speaker knows the answer, reciting facts not connected with the immediate context, and ritualizing the uses of language. Heath also pointed out that each classroom activity had its own organization and set of rules. Lesson formats, teacher-student conversations, and other learning tasks formed a classroom culture that influenced language and learning. She concluded that a significant link existed between the narrative, literacy, and communication traditions of home and those needed in school.

In another important study, Susan Philips (1972) examined the classroom language of Native American children in Warm Springs, Oregon. Teachers initially reported that children lacked appropriate language and interaction skills in the classroom and perceived these students to be overly silent and uncooperative. Philips found that the children perceived themselves to be in situations that were inappropriate for speaking. Later, when teachers understood this cultural pattern and created learning situations that more closely resembled oral participation contexts in the Native American community, student involvement increased (Philips, 1983).

And in a study on reading and text discussion behaviors of mothers with children, Williams (1999) found that the types of interactions differed greatly, despite comparable amounts of time spent reading with children and similar rates of demands for information from children. The higher-social-class group of mothers more frequently asked children to elaborate on parts of the book, connect it to their own experiences, provide explanations, evaluate the story as a text, and respond to "Do you think . . . ?" questions. During these interactions, the mothers apprenticed their children in the skill of attending to certain kinds of meaning. Not surprisingly, these types of interactions in the higher-social-class pairs strongly resemble those found in literacy activities and assessment practices at school.

These studies help us to reflect on the powerful influence that students' oral and literacy experiences outside school have on their learning in school. We need to reflect on how student backgrounds align with how we teach, what we teach, how we use language, and how we expect students to describe their learning.

DIVERSITY OF STUDENTS

Now let's zoom in on several students who experience the disconnect between background and school. These students (the names are pseudonyms) still struggle with school's differing language demands, ways of organizing and interpreting knowledge, classroom and homework expectations, and grading and feedback practices. You will likely see many similarities between the students described next and those in your own classes:

- Sara is a seventh grader who immigrated to the United States four years ago from Mexico. She had missed one year of schooling in Mexico before coming to the United States. Her family came from rural Mexico, where school days were much shorter and often canceled when it rained heavily. Few books were available at school or at home. She still scores as an intermediate English user on the state English proficiency test. She is now in mainstream English, science, and history classes with other English learners. She is a hard worker but lacks confidence in her abilities to read, write, and speak in groups. She asks very few questions even when she does not understand the assignment.

- Armando, a ninth grader who was born in the United States, doesn't like school and is easily distracted by other students. He speaks Spanish at home and in the community. His social English is fluent, but his academic English is weak, according to his teachers. The work that he does in class is just enough to receive some credit. He is not in any support classes, but teachers often say that he needs extra help, especially with his writing and test taking. He doesn't like to read or write and always prefers that the teacher read the text to him. He complains that he is not interested in any of the topics that are taught in his classes.

- Kim came from Vietnam two years ago. She is a very shy and highly motivated fifth grader. who hovers around intermediate levels in reading and writing subtests and lower on oral tasks. Her oral language has errors, but she can make herself understood in most situations. She transitioned from the beginning-English-language development program the previous semester, so this is her first exposure to mainstream classes and culture. The first year, she copied much of her written work directly from the writings of classmates. As she understood more, she took more chances with English. She had a strong academic background in Vietnam and thus comprehended many of the basic ideas being presented in her classes. Reading nonfiction was the biggest challenge for her, particularly the history textbook and the articles assigned in her language arts class.

- David is an African American eighth grader who tends to speak AAVE in most interactions. His parents, who did not go to college, work hard, and they want David to do well in school. He likes school, but does not like to use mainstream English in front of peers in his classes. He does most of his homework and often uses social and informal language in his written responses. Teachers call attention to these uses, but he usually has acceptable organization in his writing and scores well. In conversations with teachers, David uses more mainstream expressions and grammar. He knows there is a difference but does not want "to sound so white," as he says, in front of his friends.

- Lisa, a sixth grader, comes from a mixed European American and Filipino middle-class background. This is her third school in four years because her family has moved several times. She was recently tested for special education services. Teachers often recommend her for extra tutoring and for special conditions when tested. When she reads aloud, she pauses often and misreads unfamiliar words. She offers logical ideas in class, but struggles to make them clear and academic.

These students exemplify just a few of the many thousands of backgrounds that challenge and enrich the process of learning how to do school things in school ways with school language.

CAPITALS, REGISTERS, AND EXPECTATIONS

Imagine the following scenario:

It is your first day in law school. Going to law school is now a requirement for every job, including teaching. You arrive at class and sit next to folks who have studied for many years and did well on a big standardized test to be there. As the professor starts talking, you recognize the words, but they don't mean what they usually do, and each sentence in the book takes up half the page. The professor asks a question, and four eager hands shoot up around you. One person answers in long sentences and unfamiliar words. Another person adds something about previous court cases from fifty years ago. You sit there baffled and never raise your hand.

This scenario is not unlike the experiences of many students in schools around the world. They enter settings for which they lack academic capital—the valued knowledge and communication skills that get passed on to most mainstream children and are reinforced at school (Bourdieu, 1986). Different types of capital reinforce each other to help students succeed in school.

Types of Capital

Just as money and things are unequally distributed in society, so are the less visible words, skills, and knowledge that give people advantages (Bourdieu, 1986). We can think of students as having varying combinations of four overlapping types of capital: social, cultural, knowledge, and linguistic.

Social capital consists of the amounts and qualities of interactions with adults, siblings, and peers; listening abilities; empathy skills; and appropriate behaviors and responses. *Cultural capital* tends to consist of travel experiences, wealth, parent education, music listened to, games at home, being read to, reading, race, and religion-related experiences (which are especially helpful for figurative thinking). *Knowledge capital* tends to accumulate from reading, being read to, watching educational and news programs on TV, using computers, developing organizational abilities with knowledge, word memory abilities, travel, conversations with siblings and adults, and parents who ask and answer questions about the world.

I have seen cases where knowledge and cultural capital have influenced math learning. Sara and Armando, for example, lacked the experiences with math-related topics that help mainstream students visualize what they are reading in math class. They got bogged down by less important aspects of the problems, which diverted them from solving the problems. In one math book, for example, three questions in a row dealt with scores in miniature golf, baseball, and football, which are unfamiliar sports for many English learners. Other topics in the math questions included weight loss, elevators, temperatures in Fahrenheit, savings accounts, Mount Everest, driving distances in miles, basketball, a table game with a spinner, ice cream revenues, weightlifting, skiing, snow melt, and airfares. Identifying and explaining these concepts can help students do the math and equip them with cultural capital for other situations.

Linguistic capital consists of the quantity and quality of language used by parents and peers, in TV shows, and in daily discussions; of religious interactions, which can develop abilities to use abstract language; of computer experiences and games; and of books at home, whether one is reading oneself or being read to. Regional dialects also figure in. And as we shall see in more detail in chapter 2, thinking skills are assets that help students develop linguistic capital, and vice versa. Students with such capital know what, when, and how to speak and write well in school settings.

Families pass on these different types of capital to their children, who "invest them" in school and the working world. The children then pass on old and new forms of capital to their own children. As these assets build up, students store necessary knowledge and skills for when the teacher, be it in kindergarten or in eleventh-grade biology, asks them to construct new learning on top of what is already there. If a lot is already there, then learning is much less work, with much less likelihood of failure. And as is generally true in the case of financial capital, the rich get richer.

Registers

The more capital we have, the better we are at adjusting our language according to the situation and the audience. A distinctly adjusted way of talking is called a *register,* "a variety of a language distinguished according to use" (Halliday, 1978, p. 87). We all use a variety of registers in a variety of settings such as home, school, work, meetings, interviews, sporting events, and social gatherings. The register of each setting develops and is developed by its members over long periods of time. Take a moment to think about how your language is different at a party than it is when meeting with a professor or an administrator.

Mainstream social groups tend to integrate aspects of academic registers into their children's socialization more than other groups do (Gee, 1996; Heath, 1983). For example, some parents ask their children math, history, and science questions while they are eating, reading a book, or watching TV. Other parents have children recount what happened that day, and the parents do the same with each other. Whether intentional or not, such practices can give students advantages in their development of academic registers. And school designers, teachers, test makers, and textbook publishers all use their own ideas of what is proper school language (derived from their own socialization and schooling) to create expectations for how students use language each day. Academic registers (e.g., technical, medical, and educational languages) that are acquired later in life tend to shape a person's social language, or register. And schooling experiences, work environment, travel experiences, the media, and genres of reading all reshape adult social and home registers throughout life. Parents then hand down these reshaped home registers to their children (Gee, 1996). And the cycle continues.

Sometimes registers clash. As we saw with David, students are often dealing with a dual audience: they simultaneously want to please the teacher (or at least get a decent grade) and impress their peers. These audiences can conflict, as a student might not want to appear too studious, be a teacher's pet, be laughed at, or stick out too much from the expectations of a peer group. One strategy is to give the right answer to the teacher but give it in nonmainstream English. For example, in an eighth-grade science class, a student said, "A nucleus don't have no electrons in it." In this particular case, I had heard the student use the mainstream form ("doesn't have any") with me in a social conversation, but he did not and may never use this form in front of his peers. This solves his dilemma in the present, but may not help him develop more advanced uses of academic language for when he needs them.

Invisible Criteria

Diverse students can become the casualties of invisible criteria in school. This happens when we (teachers, schools, tests) assess students on things that we haven't taught (Schleppegrell, 2004). We use criteria, invisible to us and to students, that depend heavily on background knowledge and language features, many of which come from non-school experiences. We also can make wrong and harmful assumptions about students' knowledge, background, and thinking. Understanding these assumptions and the criteria we use to teach each day is imperative if we are to create an optimal classroom environment for all students.

Many of us reward home-based skills without realizing it. We unconsciously expect certain ways of talking about texts and expressing ideas in writing—ways that are often rooted in our own cultural values and beliefs. Then we reward those ways that most align with our own expectations of evidence of learning. It would be silly, as Bartolomé (1998) points out, "for teachers to expect linguistic-minority and other minority students, including working class whites, to pull academic discourses out of a hat and magically and effectively use it across class and cultural boundaries" (p. 119). Yet this is often what happens. For example, guess which of these students got the higher grade from his or her answer:

Martin: Like, to divide em, you turn the second one over and times it by the first one. But ya gotta see if any numbers fit into the top and bottom to cross em out and get em smaller so you don't get big numbers at the end. At the end you see if you can make the top and bottom as small as possible.

Leslie: In order to divide two fractions, take the reciprocal of the second one and multiply it by the first. Before multiplying, though, see if any numerators and denominators have common factors that cancel out. For example, if a 9 is above and 3 below, divide by 3 and you end up with 3 on top and 1 below. Multiply the numerators across the top and the denominators across the bottom. See if the answer can be further reduced.

Both of these students understood the content, but Leslie used more academic language. Do we grade Leslie higher because of the more advanced language she used? If so, have *we* taught that language, or did she learn it at home? This is a pair of questions that we must continue to ask ourselves. Often the answer is *yes* for the first and *home* for the second.

Teachers often have invisible criteria even for very basic practices in school. In her well-known study, Sarah Michaels (1986) found that middle-class mainstream teachers considered the narratives shared by working-class African American students to be illogical and confusing. According to "standard" English–speaking middle-class teachers, children did not follow linear lines of thought, assumed too much shared background knowledge with the audience, and signaled importance with culturally based intonation and prosodic cues. Working-class African American students, especially girls, tended to tell more episodic accounts that shifted between scenes, whereas the European American students tended to tell topic-centered stories that focused on one event. What Michaels and others have shown is that ways of interpreting meaning differ greatly, depending on one's socialization and experiences with language. We must therefore be able to validate the thinking processes and languages that students bring with them, while also explicitly teaching new forms of school language.

Many of our diverse students end up doing a lot of guesswork as they figure out what it means to "read critically," "speak clearly," "write in an organized fashion," "stick to the point," or "use your own words." Although directions and prompts such as these may seem to be common knowledge and self-evident, we must make extra efforts to be clear, offering examples and modeling. For this reason it is important to analyze patterns of school language, even in what we think are basic directions and statements. Mary Schleppegrell (2004) adds, "Students' difficulties in 'reasoning,' for example, may be due to their lack of familiarity with the linguistic properties of the language through which the reasoning is expected to be presented, rather than to the inherent difficulty of the cognitive processes involved" (p. 2). That is, the words and their organization may be a more significant issue in learning than the actual content or skills that we are teaching.

Mainstream students have acquired more than just linguistic knowledge that gives them an edge in school. They have, as Gee (1992) points out, acquired knowledge about "ways of being in the world, ways of acting, thinking, interacting, valuing, believing, speaking, and sometimes writing and reading, connected to particular identities and social roles" (p. 73). If we fail to directly teach academic ways of doing and communicating to our diverse students, what can result is the "pedagogy of entrapment," a term Donald Macedo (1994, p. 34) used to refer to situations in which schools require from students the academic discourse skills and knowledge that we don't teach.

Many educators highlight the need for teachers to directly teach students how to use academic language in school settings (Bartolomé, 1998; Delpit, 1995; Scarcella, 2003). We must strive to make the criteria visible—first to us and then to our students. We then take a close look at what we expect from students as they talk, read, write, and think about our content area. By making our expectations explicit and clear, we begin the process of accelerating their progress and narrowing the gap between them and higher-performing groups of students.

THE NEED TO VALUE *AND* CHALLENGE

So why is there a preference for academic language and literacy practices in school and work settings? The social reality is that dominant socioeconomic and political groups strongly influence what is valued in a society (Freire & Macedo, 1987).

In other words, the middle and upper classes tend to define what is intellectual, logical, linguistically appropriate, academic, and organized in a given setting. Dominant groups then set up systems (e.g., certain types of testing and teaching practices) for preserving power and limiting the access of nonmainstream groups to such systems. Although these systems supposedly evaluate abilities, much of what is tested is the cultural capital and language abilities that align with mainstream expectations. For this reason, we must continuously reflect on the power that language has to separate, marginalize, and oppress.

Another problem in schools is that teachers (along with schools and surrounding society) do not value the knowledge and language skills that linguistically diverse students bring to class. Devaluing students' ways of making sense of the world also devalues those students. I have seen many classrooms and transcribed classroom discussions that show blatant teacher bias and devaluation of student language practices. Teachers, in trying to force students to change their speech drastically, actually shut down students from speaking and participating altogether (Delpit, 1995). And all of us can be susceptible to harmful attitudes, assumptions, and expectations when it comes to student language use. Consider the following conversation from a sixth-grade English learner in a language arts class:

1. *Teacher:* Okay, what did the Egyptians believe about death?
2. *Student:* In the afterlife.
3. *Teacher:* Okay, please use a complete sentence.
4. *Student:* The Egyptians believe in the afterlife.
5. *Teacher:* Bel*ieved*, past tense. Good. Now what does that mean?
6. *Student:* Like, let's say you die and they make you a mummy and—
7. *Teacher:* Okay, you can say, "When a person died, he or she was mummified." What else?
8. *Student:* Nothin'.

We must create learning spaces for our diverse students so that they build from what they have and add the knowledge and language skills they will need in future schooling and work. We must challenge students to expand their linguistic capital. Yet at the same time, we must be willing to push back against society's narrow-minded expectations (often evidenced through tests, writing samples, and grading practices) and limited perceptions of our students' abilities. Some argue, for example, that our schools should "accept wider varieties of expression, to embrace multiple ways of communicating" (Zamel & Spack, 1998, p. xi). Our diverse students' knowledge and linguistic abilities are assets that we should integrate into how and what we teach.

Being on the Same Page

No message is ever perfectly communicated between two people. My meanings of *apple* or *honesty* or *revolution* will always differ slightly from yours. All the past events and texts and images that formed my meanings for a word are different from yours. And the meanings in the minds of our students can differ even more. This becomes a difficult reality when we begin to communicate academic, abstract, and complex topics.

When ideas are transformed into speech, transmitted, and then turned back into ideas, some things are lost in the translation, so to speak. This is more pronounced the more the speaker and listener differ, such as when backgrounds differ (e.g., mainstream and nonmainstream, young and old, male and female, rich and poor). A listener, for example, has expectations about the speaker's topic and predicts what will be said. Such predictions, along with confirmations and surprises, help the listener constantly sculpt the ideas into something meaningful. Yet a common understanding between listener and speaker is doubly difficult to achieve when communicating abstract topics between two people with very different backgrounds (e.g., mainstream teacher and nonmainstream student). Both participants need to edge closer to the middle of common understanding through the use of communication strategies.

For communication to happen, each participant in the communication process must share knowledge of the language's symbols (words, sentences, gestures) and organization. For example, educators need to know what the words *access, curriculum,* and *adaptation* mean when talking about curriculum adaptation. Shared knowledge is common for a fairly homogeneous group of people with similar backgrounds and language experiences. But in school, because most classrooms are large and diverse and because students are very different from teachers, we seldom have clear agreement on the meanings of words and their arrangements, even though we might see many nodding heads. If a teacher uses too many unknown words and complex sentences for a student to understand, then communication isn't happening. If I tell you, "The fargly merglettes grooked all the mestip," you will have no idea what I am saying, even though you might be able to answer multiple-choice questions about who did what (e.g., "What did the merglettes do?"). Too often teachers and tests assume that students know the symbols and the complex ways in which symbols are organized in school (Wong Fillmore & Snow, 2000). These assumptions hurt students later when they cannot meet academic expectations in advanced courses.

An important element of communicating meaning is shared background knowledge (Cazden, 2001). Many teachers assume that students share similar images and concepts in their heads. This assumption allows teachers to default to practices such as having students listen to lectures, read textbooks, and do worksheet activities. It also allows teachers to not say or explain what they assume students already know. In such cases, diverse students must gain much more of their learning from the words in the book or by listening to the teacher than their mainstream peers need to do. Diverse students must work much harder to fill in ideas and construct meaning.

Thus, one of our tasks as teachers is to get to know the meanings that our students have for words and terms, especially the important school-based ones. Once this happens, we get our meanings and theirs to overlap enough to reach a common understanding.

Agreeing on Importance

Another level of meaning has to do with what is considered important. That which is meaningful or significant to teachers may not be to students, and vice versa. We observe and experience life's events and ideas, from which we highlight what we consider to be important. When our students have trouble seeing what we teachers believe is important and then describing it, we must remember that they might focus on different things based on their backgrounds. For example, in one diverse ninth-grade English class that I observed, an insight emerged as the teacher and I looked at the transcripts of presentations. Students presented what they considered to be important about the book they had read. Rather than following the topic-centered, linear format that the teacher wanted to hear, students went out on tangents and focused much more on personal relationships and events that connected to their lives. This is what they considered to be important.

Similarly, a study found that 96 percent of European American student narratives but only 34 percent of African American narratives were topic centered (Cazden, 2001). We need to seek to know what students think is important as they read and learn in all content areas, not just language arts. At the same time, we need to apprentice them into new ways of looking at meaning and what is meaningful to experts in a discipline.

A common teacher tactic is to take elements of student talk and use them to shift the focus onto more academic and scientific ideas (Zwiers, 2005). The teacher shifts to what he or she thinks is important. For example, when a fifth grader responded to a story with, "Yes, last week a person asked me for money and I gave him a quarter," the teacher replied this way: "So you did the same as the main character. Why do you think the author put this part in the story? What do his actions tell us about him?"

Although the teacher could have asked the student to elaborate on his philanthropic event, she directed the discussion back to the story and the academic goal in mind, trying to get the class to think more deeply about the character. When we do this type of shifting well, we build new frames of reference for thinking and communicating. When we do this shifting poorly, we can bore, confuse, frustrate, and overwhelm our students. We must seek to validate students' current perceptions of meaning and patiently guide students into the realms of school meanings and formal ways to communicate them.

Working with Diverse Ways of Organizing Knowledge

In addition to their differences in background knowledge and ways of assigning meaning, students come to us with different ideas about organizing knowledge (Costa, 2001). In the United States, for example, a hierarchical way of organizing knowledge tends to shape the thinking and language of mainstream groups. This type of organization generally involves having a main point, supporting it with several logical reasons and evidence, explaining, and then summing it up. This is, in fact, one of the major emphases of the Common Core State Standards in reading, writing, listening, speaking, and math (National Governors Association Center for Best Practices, 2010). We also see hierarchical organization in expository texts in history and science, newspaper articles, magazines, and TV news programs. In these "texts," lack of clarity, lack of evidence, lack of focus, and extraneous language are not valued.

Hierarchical thinking requires students to understand subordinate and super-ordinate categories of knowledge. For example, a story might contain a main point, or theme, of perseverance. Subordinate points are the events and actions of the characters that support the main point. In science, the main point might be that matter changes states, while the subpoints are the examples of physical and chemical changes that occur and why. Indeed, most websites are organized in this manner, with subordinate links on every page.

Large numbers of students, however, do not organize knowledge in the same ways that teachers and textbooks do. These students have had very different home experiences, with different types of stories, messages, and categories for knowl-edge. And yet most teachers have been so immersed in hierarchical ways of thinking that it is almost impossible to see how others could organize knowledge differently. But as we get to know students, we can understand how they see the world and give it meaning. Then we can more effectively share new ways of communicating, comprehending, and organizing knowledge.

Getting to Know Students

We may come to know some students—often the obnoxious ones, teachers' pets, and higher performers—but many slip through the proverbial cracks. And these falling students need to be known the most.

We need to know how students think and communicate because we need to know where to start teaching. We need to find out what they think is important in life and why. This includes learning how they organize the facts and concepts of our content area and how they connect learning to life. Thus, in the first part of the year, we must come up with a wide range of ways to observe thinking and learning and language use (see chapter 9).

Here are a few ideas for getting to know students in order to gain insights into their language and thinking. For some activities, you can pick five, six, or seven focal students each week. After eighteen weeks you will know ninety students a little better. As you listen to or read their words, keep track of what they think is important and meaningful (as described earlier in this chapter). Here are some ideas for knowing students a little better:

• Have them write you a letter that tells their life story.

• Interview them.

- Have them record their thoughts about school and how it is different from home or from previous schools they have attended.

- Have them make a personal coat of arms.

- Ask them what they think, like, and dislike about science, math, history, stories, and other school topics.

- Read their learning logs or journals. Ask them personal questions. Ask about the types of language experiences they have at home and with friends. Ask them about their languages and how they talk in different settings.

Chapter 9 also offers ideas on how to keep track of language abilities with checklists and rubrics. As we get to know how students communicate, we must keep in mind that all languages, vernaculars, and registers have logical rules and grammars that govern them. Some languages, for example, do not have a passive voice construction, a structure commonly used in many science texts written in English. Awareness of these kinds of differences can help us better prepare students from diverse backgrounds to read these texts.

What many teachers hear and interpret about students at school is often constructed from a web of deeply rooted ways of being and seeing that cannot be quickly brushed aside and replaced. Our practices must adapt to work with, rather than against, the diversity of our students. Ultimately we must build the habit of always looking through a "sociocultural lens" to get to know our students. Purcell-Gates (1995) writes,

> How can we understand why so many children do not learn what the mainstream schools think they are teaching unless we can get "inside" the learners and see the world through their eyes? If we do not try to do this, if we continue to use the mainstream experience of reality as the perspective, we fool ourselves into believing that we are looking through a window when instead we are looking into a mirror. (p. 6)

CONCLUSION

Brilliant students have been marginalized and unrecognized (and left behind) because of their diverse languages, learning styles, and ways of thinking. This results from limited views that mistakenly equate a person's use of a mainstream register with intelligence and potential. Some argue that we must modify our expectations of language use in school and the way we teach, test, and accept student versions of language. Others argue that we should teach students the academic uses of language intentionally, knowing that students need to use the language of school to succeed later. This chapter has argued that we can and should do both.

For many students, their lives before and outside school have not sufficiently warmed them up for the thinking and communication practices of classroom learning. We must work alongside students to develop and add new forms of cultural and linguistic capital. The hard part for us is avoiding a deficit mentality, or a replacement approach, an all-too-common mentality in much teaching around the world that devalues home-based practices. We need to build on existing language use and thinking and help students add mainstream ways of using language to their repertoire of skills, just as we must add to our repertoire the various values and practices that our diverse students bring. Thus, in essence, we are promoting multilingualism and multiculturalism. The languages and cultures that we are helping students add are academic in nature.

CHAPTER REFLECTIONS

- Is "languageism" even more prevalent than racism?
- How can you connect classroom learning experiences to your students' diverse backgrounds, ways of thinking about the world, and ways of using language?
- How can you get to know your students—what they think, like, and can do in your discipline?
- What are your criteria for *important* and *meaningful* in your content area?
- What influenced your own development of academic language?

References

Bartolomé, L. I. (1998). *The misteaching of academic discourses: The politics of language in the classroom.* Boulder, CO: Westview Press.

Bourdieu, P. (1986). The forms of capital. In J. Richardson (Ed.), *Handbook of theory and research for the sociology of education* (pp. 241–258). Westport, CT: Greenwood Press.

Cazden, C. (2001). *Classroom discourse: The language of teaching and learning.* Portsmouth, NH: Heinemann.

Cook-Gumperz, J. (1986). *The social construction of literacy.* Cambridge, UK: Cambridge University Press.

Costa, A. (2001). Mediative environments. In A. Costa (Ed.), *Developing minds: A resource book for teaching thinking* (pp. 248–252). Alexandria, VA: Association for Supervision and Curriculum Development.

Delpit, L. (1995). *Other people's children: Cultural conflict in the classroom.* New York, NY: New Press.

Edwards, D., & Mercer, N. (1993). *Common knowledge: The development of understanding in the classroom.* London, UK: Routledge.

Freire, P., & Macedo, D. (1987). *Literacy: Reading the word and the world.* Westport, CT: Bergin & Garvey.

Gee, J. (1992). Reading. *Journal of Urban and Cultural Studies, 2*(2), 65–77.

Gee, J. (1996). *Social linguistics and literacies: Ideology in discourses.* London, UK: Routledge Falmer.

Gollnik, D. M., & Chinn, P. C. (2002). *Multicultural education in a pluralistic society* (6th ed.). Upper Saddle River, NJ: Prentice Hall.

Halliday, M. (1978). *Language as social semiotic.* Baltimore, MD: University Park Press.

Heath, S. (1983). *Ways with words: Language, life, and work in communities and classrooms.* Cambridge, UK: Cambridge University Press.

Macedo, D. (1994). *Literacies of power: What Americans are not allowed to know.* Boulder, CO: Westview Press.

Michaels, S. (1986). Narrative presentations: An oral preparation for literacy with first graders. In J. Cook-Gumperz (Ed.), *The social construction of literacy* (pp. 94–116). Cambridge, UK: Cambridge University Press.

National Center for Education Statistics. (2011). *The nation's report card. Reading 2011.* Washington, DC: US Department of Education.

National Governors Association Center for Best Practices. (2010). *Common Core State Standards.* Washington, DC: Council of Chief State School Officers.

Ovando, C., & Collier, V. (1998). *Bilingual and ESL classrooms* (2nd ed.). New York, NY: McGraw-Hill.

Philips, S. (1972). Participant structures and communication competence: Warm Springs children in community and classroom. In C. Cazden, V. John, &

D. Hymes (Eds.), *Functions of language in the classroom* (pp. 370–393). New York, NY: Teachers College Press.

Philips, S. (1983). *The invisible culture: Communication in classroom and community on the Warm Springs Indian Reservation*. Prospect Heights, IL: Waveland.

Purcell-Gates, V. (1995). *Other people's words: The cycle of low literacy*. Cambridge, MA: Harvard University Press.

Scarcella, R. (2003). Academic English: *A conceptual framework* (Technical Report 2003–1). University of California Linguistic Minority Research Institute.

Schleppegrell, M. J. (2004). *The language of schooling: A functional linguistics approach*. Mahwah, NJ: Erlbaum.

Wells, G. (1986). *The meaning makers*. London, UK: Heinemann.

Williams, G. (1999). The pedagogic device and the production of pedagogic discourse: A case example in early literacy education. In F. Christie (Ed.), *Pedagogy and the shaping of consciousness: Linguistic and social processes* (pp. 88–122). London, UK: Cassell.

Wong Fillmore, L., & Snow, C. (2000). *What teachers need to know about language*. Washington, DC: ERIC Clearinghouse on Languages and Linguistics.

Zamel, V., & Spack, R. (Eds.). (1998). *Negotiating academic literacies: Teaching and learning across languages and cultures*. Mahwah, NJ: Erlbaum.

Zwiers, J. (2005). *Developing academic language in middle school English learners: Practices and perspectives in mainstream classrooms*. Unpublished doctoral dissertation, University of San Francisco.

Chapter 2

Language Skills Required by the Common Core State Standards

All that glitters is not bold.

So what *is* academic language? It has been around for millennia; we use it all the time, but we still have trouble defining it. Its complexity, versatility, and diversity make academic language difficult to grasp. It varies widely across regions, content areas, grade levels, textbooks, and teachers. Nevertheless, some common features of school language have emerged from my research and in the writings of classroom language scholars. These features are described in this chapter. The following pages may have more linguistic terms than you wish to take in at the moment, but they will leave you with a much better idea of what makes academic language academic.

A BRIEF HISTORY OF ACADEMIC LANGUAGE PROFICIENCY

Several decades back, a well-known researcher of bilingualism, Jim Cummins, used the terms *basic interpersonal communicative skills* (BICS) and *cognitive academic language proficiency* (CALP) (Cummins, 1979) to expose a widespread problem that he was observing. Schools were assuming that students were academically proficient because they were fluent in the social and everyday uses of English and then placing large numbers of students in mainstream classes without language support. These students performed poorly, Cummins argued, not only because they lacked academic language preparation but also because their teachers lacked preparation to teach them this language. This is still happening to many diverse learners (Bartolomé, 1998; Scarcella, 2003; Valdés, 2001).

Social language (BICS) tends to be less complex and less abstract and is accompanied by helpful extralinguistic clues, such as pictures, objects, facial expressions, and gestures. Social language is used to build relationships and get things done in less formal settings, such as the home, parties, sporting events, and shopping. Academic language (CALP) tends to be complex and abstract, lacking extralinguistic support. A conversation with a friend about a recent sports event would involve much social language, whereas listening to a lecture on globalization would be more academic.

Other ideas of academic language emerged. Dutro and Moran (2003) defined *academic language proficiency* as the abilities to construct meaning from oral and written language, relate complex ideas and information, recognize features of different genres, and use various linguistic strategies to communicate. Díaz-Rico and Weed (2002) offered a helpful metaphor. They considered academic language to be a cognitive toolbox—a set of thinking skills and language abilities used to decode and encode complex concepts. And my short definition of *academic language* is this: the set of words, grammar, and discourse strategies used to describe complex ideas, higher-order thinking processes, and abstract concepts.

The new standards, particularly the Common Core State Standards for English language arts, math, and literacy across subjects, have served to further shape ideas of academic language and its uses. For example, notice the challenging language functions and thinking skills that recur in the following excerpts from the standards:

"Supporting ideas with evidence from text."

"Determine how themes and main ideas are conveyed through particular details in the text."

"Analyze how chapters, sentences, and words contribute to the development of the key ideas in texts."

"Build on others' ideas and express own ideas clearly in a range of collaborative discussions."

"Determine whether earlier events caused later ones or simply preceded them."

Even in this short list, there are a variety of ways in which students need to use very academic language to both learn and show their learning.

General and Specialized Language

Every student starts with a foundation of language that he or she has been building from early childhood (see figure 2.1). This foundation represents the language and thinking of family, home, culture, and community. During the school years, students construct other levels of general and specialized language from this foundation. An important layer is the general academic language of thinking and literacy that is used across the disciplines. This layer then overlaps with more

Figure 2.1 Overlapping Variations of Language That Develop over Time

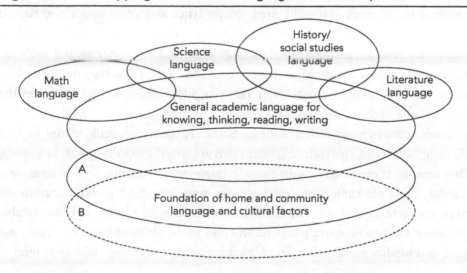

specialized variations of thinking and language, four of which are prominent in school: math, science, history or social science, and literature (in the upper circles). Over time, all of the circles expand and even contract, depending on where we are and with whom we interact. Later, students often pick an area that becomes even more expanded with technical and professional language of the discipline. This area often becomes their field of study and eventual field of work.

Students come to school with a wide range of language and thinking variations circles. Student A in figure 2.1, for example, has more developed math and history language abilities, signified by more overlap with the general academic language oval. For some students, their general academic language is well developed, having significant overlap with their home and community language foundation. Yet if the student has the dotted-line foundation in figure 2.1, as student B does, he would have less support from home and cultural factors for school's ways of doing things. This would mean less alignment and more mismatch of learning and language, as described in chapter 1. Ultimately all students must build up each of their circles (spheres) of language and thinking.

Tools and Skills

We must consider language as dynamic, not static. Language gets things done; it helps us act, and it is action (Walqui & van Lier, 2010). One way to foster students' abilities to get academic things done with language is to think of language as an evolving set of tools and skills used to construct and communicate ideas. To construct or communicate an academic idea, a student chooses and uses tools— the words, phrases, grammar, and message organization strategies. But tools are not enough; students must know how to use them. To do this, they use their skills to combine the tools in constructing coherent ideas and messages that meet the needs of the audience or task.

Tools come in many different forms. Some are content-specific words, such as the long, boldfaced, and technical words that are specific to a discipline. In science, for example, these words might include *respiration, transpiration, meiosis,* and *habitat.* Most academic words and phrases actually extend across a continuum from concrete to abstract. For example, names, events, places, and illustratable processes tend to be more concrete, whereas more philosophical, complex, and hard-to-visualize words (*democracy, photosynthesis, balancing equations*) tend to be on the abstract side. Many important abstract terms are what Beck, McKeown, and Kucan (2013) call tier 2 words, which are "general but sophisticated words" used across a variety of domains that mature users use to communicate complex thoughts (p. 18)—for example, *feature, require, tend, dimension, reality, correspond, inevitable, represent, account,* and *reflect.* In middle grades and early high school especially, students need to know and use many new terms on the abstract side of the continuum.

The importance of academic vocabulary knowledge is obvious and well documented (McLaughlin et al., 2000; Moats, 2000; Stahl, 1999). Indeed, it is one of the six major pedagogical shifts for English language arts and literacy that have surfaced in Common Core resources (EngageNY, 2013). Yet there is a danger of overfocusing on individual words, particularly if that focus is on accumulating definitions to do well on tests. When this happens, connected and in-depth understandings of content concepts and practice in disciplinary thinking get pushed aside. Each lesson should be a place for students to improve their understandings of key ideas and hone their practices in the discipline. They must be able to work on their skills of communicating ideas.

A key skill for constructing ideas is using the many tools that logically and clearly connect sentences and paragraphs. Some of these tools are connectives, such as *therefore, however, whereas,* and *because;* prepositions, such as *behind, between,* and *without;* and pronouns, such as *each other, themselves,* and *it.* Students must know when and how to use these tools to make messages clear to others and to themselves. Another skill is being able to use terms that describe higher-order thinking skills (Scarcella, 2003) required in school tasks, tests, and texts. These tools, such as *differ, boils down to, contrast, outweigh, led to, ramifications, analyze, theory, estimate, filter, model, link, evidence, establish, consequences,* and *aspects,* tend to be shared across content areas (see a longer list of these in appendix B). Other skills for constructing ideas and messages are described in later chapters.

FUNCTIONS OF ACADEMIC LANGUAGE

Describing academic language is yet another case of fish trying to describe water. Most of us educators have been so immersed in school language that we have trouble recognizing the tools, skills, and other features used to describe and communicate academic messages. Many years of immersion prevent us from seeing such language and describing it to our "student divers." Many of the expressions seem straightforward, but as you have likely observed, a student's misunderstanding of even a few terms or grammatical structures in a text can severely hinder his or her comprehension or communication.

Academic language serves three interrelated and broad-ranging functions found throughout the Common Core and other standards: it describes complexity, higher-order thinking, and abstraction. These overlapping purposes take different forms in each content area and at each grade level.

To Describe Complexity

One of the main functions of academic language is to describe complex concepts as clearly as possible (Schleppegrell, 2004). Complex ideas and relationships abound in many different forms in all content areas. For example, in science there are complex relationships among the systems in the human body, complex calculations in chemical reactions, and complex geological forces that change the planet. In history there are complex historical figures who were both "good" and "bad," complex causes and effects of major events, and complex and conflicting historical records. In math there are complex ways to solve word problems, complex tables and charts to interpret, and complex applications of math to real-world situations. In language arts there are complex relationships between characters, complex plots and literary devices to interpret, and complex ideas to organize and express in writing. You get the point.

And to complicate matters, complexity deepens as students reach upper levels of education and the world of work. In the working world, for example, there are complex causes and effects, relationships with clients and coworkers, business models, politics, computer programs, presentations to give and attend, project flowcharts, lab experiments, financial reports, and so on. In each of these, people struggle to skillfully use the tools of language to make them as clear and accessible as possible.

To Describe Higher-Order Thinking

Academic language is used in school to describe complex thinking processes, often called higher-order thinking skills. These include cognitive processes that are used to comprehend, solve problems, and express ideas (Facione, 1990; Swartz, 2001). Many lists of thinking skills have emerged over the years, the most famous one being that of Benjamin Bloom and his colleagues (Bloom, Engelhar, Furst, Hill, & Krathwohl, 1956). They proposed six levels of thinking that progress from knowledge to comprehension to application to analysis to synthesis to evaluation. Other researchers have argued that classrooms also use language for the following cognitive functions: analyzing, seeking information, comparing, informing, explaining, predicting, classifying, justifying, hypothesizing, solving problems, synthesizing, persuading, empathizing, interpreting, evaluating, and applying (Valdez-Pierce & O'Malley, 1992; Wiggins & McTighe, 1998).

Even a cursory analysis of the Common Core, Next Generation Science, and new English Language Development (ELA) standards yields a wide range of thinking skills. Common Core ELA/Literacy standards, for example, emphasize interpreting themes and evaluating evidence, supporting arguments, identifying themes in texts, building on ideas of others, and synthesizing ideas from multiple sources (National Governors Association Center for Best Practices, 2010). The new science standards tend to emphasize describing, classifying, formulating hypotheses, planning and carrying out investigations, proposing different solutions, interpreting data, generalizing, and communicating one's findings (Achieve, 2013). In the CCSS ELA/Literacy standards for history and social science, students need to describe, explain, justify, give examples, compare primary and secondary sources, analyze, and evaluate (National Governors Association Center for Best Practices, 2010). And the CCSS math standards emphasize large amounts of explaining one's reasoning; critiquing the reasoning of others; supporting arguments; applying; making conjectures; and using models, tools, and language strategically to solve problems and understand the concepts. Chapter 4 offers an in-depth look at thinking skills in each content area.

Most of the resources on cognitive skills, however, have not emphasized the importance of understanding and teaching the language that describes them or the implications for English learners and other diverse students. Although students use these thinking skills beyond the classroom walls, they often need significant bridging from the ways they use and describe their thinking outside school to the ways in which school expects and values.

To Describe Abstraction

A third function of academic language is to describe abstract concepts—ideas or relationships that we cannot easily act out, point to, or illustrate with images, as can often be done in home and social settings. For example, in the sentence *On the other hand, the two scientists had differing views on the topic of evolution,* the term *views* refers not to being up on a ledge with a view, which can be observed, but to the scientists' thoughts on evolution, which are also abstract. The reader should then expect an explanation of how their views differed. The reader must also know that *on the other hand* is a cue that changes direction in a text, similar to the words *but, however,* and *yet.* This abstract, compare-and-contrast thinking, which kicks in fairly automatically for fluent readers and thinkers accustomed to such texts, is not automatic for everyone. These concepts are hard for many students to visualize (Snow & Brinton, 1997).

One of our jobs as teachers is to build automaticity in the comprehension and use of academic language cues. This means helping students see words that trigger certain types of abstract thinking. Take, for example, the following abstract phrases: *the long-term effects of a major war; evidence that supports the opposing position in a debate; interpretations of a character's words or actions;* and *the similarities between two cultures.* Looking at these examples, we see that understanding the abstraction depends on one or more of the cognitive skills: cause-and-effect, persuasion, interpretation, and comparison. We must create classroom situations and tasks that train students to see this language, to understand the abstract thinking behind it, and then to engage in similar types of thinking in practice activities.

Each content area, of course, has its large share of abstraction. And with each new year of school, students' minds must engage in even more visualizing, connecting, and reasoning of concepts. Math, for example, is an abstract discipline in upper grades because it uses symbols and invisible logical relationships.

For example, here's a prompt:

Find the roots of the equation $12x^2 + 5x - 2 = 0$ by factoring.

A student has to know what a root is, what an equation is, how to factor, and how variables can signify different numbers—abstract processes and relationships.

History concepts, such as cause, effect, bias, empathy, learning from the past, political systems, economic forces, and social movements, are also abstract. In science, abstraction abounds in such target concepts as adaptation, atoms and molecules, elements, energy, chemical bonds, biological systems, and gravity. Finally, in language arts, there is abstraction in applying a novel's themes to real life, comparing characters' actions to our own, using figurative language, interpreting the author's message, looking for text evidence to support one's ideas, and responding to literature by writing essays.

John Dewey (1910/1997) pointed out long ago that abstractness depends largely on a person's familiarity and expertise with a topic. For example, if a physicist has lived and breathed particle physics for several decades, the topic might be quite concrete to him or her but very abstract to a person who is not a physicist. The level of shared background knowledge, therefore, is a key factor in understanding and communicating abstraction. Things that are directly connected to common social life tend to be more concrete, even though they might appear to be abstract to an outsider. For teachers this means that we need to understand that what is concrete to us is perhaps not concrete to our students. Content concepts, definitions, and clear mental images that are obvious to us might not be to students, especially diverse students. We must remember how much better we know a topic, often because we have taught it five times a day for many years. We might be especially interested in it, too. For students who lack considerable background knowledge about a topic, school is often their first exposure to the topic's language, thinking, and basic concepts. Putting so many new pieces together is quite abstract for them.

FEATURES OF ACADEMIC LANGUAGE

Now that we have a better idea of what academic language does, we can look at how it does it. That is, we can gain a better understanding of the features that are commonly used to describe complexity, higher-order thinking, and abstraction. Not all of the following features of academic English apply to all languages, though. Some languages, for example, do not use passive voice, or they use figurative expression in different ways from English. This is important to keep in mind, especially when students come with already-developed academic versions of a non-English home language.

Using Figurative Expressions

Figurative expressions are often employed to describe abstract concepts. Figurative language includes metaphors, analogies, idioms, and other terms that use concrete and common ideas to describe abstract concepts and relationships. They are commonly found in works of literature, but they are also very prevalent (more than we think) in articles, letters, speeches, lectures, and conversations. Some texts are saturated with figurative terms.

It is important to keep an ear open for figurative terms that are used in our classes. The following are a few terms that have emerged in my classroom observations: *boils down to, sidestep the issue, read between the lines, on the right track, outweigh, the gory details, that answer doesn't hold water, a thin argument, dissemination of knowledge, read into, set the stage, zoom in and zoom out, a keen insight, crux of the matter, see eye to eye, on the same page, point of view,* and *dissect the article.* When we look closely, we see that figurative terms are much more common than we think, and many students, especially English learners, get tripped up by these expressions to the point where they do not grasp the messages.

One group of figurative expressions found throughout academic messages is clichés (also called dead metaphors). A cliché is an expression that has been used so much that the original idea or image isn't present in the mind of the speaker or writer. For example, users of *grasp the concept* or *shed light on the subject* typically do not think about grasping anything with a hand or shining lights. These expressions are automatic and woven into normal speech. In this book, there is a host of metaphorical clichés that you may not have noticed because they are so automatic to teachers (feel free to count them for me). Many of these terms were learned outside school. We should teach such terms and the thinking that supports them so that the use of figurative expressions eventually is automatic for students as well. Along the way, we must teach students when such expressions are appropriate to use and when they are not.

Many words have dual or multiple meanings, one being more common and concrete and the others being more academic, abstract, and technical. Examples are *defend, blossom, voice, vision, support, structure, claim, overhaul, root, dissect, assemble, frame, background, class, concrete, components, employ, explore, viewpoint, space, ignited, turncoat, catalyst, harbinger, reflect, key, pattern,* and *exhibit.* To use and understand these terms, students need to have mental flexibility and openness to connecting ideas to background knowledge, understanding the context, and making the leap to verbal or poetic interpretation. Notice the figurative descriptions of abstract ideas in the following paragraph from an educational article:

> As we stand on the threshold of a pluralist future, it will be important to hold a steady gaze on the belief that exemplary biliteracy programs will embody more than a focus on teaching the mental processes of reading. Rather, the potential is great for multi-pronged efforts with many layers of goals. In addition to nurturing the cognitions of reading, educators will be afforded the opportunity to use literacy lessons to better assist acculturation by helping various ethnic communities to understand, know, and respect the multiplicity of heritages. (Fitzgerald, Garcia, Jimenez, & Barrera, 2000, p. 520)

How many figurative and abstract terms did you find in the preceding paragraph? If you said "lots," good enough. There are many not-so-obvious figurative terms in the texts that students see and hear every day. For this reason, I cannot overemphasize the importance of teaching students to think figuratively in all content areas. Ultimately these abilities allow students to construct theories, explanations, and abstract concepts by expressing everyday language in specialized ways (Schleppegrell, 2004). When students become fluent in this type of thinking and start using the language for their own messages—and even inventing them on their own—then they will be able to perform better in academic settings.

Academic texts often use a variety of synonymous terms to say the same thing because authors want to avoid sounding overly repetitive. Readers must know the different synonyms and be able to figure out that they all mean the same thing. Many of these are new words for diverse learners. For example, I might read this: "The likelihood of an earthquake in that region is high. The chances of seismic activity have increased each year since 1950." Notice that *likelihood* and *chances* mean the same thing, as do *earthquake* and *seismic activity*. Readers must avoid getting sidetracked by a variety of synonyms as they construct the main ideas of a text.

Being Explicit for "Distant Audiences"

Being *explicit* means that the speaker or writer does extra things to explain and clarify concepts for listeners and readers who are not familiar with the topic. These listeners and readers are, in a sense, a "distant audience." Academic language helps the audience (listeners or readers) understand a message, even when they cannot interact with the speaker or writer. Most written texts, for example, are written by authors many miles and years apart from their readers. The authors write the books for a variety of distant audiences with wide ranges of backgrounds and knowledge. They need to be explicit, explaining as they go, to help as many readers as possible understand as clearly as possible. In other words, they cannot assume large amounts of shared background knowledge.

Students need to learn to speak and write using explicit language. This is difficult, though, when the audience is made up of other students who also studied the topic and the teacher who taught it. In one study, for example, the fifth-grade students were more likely to use explicit language (i.e., academic language) in their utterances when they were communicating to an authentic audience of people who had not shared the same classroom experiences (Bartolomé, 1998). We need to keep in mind that the more time that speakers spend together communicating about common experiences, the more meaning they tend to take for granted. One solution to the "too much in common" issue is to have outside people form the audience for presentations. This may take the form of writing letters, making reports to city boards, and presenting to parents, community members, and other students, teachers, and staff in the school. This outside audience forces students to be more explicit and, with proper questions by the audience, trains them over time to figure out what needs to be explicit.

Many mainstream students have had experience at home with making messages explicit. I know parents whose children put on skits that they have written and answer questions at the dinner table that sound like oral presentations. The parents ask students to elaborate on their answers, even though the parents know what the children will say. Nonmainstream students can lack this extra home practice with explicit communication because they use language predominantly for interpersonal and practical purposes. And some students know how to make their messages more explicit; they just don't always know when or why they need to do so or what they should clarify. When we ourselves have a clearer idea of what we mean by *explicit* and the specifics of what we want from students, we can better train them. Much of this we already do, as in the following example from a fourth-grade class:

1. *Lilia:*   He wanted to fight for freedom.
2. *Teacher:*   Who?

3. *Lilia:*   That guy on the horse in the book I read.
4. *Teacher:*   I haven't read the book. Can you explain?

Explicit academic messages avoid the use of vague referents, confusing pronouns, and isolated deictic (pointer) terms such as *this* and *that*. For example, if a student says, "I think she did that because she knew he was going to be there, not because she believed what they said," a teacher would likely require more explanation of who *she* was, what *she* did, who *he* was, where *there* was, and what *they* said—even though the other students who read the book might have understood the statement.

School language should leave little room for misinterpretation (Schleppegrell, 2004). Meanings of words and clauses must be clear. For example, if *this* is used to start a sentence, it should be followed by a word that refers to something specific in the previous sentence: *The scientist finally found a way to identify the correct enzyme. This discovery changed the way we look at the disease.* Thus, we must continually seek to train students to be extra aware of what their audience needs to know, which usually means training them in being hyperclear as they talk and write.

Remaining Detached from the Message

The speaker or writer of academic messages is often detached from the message; that is, the person does not use many feelings, opinions, or personal stories. Instead, logical reasons and evidence are emphasized (Valdés, 2004). The message needs to hold up its own weight and not be overly connected to the person communicating it. This detachment, though, is particularly challenging in upper elementary classrooms and intermediate levels of English language development, when students are transitioning from writing and speaking tasks that tend to emphasize personal accounts and connections to tasks that are more expository, more scientific, and less personalized.

Supporting Points with Evidence

Academic talking and writing require an acceptable amount and quality of evidence, examples, or data to back up one's positions and opinions. *Acceptable amount* and *quality,* of course, are subjective terms that will vary among experts and teachers of a discipline. Therefore, as discussed in chapter 1, we need to thoroughly understand the types of supporting information that experts in each content area value. We need to discuss with students not only the need for supporting evidence but also what makes some information more supportive than information. For example, using data from certain websites or newspapers is not sufficient in many fields. We must model and apprentice students to always have the "How can I best support my claims?" mentality as they talk and write.

Conveying Nuances of Meaning with Modals

Starting with basic verbs, an academic speaker or writer then modifies that verb or attaches other auxiliary or modal verbs to change the meaning. Modal verbs, for example, combine with "regular" verbs to convey nuances in meaning—for example, *The people could look for shelter elsewhere.* Without the modal *could*, the sentence meaning would change. Other modals are *would, can, will, shall, might, may, must, should,* and *ought to.* Speakers and writers use these to convey such nuances in meaning as intent, obligation, ability, probability, permission, possibility, and conditionality. English learners often "have trouble sorting out the subtle shades of meaning conveyed by modal verbs and may deliver a stronger or weaker message than intended" (Coelho, 2004, p. 78).

The important modal *would* is often used in conditional statements. Conditional statements (*If . . . would, If . . . then*) allow a student to consider situations beyond personal experience through the use of predictions, cause-and-effect inferences, and hypotheses. Such hypotheses give students a chance to visualize and generate logical but yet unproven connections between ideas. Most students probably learned if-then clauses early on at home (e.g., "If you touch that, then you'll be in trouble"). Students then expand its basic meaning to meet school demands.

Of course, this is a very important skill in life and school, including the following content areas:

- *For the scientific method:* "If I were to add this to the mixture, what would happen?" "If we cool this solution, then will it form a precipitate?"

- *For alternate possibilities in history:* "What would have happened if the Germans had repelled the invasion?" "If a firestorm hadn't destroyed the palace, then perhaps China would have colonized the world."

- *In narrative interpretations:* "How would you feel if you were in her shoes?" "If the character had been a woman, would the people have respected her less?"

- *In math problem solving:* "If we put a zero in the denominator, what would happen?" "Could we solve this if gravity were not a constant?"

A student who hears the conditional needs to be able to logically connect the *if* clause with the *would* clause by using cause-and-effect thinking. This is a difficult task for some English learners because the verb tense does not always match the meaning (Coelho, 2004). For example, *if they went to Spain* appears to be in the past tense, but it actually refers to something that has not happened or may never happen.

Softening the Message with Qualifiers

Qualifiers, or hedges, help an author show an awareness of his or her own limited knowledge and views about a topic, exceptions to his or her claims, and other perspectives, perceptions, ideas, and opinions about the topic. These devices are generally used to lessen the force or universality of a claim (Gee, 1996). (For example, I just used the word *generally*.) Qualifiers include such expressions as *most, perhaps, usually, seldom, often, likely, mostly, presumably, relatively, theoretically, suggest that, tend to, imply that, some, few, somewhat,* and *seems to*. These terms soften a message to avoid the use of all-or-nothing statements that might contain or imply such expressions as *all, none, always, never, is,* and *is not*. Hedges also help show a person's humility with respect to the topic.

Other qualifiers are found more often in spoken utterances: *just, mainly, fairly, sort of, pretty, I mean, maybe, kind of, well, around, more or less, see it as, believe that,* and *consider it to be*. Some of these terms, though, are not appropriate for academic writing, and we must help students come up with alternatives (while acknowledging their efforts to hedge). For example, one student in history wrote, "Well, *we thought* she was, *like,* a symbol of faith. She *seemed* pretty religious and *maybe* that's why they killed her." In addition to *we thought, seemed, pretty,* and *maybe,* even the infamous word *like* is used as a qualifier in this excerpt from this seventh grader.

Using Prosody for Emphasis

A large portion of oral communication depends on intonation and other prosodic cues (Celce-Murcia & Olshtain, 2000). The term *prosody* covers the many ways in which words and messages are spoken to emphasize or deemphasize certain parts of a sentence or paragraph. A common example in English is the rising intonation used in a question (*Do you understand?*). Other prosodic strategies include changing loudness and pitch, stressing syllables and words within a sentence, changing the length of words and syllables, speeding up and slowing down, and pausing for punctuation and syntax.

As a quick example, read excerpt A with an emphasis on the words in bold and monitor your comprehension. Then read excerpt B and underline the words that you would emphasize while reading aloud to a class.

> A: Native English **speakers** do not **decode** the spoken **stream** one word at a **time**, from left to right in a sequential **fashion**. Instead, "the stressed **syllable** is picked out of the **speech** stream and is used to **search** the mental **lexicon**. Feasible **candidates** are selected from the mental **lexicon** on the basis of this **syllable**, and are **then** judged by how well they **fit** with the un**stressed** syllables that **appear** to their left and right." (Dalton & Seidlhoffer, 1994, p. 39)

> B: Native English speakers do not decode the spoken stream one word at a time, from left to right in a sequential fashion. Instead, "the stressed syllable is picked out of the speech stream and is used to search the mental lexicon. Feasible candidates are selected from the mental lexicon on the basis of this syllable, and are then judged by how well they fit with the unstressed syllables that appear to their left and right." (Dalton & Seidlhoffer, 1994, p. 39)

Now see how well the terms that you underlined in excerpt B match up with the terms in bold in excerpt C:

> C: **Native** English speakers do not decode the **spoken** stream **one** word at a time, from **left** to **right** in a sequential fashion. **Instead,** "the **stressed** syllable is picked **out** of the speech stream and is used to **search** the mental lexicon. **Feasible** candidates are **selected** from the **mental** lexicon on the **basis** of this syllable, and are then **judged** by how well they fit with the un**stressed** syllables that appear to their left and right." (Dalton & Seidlhoffer, 1994, p. 39)

Incorrect stress (as you likely experienced in excerpt A) can often lead to breakdowns in communication. Try reading excerpt B without any prosody, in a monotone at a constant pace. You will notice that the lack of prosody can make a big difference. You can try this type of activity with a text in your class.

Prosody is particularly challenging for English learners because other languages can have very different prosodic features from those of English. Students must learn the intonation patterns of longer, more complex sentences. For example, they must learn that subordinate clauses often receive less emphasis and are said more quickly than the main clauses of a sentence. Moreover, diverse learners must learn not only the new ways of using prosody in social settings but also its different uses in academic settings. Sarah Michaels (1986), for example, found that the intonation patterns and pace that students used when they shared in class differed from those used in casual conversation.

We use prosodic cues automatically when we listen and speak, and even when we read and write. For example, as you read this paragraph, you emphasize certain words in your mind—as I did when I wrote it. Your prosody while reading and my prosody while writing are likely very similar. When it is not similar, however, as is the case with many diverse listeners or readers of academic texts, communication suffers.

FEATURES OF ACADEMIC GRAMMAR

Grammar is the broad set of rules that govern language in a community. One of grammar's subfields is syntax, which is the set of conventions for putting words and phrases together into sentences. (The term *grammar* in this book refers mostly to syntax.) Well-developed grammatical competence can show others that the student is a proficient speaker and writer who is capable of understanding, expressing, and participating in community decisions (Delpit, 1995). A lack of grammatical development can significantly hinder students in future years of schooling (Dutro & Moran, 2003). Following are several grammatical features that separate academic language from everyday language.

Long Sentences

Unlike informal language, which uses a variety of linking strategies such as intonation and pace to create a coherent message, academic texts tend to be complex in their organization of clauses and phrases. Each message that we read or hear is essentially a series of clauses strung together. Each clause, which is a chunk of words, represents relationships, experiences, or ideas. Each links with previous and subsequent clauses, building up the intended message (Schleppe-grell, 2004). Of course, the clauses, their links, and their presentation all depend on the people involved, the purposes, and the setting.

Long sentences often have multiple clauses. Consider this sentence from the Federalist Papers:

> This idea admits not of precise demonstration, because there is no rule by which we can measure the momentum of civil power necessary to the government of any given number of individuals; but when we consider that the island of Britain, nearly commensurate with each of the supposed confederacies, contains about eight millions of people, and when we reflect upon the degree of authority required to direct the passions of so large a society to the public good, we shall see no reason to doubt that the like portion of power would be sufficient to perform the same task in a society far more numerous. (Hamilton, 1787)

Notice the length of the sentence, the embedded clauses between commas, and the overall cognitive load the reader must bear to process it. Long sentences demand that readers or listeners fit more words and thinking into their heads. Students must be trained to quickly and automatically break down long sentences and process and interpret the clauses. They must recognize what is subordinate and, more important, what is the main point of the sentence in the main clause. (Chapter 7 offers strategies on how to teach students to read long sentences.) Subordination is a hard-to-use tool because it represents hierarchical relationships between clauses. For example, in the sentence *Although several precautions were taken, the key was lost,* the first clause modifies the second, more important clause. Extra clauses, of course, mean extra things to think about in one sentence. Many subordinate clauses begin with words such as *although, because, before, if,* and *despite.* We can train students to notice these words and organize their thoughts accordingly. (The use of embedded clauses is discussed in more depth in chapter 8.)

Authors of academic texts also make sentences longer (and make us hold more in our heads) with lists. The most difficult passages are lists of abstract items for which each item has multiple words. In the following example, notice the passive voice, the long list of abstract subjects, the abstract verb, and the abstract object—all in one sentence: *The transformation was complicated by their lack of understanding of the political ramifications of the law, the recent clashes with the ruling party, and the demands of those oppressed by the old regime.* Often when "academicness" rains, it pours.

Passive Voice

In academic talk and writing, a common verb structure is the passive voice, which is used when the focus is on the objects or persons affected by the action rather than on the actor. Academic English, for example, uses passive voice much more than everyday English uses it. This is particularly true in science (Lemke, 1990) and mathematics (Spanos, Rhodes, Dale, & Crandall, 1988). Passive voice tends to place more emphasis on the object than the subject. Often the subject is never named. For example, in *The radius is then plugged into the formula for the area of a circle,* there is no subject. Notice how normal and straightforward this seems to us; we automatically know that the radius is a number that is manipulated by someone—anyone—who knows how to do the math.

A challenge for many English learners is that their languages have no passive voice. Learners may confuse the actor with the object of the action. For example, a learner might think that the cells are doing the removing in the clause *the cells are then removed from the slide.* And even when students do begin to understand passive construction, it takes more time for them to be able to use it in speech and writing (Coelho, 2004).

Nominalization

Another academic grammar tool is *nominalization,* which means turning verbs or adjectives into noun phrases that then become the subject or object in a clause or phrase. The purpose of nominalization is to condense what can often amount to lengthy explanations into a few words. Examples include *revolution, refraction, personification, cancellation,* and *renunciation.* Another example is the word *nominalization* itself. (It is a nominalization of the process of nominalizing.) Nominalization essentially "allows a lot of information to be packed into the Theme/Subject position which otherwise needs a whole clause to express" (Harvey, 1993, p. 36).

What this means for students is that they need to process more ideas per clause, often with increased levels of abstraction. For example, the sentence

The condemnation of dissenting perspectives led to revolution contains three abstract nominalizations: *condemnation, perspectives,* and *revolution.* Students must fit the complex meanings of all three words into their heads, while also putting them together in the sentence. Nominalization is one of many ways in which academic language describes abstract processes, concepts, and relationships between ideas that are too complex or abstract to show with images or movement (Dutro & Moran, 2003). And without extra support and practice in compact language such as nominalization, many students fail to comprehend the main points of challenging texts, especially students who lack practice with mainstream English (Snow & Brinton, 1997).

For example, a common practice is to begin a sentence with a condensed description of information from the previous sentence. This compressed information usually takes the form of a noun phrase through the process of nominalization—for example, *The virus adapted to survive outside the body. This mutation allowed it to be passed on by casual contact.* The word *mutation* is a nominalized version of the action in the preceding sentence. Academic texts condense sentences, paragraphs, and even chapters, requiring readers not only to understand what was condensed but also to quickly incorporate it into background knowledge in order to then use it as the subject of the current argument. The main purpose of nominalization in many scientific texts is to develop chains of reasoning that lead clearly from one conceptual step to the next (Schleppegrell, 2004).

Nominalizations challenge the reader to keep track of multiple abstract relationships throughout an academic text. The referents *this* and *these* are often followed by a nominalization and more information about it in the rest of the sentence. This cycle builds as each new idea is condensed into a nominalization. (I just did this with *This cycle.*) Consider the following examples of the use of referents, which are italicized:

> Many alloys are made by melting metals and mixing them together in carefully measured amounts. Since the beginning of the Bronze Age, *this technique* has been used to make copper alloys. Some modern alloys are made by mixing the elements as powders and then heating them under high pressure. *This process* uses less energy because the metals blend at lower temperatures. (Padilla, 2001, p. 644)

Condensed Complex Messages

Because complex texts pack a lot of meaning into a word or phrase, students must process more ideas per sentence. This technique allows proficient readers to free up thinking space for processing the main points that the author or speaker intends to communicate. For example, if my listeners and I already know what *photosynthesis* means, I can use the word without describing each of its component processes. Embedded clauses help the speaker or writer save space. Yet nonproficient readers, having to think about and figure out much more in each long sentence, don't always have the "free space" to focus on the main points. In other words, readers of academic texts must bear an increased cognitive load.

Despite condensing, which should make texts shorter, academic texts tend to have longer sentences because of the extensive use of clauses. Students must learn to "engage in increasingly advanced literacy tasks in which language is typically structured in ways which condense information through lexical choices and clause structures that are different from the way language is typically used in ordinary contexts of everyday interaction" (Schleppegrell, 2004, p. 4).

In other words, students must learn new ways of understanding the world, organizing its meanings, and communicating them to a wide range of people.

One form of condensation, very familiar to teachers, is the use of acronyms. Acronyms, which are found more often in workplace settings, condense longer phrases into one nonsense word or letter set made up of initial letters of a phrase or title. The words in the phrase or title are often complex and abstract as well. Consider the acronym SDAIE, which stands for *specially designed academic instruction in English*. The meanings of *specially* and *academic* are complex and subject to wide interpretation, yet many people widely use the term SDAIE, assuming a shared understanding. Other acronyms are ELD (English Language Development), IEP (Individualized Education Program), IRS (Internal Revenue Service), and FEP (Fluent English Proficient).

Clarity

A primary goal of academic language is clarity. Striving for clarity consists of making an academic message as efficient and effective as possible for the intended audience. Clarity, of course, is subjective and varies across settings and people. We need to pay close attention to all that makes messages clear in our disciplines. (Chapter 4 has several ideas for achieving clarity in different disciplines.)

Students can try to be overly academic, but this is often at the expense of clarity. We all have read papers and books whose authors have overcomplicated the language of a text or speech to the point of sounding pretentious or stilted. They use sentences that are too long, they use too many clauses and "SAT words," and the message ends up being too concentrated or muddy to make sense to the reader or listener. Therefore, although most of us would rather have students err on the side of being overly academic, we must take care to model and apprentice them in the use of the clearest language possible to get messages across in academic settings.

CONCLUSION

Academic language builds from a foundation of home and community communication experiences and then branches out into more specialized forms of language. It is much more complicated than a set of big and bold vocabulary words that students must learn for Friday's quiz. Students need to learn not only the key words but also how to explain and link these terms together with more subtle expressions and grammar. Academic language serves several broad and overlapping functions: to describe complexity, higher-order thinking, and abstraction. To carry out these functions, authors and speakers use a variety of features that work together to clarify a message. For example, in just one sentence, you might see figurative expressions, dependent clauses, passive voice, and nominalization.

Building up students' mental muscles to quickly and automatically handle these features is a primary responsibility that we have as teachers. But academic language for most teachers *is* our everyday language, which makes it hard to notice—and therefore hard to teach. As we teach and interact with students, we must work on two dimensions: our own language and communication behaviors and those of our students. We explore this dual emphasis in the next chapter.

CHAPTER REFLECTIONS

- What are the complex and abstract concepts in your content area?
- What are some of the common academic language features in your content-area texts and assessments?

- What are the main content-area thinking skills needed in your discipline?

- How do you prepare students to use the language that you want to hear and read?

References

Achieve. (2013). *Next Generation Science Standards*. Retrieved from http://www .nextgenscience.org/search-standards-dci

Bartolomé, L. I. (1998). *The misteaching of academic discourses: The politics of language in the classroom*. Boulder, CO: Westview Press.

Beck, I., McKeown, M., & Kucan, L. (2013). *Bringing words to life: Robust vocabulary instruction*. New York, NY: Guilford Press.

Bloom, B. S., Engelhar, M. D., Furst, E. J., Hill, W. H., & Krathwohl, D. R. (Eds.). (1956). *Taxonomy of educational objectives: The classification of educational goals. Handbook I: Cognitive domain*. New York, NY: David McKay.

Celce-Murcia, M., & Olshtain, E. (2000). *Discourse and context in language teaching: A guide for language teachers*. Cambridge, UK: Cambridge University Press.

Coelho, E. (2004). *Adding English: A guide to teaching multilingual classrooms*. Toronto, Canada: Pippin.

Cummins, J. (1979). Cognitive/academic language proficiency, linguistic interdependence, the optimum age question, and some other matters. *Working Papers on Bilingualism*, *19*(1), 121–129.

Dalton, C., & Seidlhoffer, B. (1994). *Pronunciation*. New York, NY: Oxford University Press.

Delpit, L. (1995). *Other people's children: Cultural conflict in the classroom*. New York, NY: New Press.

Dewey, J. (1997). *How we think*. Boston, MA: D. C. Heath. (Original work published 1910)

Díaz-Rico, L., & Weed, K. (2002). *The crosscultural, language, and academic development handbook: A complete K–12 reference guide*. Boston, MA: Allyn & Bacon.

Dutro, S., & Moran, C. (2003). Rethinking English language instruction: An architectural approach. In G. García (Ed.), *English learners: Reaching the highest level of English literacy* (pp. 227–258). Newark, DE: International Reading Association.

EngageNY. (2013). *Common Core toolkit.* Retrieved from http://www.engageny .org/resource/common-core-toolkit

Facione, P. (1990). *Critical thinking: A statement of expert consensus for purposes of educational assessment and instruction.* Millbrae, CA: California Academic Press.

Fitzgerald, J., Garcia, G., Jimenez, R., & Barrera, R. (2000). How will bilingual/ESL programs in literacy change in the next millennium? *Reading Research Quarterly, 35,* 520–523.

Gee, J. (1996). *Social linguistics and literacies: Ideology in discourses.* London, UK: Routledge Falmer.

Hamilton, A. (1787). Number 13: Advantage of the Union in respect to economy in government. *The Federalist Papers.* Retrieved from www.foundingfathers .info/federalistpapers/fedindex.htm

Harvey, N. (1993). Text analysis for specific purposes. *Prospect, 8*(3), 25–41.

Lemke, J. (1990). *Talking science: Language, learning, and values.* New York, NY: Ablex.

McLaughlin, B., August, D., Snow, C., Carlo, M., Dressler, C., White, C., . . . & Lippman, D. (2000, April). *Vocabulary improvement in English Language learners: An intervention study.* Symposium conducted by the Office of Bilingual Education and Minority Languages Affairs, Washington, DC.

Michaels, S. (1986). Narrative presentations: An oral preparation for literacy with first graders. In J. Cook-Gumperz (Ed.), *The social construction of literacy* (pp. 94–116). Cambridge, UK: Cambridge University Press.

Moats, L. (2000). *Speech to print: Language essentials for teachers.* Baltimore, MD: Brookes.

National Governors Association Center for Best Practices. (2010). *Common Core State Standards.* Washington, DC: Council of Chief State School Officers.

Padilla, M. (2001). *Focus on physical science.* Needham, MA: Prentice Hall.

Scarcella, R. (2003). *Academic English: A conceptual framework* (Technical Report No. 2003–1). University of California Linguistic Minority Research Institute.

Schleppegrell, M. J. (2004). *The language of schooling: A functional linguistics approach.* Mahwah, NJ: Erlbaum.

Snow, M., & Brinton, D. (1997). *The content-based classroom: Perspectives on integrating language and content.* New York, NY: Longman.

Spanos, G., Rhodes, N., Dale, T., & Crandall, J. (1988). Linguistic features of mathematical problem solving: Insights and applications. In R. R. Cocking & J. P. Mestre (Eds.), *Linguistic and cultural influences on mathematics learning* (pp. 221–240). Hillsdale, NJ: Erlbaum.

Stahl, S. (1999). *Vocabulary development: From reading research to practice.* Cambridge, MA: Brookline Books.

Swartz, R. (2001). Infusing critical and creative thinking into content instruction. In A. L. Costa (Ed.), *Developing minds: A resource book for teaching thinking* (pp. 266–274). Alexandria, VA: Association for Supervision and Curriculum Development.

Valdés, G. (2001). *Learning and not learning English: Latino students in American schools.* New York, NY: Teachers College Press.

Valdés, G. (2004). Between support and marginalisation: The development of academic language in linguistic minority children. *Bilingual Education and Bilingualism, 7*(2 & 3), 102–132.

Valdez-Pierce, L., & O'Malley, J. M. (1992). *Performance and portfolio assessment for language minority students.* Washington, DC: National Clearinghouse for Bilingual Education.

Walqui, A., & van Lier, L. (2010). *Scaffolding the academic success of adolescent English language learners: A pedagogy of promise.* San Francisco, CA: WestEd.

Wiggins, G., & McTighe, J. (1998). *Understanding by design.* Alexandria, VA: Association for Supervision and Curriculum Development.

Chapter 3

Cultivating Academic Language Acquisition

Academic language doesn't grow on trees.

As the opening quotation suggests, fostering language growth requires hard work and patience. We cannot just do business as usual and expect the thinking skills and language to magically sink in. For our diverse students especially, we must do more than what we normally do with our lessons and interactions in order to accelerate their academic development. Chapter 2 gave a little more background on what academic language is; this chapter looks at how it is learned and cultivated. After looking at several language acquisition principles (input, output, negotiation of meaning), the chapter describes how to interact with students in ways that model and support the acquisition of academic language for the new standards.

LANGUAGE ACQUISITION BASICS

Until the early 1960s, language learning was predominantly viewed as a behavioral process in which words and rules were learned and then pieced together through stimulus and response. Then Noam Chomsky's ideas (1965) began to undo the behaviorist claims that language was learned solely by reinforcement. Chomsky (1980) argued that the brain has innate abilities to take in and process language, implicitly learning the language's rules and features.

Processing Input

Stephen Krashen (1985), building on Chomsky's ideas, argued that a second language is acquired much like a first language—by hearing or reading understandable pieces of it in authentic contexts, which he called *comprehensible input*. He argued that people acquire other languages in much the same way that children acquire a first language: by listening to it and being exposed to increasingly challenging vocabulary and grammar. For example, an Italian might say to me, "*Loro sono molto stanchi*" ("They are very tired"), as he points to a group of people and makes a tired expression on his face. He uses a new word (*stanchi*), but helps me understand it with contextual clues. As I see new forms of language multiple times, my brain begins to hold on to it.

Of course, making input understandable is more difficult to do when describing abstract and complex concepts like those taught in school. The input that students receive can often be incomprehensible due to the newness of the concept, the language, or both.

One of the most powerful types of input comes from reading challenging texts (Wong Fillmore & Fillmore, 2011). The Common Core State Standards, in fact, place a heightened emphasis on preparing students to read complex texts at grade level (National Governors Association Center for Best Practices, 2010). The standards emphasize focusing on the text itself, asking text-dependent questions to zoom in on the text's evidence and author's purpose for writing it. Of course, using grade-level texts with English learners requires extra scaffolding and formative assessment, topics that are further discussed in chapter 7.

Producing Language

Producing language (output) pushes learners to process the new language at deeper and more lasting levels than just listening to it (Swain, 1995). Swain noted situations in which students needed to challenge themselves to take the needs of listeners into account, focusing not only on what they are saying but also on how they are saying it. Producing output made a positive difference. In most of the classrooms studied, students needed more opportunities to produce longer stretches of academic talk for the positive effects to take place. These positive effects can happen when the overall linguistic goal of a group task requires learners to produce more complex language than they would use on their own. (See chapters 5 and 6 for ideas that scaffold students' academic talk.)

Studies have pointed out the significant differences between input and output, also arguing that just taking in language is not enough for acquisition (Carroll, Tanenhaus, & Bever, 1978). A listener focuses on meaning, which is recoded into the brain in a simpler syntactic form than the original message. Such recoding can later be expanded by the listener in the form of output, but will likely not be in the same form as the original input. Reading is a similar process. For example, you are probably summarizing the gist of this paragraph right now. Yet if you were to reproduce it five minutes from now, you would not do so with the same vocabulary and grammatical structure (if you remember it at all).

Thus, a fundamental difference between listening and speaking (and between reading and writing) is that a listener (or reader) can bypass much of the grammar by focusing on meaning (Rivers, 1994). Speaking and writing, in contrast, require students to develop control of grammar and syntax enough to clearly reexpress the message to a particular audience in proper ways. A simple illustration might be riding in a friend's car to a new destination (receiving language) versus driving there on your own (producing language). When someone else drives, you can enjoy the scenery and still get to where you want to be. When you drive (produce language), you need to focus on directions. This involves more work and stress, but you are more likely to remember the way the next time you go there.

Negotiating Meaning

Long (1983), after studying conversations at length, argued that negotiation of meaning is a critical aspect of language acquisition. Negotiation of meaning is the process by which participants come to a mutual understanding. This is what we do when we have different ideas of what words mean during communication. *Negotiating meaning* means using verbal and nonverbal strategies to interpret, express, expand, and refine the many ideas, thoughts, and subtle variations in meaning in a conversation (Hernandez, 2003). These are the things we do so that we are "on the same page," as chapter 1 described. For classroom purposes, several important negotiation strategies that we can develop are comprehension checks, confirmation checks, and self-repetitions (Long, 1987).

Clarification checks are little words and phrases that speakers interject in their messages, such as *Right? Got it? Clear? Understand?* These allow the listener to ask questions about meanings of words and concepts during the message rather than after, when it is too late. Listeners make confirmation checks when they interject and paraphrase what the speaker has said to confirm comprehension: *So what you mean is . . . In other words . . . I think I get it. It's when . . . Are you saying that . . . ?* Self-repetitions are statements by speakers that repeat a message to emphasize certain parts and make sure the message is understood. Because one-way communication tasks (e.g., lectures) cannot help students become skilled at modifying their messages to make them more understandable, two-way tasks tend to be more effective.

Throughout the rest of this chapter, there are boxes with featured teacher comments. This is a way to help teachers build what I call "comment habits" that encourage students to talk, clarify what they say, listen to others, and build on what others say. These are little comments that can make a big difference in the cultivation of democratic discussion processes in a classroom. Of course, these responses are also small symbols and extensions of who we are and how we think. They show students how to relate to other people such that students might also appropriate these ways of treating others when they are in positions of authority and "teachership." (Additional in-depth analyses of similar comments are found in Johnston, 2004.)

Modeling Academic Language

Academic language has many features that make it like a new language for many students. English learners in particular need to learn new words for new concepts, new meanings for known words, and new grammar patterns that are valued in school (Scarcella, 2003). Not long after learning the everyday concrete meanings of words like *slope, underground, run, base,* and *slings and arrows,* students are required to learn their second and even third meanings. For this reason, they need extensive modeling of academic language.

Just using academic language, which we teachers tend to do automatically in class, can be a form of modeling, but it is not enough. We need to do extra things to highlight and build "extra-important language." This is especially important for second-language learners, for whom there is much more new language than for their mainstream peers. An analogy might be a novice birdwatcher going birdwatching with several experienced birdwatchers. The experienced bird-watchers know which birds are common to the area and do not take note of them. For the novices, most of the birds are new, and they have difficulty picking out the uncommon birds for the area. As they take time and energy to note the many common birds, they may miss the important ones. In school, mainstream speakers get to focus on fewer new terms and grammatical structures, while English learners, for example, need to filter through many more new words and terms, often not sure what is "new" for that day.

Three forms of language modeling are found in the following transcript from an eighth-grade science class. See if you can pick them out. (In the dialogue excerpts throughout this book, students A, B, C, and D are mainstream English speakers; students E, F, G, and H tend to be intermediate-level or early-advanced-level English learners and speakers of nonmainstream vernacular versions of English.)

1. *Teacher:* What does the third prong of an electric plug do? It conducts electric current from . . .
2. *Student E:* From us electro . . . shocked.
3. *Teacher:* Yes, it helps prevent us from getting electrocuted, true. But electrocution happens when . . .
4. *Student F:* When you touch a wire, the electricity goes through you.
5. *Teacher:* Yes, we might say a person creates a short circuit *through which* the electric current flows. Let's say it . . .
6. *All:* A person creates a short circuit *through which* the electric current flows.
7. *Teacher:* And human cells have ions, which make our bodies have low resistance to electric current. Who in here has low resistance to electric current? *(most hands are raised)* What about you? Do you have low resistance to electric current?
8. *Student E:* I guess.

9. *Teacher:*   But the third prong can help you! The third prong has even lower resistance, so the electric current flows through it into the ground instead of through you!

The teacher used three forms of modeling in this excerpt: sentence starters, pace and emphasis, and teacher repetition. Sentence starters are most commonly used to help students write, but they are also used to guide students in clarifying what they are trying to say. In lines 1 and 3, the teacher used sentence starters as model language prompts. Student E didn't reply with the starter and gave a related answer that the teacher then used to try to get back to the original line of concept. (This synthesizing and redirecting of tangential comments is one of the tips for leading classroom discussions found in chapter 5.)

In line 5, the teacher used pace and emphasis to model the sentence by saying it slowly and loudly, and then explicitly asked students to repeat the line in order to hear them say the words in unison in line 6. She was especially focused on teaching the prepositional phrase *through which,* which isn't commonly used in everyday speech. Finally, in line 7, the teacher repeated the phrase *low resistance to electric current* three times to help it stick in the students' heads. She effectively wrapped up the conversation by getting back to the original idea of the third prong.

Table 3.1 borrows ideas from chapter 2 to categorize thinking skills and academic communication strategies to model. As we get to know students' strengths and weaknesses, we can identify what we need to teach. We can choose two or three skills from each column in table 3.1 to work on over a period of time. Chapter 9 goes into detail on how to use these in assessments.

Modeling with Think-Alouds

A powerful way to model the language used by experts in a discipline is to think aloud. We demonstrate a think-aloud (Davey, 1983; Farr, 2001) when we stop occasionally to model our thinking processes aloud to students while we do something academic. For example, we might think aloud when reading to students, solving a problem, planning a lab, writing up a lab, watching a video, or creating a chart. The key is to give students a window into expert thinking (more expert than theirs) and the language used to describe it. We model what it

Table 3.1 Academic Language Skills to Model, Teach, and Assess

Describing Complexity, Abstractness, and Thinking	Academic Vocabulary and Grammar	Audience
Clearly describes complex relationships	Uses new vocabulary	Makes language explicit for distant audiences
Uses language to explore and question abstract ideas (e.g., freedom, justice, truth, science)	Uses qualifiers and hedges to soften message	Matches language to audience and purpose
Can persuade others with language	Keeps thoughts ordered, logical, and consistent	Varies pitch, tone, and pace of speech
Can generalize, apply, and hypothesize	Uses such connectives as *although, despite, so that,* and *on the other hand*	Focuses on deeper meanings rather than on surface features of language
Summarizes and synthesizes group ideas	Uses subordinate clauses	Reads the audience and self-corrects if there is confusion
Encourages analysis of issues	Distinguishes and defines complex terms	Elicits opinions, ideas, and responses from others (e.g., asks questions of the group)
Describes different perspectives	Uses academic idioms, analogies, and metaphors	
Distinguishes between relevance and irrelevance	Reacts to inappropriate language	
Supports opinions and assertions with evidence		
Makes links between ideas, texts, and life		

means to be, think like, talk like, read like, write like, and act like a content expert. Students become our apprentices, whether we are mathematicians, biologists, authors, literary critics, historians, artists, or physicists. We give students the inside scoop on what the discipline's language looks and sounds like, providing them with the various codes used in the discipline.

Here is an example of a teacher modeling the process of solving a problem from an eighth-grade math test.

> ## TEACHER EXAMPLE: MODELING PROBLEM SOLVING
>
> "Okay, the problem says that a rectangle is three times as long as it is wide. This means that if the width is one finger long, then the length is three fingers long. Then it asks what the ratio of the width to the perimeter is. Okay, I will draw it first. For the long side I will put 3, and for the width I will put *w*. Now they didn't give me measurements, so I can't figure out an actual perimeter and then use it. They want a ratio, like a fraction. But ratios have two numbers with a colon in between. Three to one would be too easy and that would be, hmmm, the ratio of the length to the width, I think. They want the width to the perimeter. So for perimeter, I sum up all the sides. I get $w + w + 3w + 3w$. That's $8w$. So I put w on one side and $8w$ on the other, I think. But I don't want variables in the ratio, so just like a fraction's denominator and numerator, I cancel them out. I am left with 1:8."

Notice the many content-area terms (*perimeter, ratio, measurements, fraction, variables, denominator, numerator*) and general academic terms (*as long as, this means, if-then, it asks, will put 3w, actual, would be too easy, on one side, they want, I don't want, cancel, left with*), which are all used together to describe the problem-solving process. This teacher also made the language much more understandable by using extra intonation and movement. As students begin to comprehend this language of the discipline's thinking, they begin to acquire it in bits and pieces. Their brains soak in the new terms to make sense of new ideas as they listen to and watch our modeling.

Scaffolding Thinking and Language

Modeling is not enough, of course. Students need to work with academic language in supported ways to acquire it effectively. Psychologist Lev Vygotsky (1978) pointed out that children internalize the thinking and language patterns of more proficient speakers. This happens when new language and concepts are just above the student's current levels of proficiency. Vygotsky called this concept the *zone of proximal development* (ZPD). His insights provided a theoretical foundation for Jerome Bruner's studies of child language development (1986). In his research on mothers and their children, Bruner described their shared learning experiences using the term *scaffolding*, which has since become a popular metaphor for an apprenticeship-style support of learning.

Scaffolding provides high levels of language support in the early stages of learning and gradually takes the support away so that the learner develops independence. The trick is in providing the proper amount of support—not too much and not too little—all along the way. This is also known as the *gradual release of responsibility* because the learner gradually takes on more responsibility and independence.

Think of scaffolding as coaching a sport. A coach models, scaffolds, and provides feedback to players as they practice and even as they play games. He or she explicitly explains strategies and techniques, and then organizes more realistic practice sessions to prepare for games. As a basketball coach might model a shot, we teachers must model our thinking and language to help students take on new academic frames of reference. If we notice that students fail to understand or use a skill, we increase our support. And when we see that students are developing competence, we withdraw our guidance. We work alongside students as they hone their language skills every day of the very long learning season.

Gestures and Facial Expressions

Gestures, facial expressions, and other nonverbal movements are communication strategies that help emphasize and clarify difficult language. Research and experience show that strategies that go beyond the verbal are helpful for lasting learning (Druyan, 1997; Marzano, Pickering, & Pollock, 2001). Movements make academic communication more animated, similar to social interactions. They also help students form images in their minds of the abstract concepts being communicated. I once observed a science teacher who used the term *perspective* and got up on a table to look down with both hands around her eyes, forming binoculars. A seventh-grade history teacher often emphasized the words *however* and *yet* as she moved one hand in an arc in the opposite direction. She performed this action every time she used terms that contradicted a previous point. She did this in the following dialogue.

Teacher: The Romans continued to persecute the Christians. However *(hand motion),* they stuck to their beliefs. So what happened?

Student E: They got killed.

Teacher: Yes, many were killed and became martyrs. Nevertheless *(hand motion),* what happened?

Student A: More people became Christians.

Students should also do the movements, gestures, and facial expressions to reinforce for them the basic academic language devices in a text that preserve its cohesion and coherence. These small but important pieces of language are similar to major direction markers on a trail: if you miss one, you can easily get lost. For example, the better a student understands how the transition *nevertheless* makes a listener or reader expect a contradictory argument or example, the more effectively the student will maneuver through the text. Actions, like those described in table 3.2, can help.

You can create a wall chart like table 3.2 to help students keep track of the language and actions. As you notice key terms, ask students to come up with actions to help you fill in this chart throughout the year. Encourage students to use the terms in their writing. If they use a term too often in speech or in writing, tell them to refer to the chart for other options. Every so often, perform a quick check: say the words and see if students can do the motions, or do the motions and see if they can say the words. Tell them to avoid looking at the chart as you stand on the other side of the room.

Some gestures seem to be culturally bound and tend to confuse diverse learners. I watched one teacher use the term *pacify* and make a peace sign with her fingers.

Table 3.2 Academic Language Actions

Language	Action or Expression
For this reason, because of this, thus, hence, therefore	Hands make forward pushing motion.
And, furthermore, moreover, in addition	Hands make a rolling motion forward.
In conclusion, in essence	Both hands start with fingers spread, then close to make a ball.
For example, for instance, to illustrate, let's say	Put index finger at the tip of little finger on other hand.
On the other hand, nevertheless, on the contrary, then again, even though, despite, granted, of course, however, but, yet	Move hand, palm down in one direction and then make a 180-degree arc to palm up; walk one way and turn around; look at the hand that is out and then put out the other and look at it.
Similarly, likewise, in the same way	Put both hands up with crossed fingers.

Looking around the class, most of the mainstream students understood the gesture, yet the diverse students had quizzical looks on their faces. I asked them later about the gesture; they thought it meant the number 2. A sixth-grade science teacher acted out the word *erratically* by waving her arms and making a random sound. Later I asked several English learners what *erratically* meant, and only one out of four knew it. In another instance, a language arts teacher used the term *promise* when referring to a court oath and then made an X with her finger over her heart ("cross my heart and hope to die"). This gesture needed further explanation as well.

Linguistic Enabling

The overuse of scaffolding is what I call *linguistic enabling*. This happens when teachers use behaviors that do not push students to reach higher levels of learning and language development. In order to affirm student responses and to avoid placing unnecessary stress on students, teachers sometimes do two things: (1) they do not use enough academic language when they model and scaffold content-area thinking and doing, and (2) they too often accept oral and written responses that are not sufficiently academic in nature. These behaviors do not build the scaffolds high enough or gradually take them down, which prevents both the accelerated learning and gradual independence that we want to see.

Teachers enable for several possible reasons: they don't want to offend students or discourage their participation, they want to speed the class along and focus on content, or they simply lack awareness of the nonacademic nature of the responses. Enabling is easy to do, as we tend to focus on getting students to learn the content by any and all means. But language *is* content. We need to find the balance between just enough academic language and not too much, similar to Vygotsky's (1978) ZPD. We must always nudge students to higher levels of language and not be satisfied with content understanding that is displayed only with nonacademic language.

I have observed teachers (and myself) who have missed out on opportunities to challenge students to use more academic ways of expression, even when there was time to do so (e.g., with group and pair work or while writing). In the following discussion, which develops perspective taking and empathy in a history class, the teacher (in lines 3, 7, 10, 14) neglects to challenge students to produce more elaborated and academic responses:

1.	*Teacher:*	So do you think that Dante was popular with some of the people in Florence? You think he made friends?
2.	*Student E:*	No.
3.	*Teacher:*	Why don't you think he made friends? What did he write about?
4.	*Student E:*	Their sins.
5.	*Teacher:*	Yes, he wrote about real people and all the bad things they did. That's like me writing a book about Juan and all the bad things he has done and letting everyone read about it, whether true or not. Would you like that?
6.	*Student E:*	No.
7.	*Teacher:*	How might people feel in each place?
8.	*Student A:*	For paradise, it would be better than being in hell.
9.	*Student F:*	Freedom, or free? Love?
10.	*Teacher:*	Okay, keep going.
11.	*Student E:*	Safe?
12.	*Student B:*	In purgatory, scared? Maybe that's for inferno.
13.	*Student C:*	Sorrow? Humble?
14.	*Teacher:*	What do those mean in your life?

In line 5 the teacher did not ask student E (an intermediate-level English learner) to connect the writing about sins to Dante's lack of friends; rather, she does it for him. Then she did not ask him for reasons when he said no in line 6. The teacher responded, "Okay, keep going," in response to interesting ideas that student F offered in line 9. The teacher seemed primarily focused on getting the answers as quickly as possible. Then in line 14, the teacher prompted a mainstream English speaker to elaborate on her response. We must be careful not to rob our diverse students of the opportunities to think more deeply and respond academically, even when we think they will struggle to formulate their answers and even when we think we don't have the time. Such struggling leads to learning, especially when we are there to support their responses.

In the area of writing support, research shows that English learners and underperforming writers tend to be given easier, less academic, more personal writing assignments (Applebee, 1984). I have compared teacher responses to the writing of mainstream speakers with responses to the writing of English learners (Zwiers, 2005). For less proficient speakers, teachers provided far less thoughtful feedback on their comments and instead focused much more on mechanics. For the more proficient speakers, the teachers asked more probing questions, gave more positive comments, and used more elaboration phrases. This is highly problematic because the students who can benefit the most from more academic teacher responses are not getting them in many classrooms.

BUILDING HABITS OF CONNECTION

The process of scaffolding builds from what students already know and can do. We know that we must connect new learning to students' background knowledge, but when things get busy (and they do that first week of school), effective connecting is a struggle. And for diverse students, connecting learning can be even more challenging—and more important. For effective teachers, this is a habit that automatically kicks in at the right times. This section offers a few ways to build habits of connecting thinking, content, and language to students' lives.

Connect with Metaphors

Metaphors (and analogies) use known ideas to describe and clarify new ideas. The use of metaphors involves recognizing similarities between two seemingly dissimilar things. For example, in the following dialogue, the teacher compares a person to a leech. Physically people and leeches don't have much in common. But as the teacher and students work through the similarities and connections, abstract understandings begin to form. Metaphors and other analogies provide pivot points and conceptual anchors that help abstract understandings to grow and stick. The fifth-grade language arts teacher prompted metaphorical thinking, which helped a student figure out how the term *leech* related to the actions of a character:

1. *Student A:* I don't get why you called him a leech.
2. *Teacher:* Well, what do leeches do?
3. *Student A:* I think they suck blood from animals or something.
4. *Teacher:* Okay, and what did Mr. Reed do?

5. *Student A:*   Well, he kept stealing money from the club. Oh, so taking money was like the leech taking people's blood?

6. *Teacher:*   Do others of you agree?

The use of metaphor can help not only in the interpretation of literature but also in understanding content-area concepts. I have learned many complex concepts in science, math, and social studies through metaphor. For balancing equations in algebra, for example, I think of two twins on each side of the equation who must be treated equally and immediately; for antibodies in science, I think of little soldiers who react and surround enemy germs; for history, I think about how a single child grows and learns as symbolizing how a civilization grows and learns. Of course, it can be just as important for a student to recognize when and where metaphors break down, which, luckily, is also powerful for remembering certain aspects of the concept.

Here are some language starters for metaphorical thinking:

- *It's like . . .*
- *Imagine a . . .*
- *It's similar to . . .*
- *How is the . . . like the . . . ?*
- *But the analogy [or metaphor] breaks down when we look at . . .*
- *Think about a . . . Then picture it with . . .*

Connect with Examples

Appropriate examples can clarify complex concepts for students, but examples need to be familiar to them. We must remember that students often watch different TV shows, listen to different music, celebrate different holidays, and do different things than teachers do. This means that we must know our students so that the examples we use connect to them. The ninth-grade science teacher in the following excerpt explained gas pressure by using the example of a bicycle tire:

1. *Student E:*   I don't get it—why gas flows from an area of high pressure to low.

2. *Teacher:*   Think of a bicycle tire. When it is inflated, it has a lot more molecules bouncing around, colliding. The tire keeps them in. But when you hit a nail and get a hole, more air molecules inside the

tire hit the hole than molecules outside the tire. The tire molecules win and escape until there is an even amount inside and out.

3. *Student F:* So more molecules gives a thing more pressure?

4. *Teacher:* Yes, and then when you patch the hole and pump it up, the pump compresses, or squashes, the normal air into a small space where there are more molecules outside the valve now. So what happens?

5. *Student F:* So I think the pump's molecules win and enter the tire to pump it up.

6. *Teacher:* Yes.

Teachers use examples to give a more concrete picture of complex and abstract descriptions of concepts or processes. Another science teacher referred to the giraffe's development of a long neck when she was explaining the abstract concept of adaptation. An economics teacher used the example of an iPod to describe supply, demand, and marketing strategies. As often as possible, I have students come up with their own examples. This encourages them to make their own connections—a skill that they will need to use more and more in school and the rest of life.

Using examples not only helps clarify content but also, and perhaps even more important, models for students the process of supporting their claims and opinions with examples, explanations, and evidence.

Personify

What I call personifying is a fun and effective way to connect learning to students' background knowledge (Zwiers, 2006). Personifying, which is similar to role playing, means to step into the mind-set of another person or an object and then say or do what the person or object would say or do. Teachers do this to bring the content closer to students and make it more tangible, dramatic, and exciting. Teachers *and* students should participate.

Personifying seems to be effective for two reasons: (1) it makes the content more relevant and fun for students, connecting to their lives in some way, often through the use of slang and exaggeration (e.g., "I can't hang out at the party tonight. I'm going through mitosis!"), and (2) it allows students to feel safe in answering with new language, knowing that their thoughts on a topic will not be shot down as wrong. ("Okay, Kim, you are one side of the equation; your sister is the other. How would you feel if we added thirty-seven dollars to her side?") The following teacher example about squids in a seventh-grade science class shows personifying.

> ## TEACHER EXAMPLE: PERSONIFYING IN SCIENCE
>
> "Squid are predators, and they catch fish. So if I'm a squid, as I swim through the ocean and I see something I want to eat, I shoot my tentacles out and grab onto the fish and use my eight arms to wrap around it [the teacher grabs a student's head]."

There are other advantages of personifying. First, it gives students exposure to the hypothetical-conditional *if-would* grammatical structure. Here's an example: *If I were the king and you were the feudal lord, what would you say in this case?*

Second, personifying helps students build the cognitive skill and language of seeing different perspectives. Some examples: *Put yourself in the shoes of the main character in the story. Imagine you are Napoleon. How would you feel if you were a clone?*

Third, personifying helps students remember abstract concepts by connecting them to more concrete experiences. One student commented after a test, "I pictured the teacher acting like a king that one day to remember the answer."

We must make sure that diverse learners have enough background and exposure to understand our personifications, examples, and analogies. One history teacher often referred to television shows that few English learners had watched. A language arts teacher referred to being stuck in the snow: "Imagine you are sitting on the snow without thick pants or gloves." But many students in her class had come from warm climates and had not experienced snow; neither had many others who had been born in the United States.

Use Language to Authentically Do and Think

The later stages of scaffolding involve doing something with learning. In the real world, facts and concepts are usually learned to create a larger product or performance that demands much more thinking than just memorizing pieces of information. To prepare students for real-world thinking, we need to let them use what they learn, not just pile up facts and rules inside their brains. So even if standards say such things as "Know the . . . Trace the . . . Understand the . . . ," we need to remember that students will learn such knowledge much better when they actually do something interesting with it.

As students engage in literacy and learning tasks in the discipline, they build up abilities to recognize patterns to then apply language skills in new ways. In effective classrooms, students go from being novices who use much of their energy for attending to new facts and skills to being more like experts who can quickly recognize patterns and sharpen their skills as they apply them to new and more complex understandings. This sculpting of learning, rather than just the stockpiling of it, is described more in detail in chapter 9.

BUILDING HABITS OF COMMUNICATION

Teachers model appropriate ways to be, act, and talk in a community of learners. What we say and how we say it (our body language, sighs, rolled eyes, silences, facial expressions, and tones of voice) are all under the watchful eyes of students. They will emulate such communication habits in the long run, often without our realizing it. If we can make some of the following habits part of our automatic repertoire, good things can happen in the learning, identities, and language growth of our students.

Use Controversial or Provocative Statements

Students often like to argue, and they like to be right. A statement that invites disagreement from students can ignite thinking and the need to use academic language. This procedure is particularly helpful in light of the CCSS emphasis on argumentation and supporting ideas with evidence.

Controversial ideas and their supports tend to stick; they have more anchor power for the facts and concepts that are often tested. For example, when my students learned that people often lie about history, they were more interested in seeking out the truth, questioning sources, and thinking critically about textbook accounts. If real-world folks are currently wrestling with an issue, then students might be interested in it, too. They usually want to put their thoughts into the mix rather than just be a receptacle of facts. Here are a few examples of provocative statements:

Math: "You cannot divide by 0." "Statistics often lie." "Algebra is more important than calculus."

History: "The American Civil War happened in order to end slavery." "Columbus Day should not be a holiday."

Science: "The Earth is round." "Volcanic eruptions are helpful." "A fish out of water always dies."

Language arts: "Computers have made life easier." "Love at first sight exists." "Humans are born evil."

I have seen many instances in classrooms where a controversial topic could have been used and analyzed, but was not. One science teacher presented a slide show on the traits of viruses. I suggested starting class the next day with a statement such as "Headline news: defendant claims that the virus he killed was never alive," and have students respond to it. History is also full of questions and controversies, many of which are not included in history books. These are the ideas that make history interesting. And most literature is full of ethical and philosophical controversies that are waiting to be tackled.

FEATURED TEACHER COMMENTS

What are other possible perspectives on this? What are other opinions?
The tension between multiple perspectives can energize thinking and create opportunities for effective learning of academic language. This often happens because students get wrapped up in the issue, stepping for a moment outside the typical school chores and reward-based tasks. Students want to argue their views effectively and logically, but to do so they must resolve conceptual conflicts. They must disagree and confront the disagreement of others in academically appropriate ways. By doing so, they develop their thinking.

Hearing multiple perspectives helps students understand and empathize with others who do not share similar backgrounds (Johnston, 2012). Students can (and need to) see through the eyes of others, such as those of different religions, socioeconomic classes, cultures, and time periods.

Coshape Conversations

We can work individually with students to make their conversation more academic. This strategy, though it may seem insignificant, is perhaps one of the most difficult and complex things we do as teachers. It is also particularly helpful for nonmainstream students, many of whom have had little exposure to school-type conversations—either listening to them or participating in them.

Everything a student says has meaning, and we can help solidify this meaning as we also offer different ways to describe and communicate it. Notice in this example from a fifth-grade class how the teacher recasts student responses in more academic ways and gets the student to hypothesize:

1. *Teacher:*   What are you working on?
2. *Student E:*   We're makin' a thing about the plant growing.
3. *Teacher:*   Oh, you are making a graph to show the growth rates of the plants.
4. *Student E:*   Uh, and they not the same.
5. *Teacher:*   Wow, I wonder why they differ, why they grow at different rates. Any ideas?
6. *Student E:*   Maybe light change their rates.
7. *Teacher:*   Hmm. Yes, maybe the different amounts of light influenced their growth rates.

This type of scaffolding does not have steps, and much of it is improvisational, given that we need to respond to what the student says. The following are several points to remember:

- Adjust your language to the student's level and slightly bump up the level of vocabulary, syntax, and message organization features.
- Do not entirely control the conversation; let the students have some control over the direction as well.
- Be supportive, accepting, and patient.
- Focus on meaning and communication.
- Model correct pronunciation and intonation to clarify the messages when needed.
- Subtly repeat key words in the conversation.
- Make every effort to understand what the student is saying.
- Ask understandable and answerable questions that go deeper than asking for facts.
- Animate the discussion with appropriate expressions and gestures.

Repeat Student Responses for Emphasis

Repeating a student response can be done at times to emphasize its importance or highlight the vocabulary or grammar the student used. Repetition also allows language learners to hear the response a second time. We can augment the repeated message with gestures and emphasis on its key words. I have also written phrases on the wall as models after repeating student utterances. We must be careful to repeat responses from a range of students in the class rather than just the most verbal ones. And during class discussions, we must not allow students to depend on us to repeat responses, which reduces the authenticity of the conversation and does not give students practice in projecting their voices in group settings.

> ### FEATURED TEACHER COMMENTS
>
> *Interesting! Say it again so we can remember it. Hmmmmm. I will also write it down! That might be a thesis for an essay! Tell us more.*
>
> I use these comments to keep conversations going and validate the insightful ideas that students produce. These are often combined with some silence, especially if I write down the idea, which gives students time to put their next thoughts into words.

Rephrase Student Responses

Rephrasing (also called recasting) means to correct a slightly erroneous response or to change a response while still retaining the central meaning (Long, 1996). Teachers often do this to upgrade the vocabulary terms or academic language that the student used. By rephrasing with more developed clauses and sentences, students can hear their own words being used in new academic frames. This is a form of modeling. In this example, taken from a sixth-grade history class, notice how the teacher rephrases the student's response to clarify it, make it more explicit, and funnel it into what the teacher considers the purpose for the text:

1. *Teacher:* So, what's the topic?
2. *Student E:* People lookin' at daily life things?
3. *Teacher:* Yes, how archaeologists study . . . let's use the word *artifacts*. How archaeologists study artifacts to . . .

4. *Student E:*   Find out.

5. *Teacher:*   What's a better word? What do you do in school?

6. *Student E:*   Learn?

7. *Teacher:*   Let's put that for the topic: "How archaeologists study artifacts in order to learn about daily life in the past." Why do they study artifacts? In order . . .

8. *Student E:*   In order to learn about the past?

This teacher did more than just rephrase to upgrade vocabulary and grammar. The teacher helped the student improve her sentence-building abilities in order to generate the topic of the article in line 7. She stressed the term *in order to* as she helped the student write the title and then prompted the student to use it in her answer in line 8.

Many teachers already rephrase automatically, but this happens more often at the word level, not the sentence level. Usually rephrasing consists of just substituting a more appropriate vocabulary word. Teachers begin with a positive signal of acceptance, such as *Yes, Okay, Oh,* or *I see.* Then they rephrase the student's response with the new term. For instance, if the student says, "I saw the cell move quick," a teacher might respond with, "Oh, you observed the cell move quickly."

Yet without additional feedback, rephrasing can confuse students. They might not know if their answer was incorrect, their language was incorrect, or both were correct and the teacher was just improving the sentence. Lyster and Ranta (1997), studying recasts in second-language teaching, found that teachers tended to use recasts implicitly and in isolation and that this was not effective at improving student uptake (self-correction). Recasts were more effective when they were used with metacognitive feedback (talking about language) and clarification requests.

Granted, more research on rephrasing for academic language acquisition needs to be done, but for now we can (1) reflect on how much we use rephrasing and how effective it is, (2) be more explicit in the beginning of a course about how and why we will rephrase student responses, (3) use rephrasing in combination with other types of modeling and feedback, and (4) be extremely sensitive to how students respond to our rephrasings because some students may feel that their answers or their language (or both) are not being valued.

Have Students Paraphrase

Another scaffolding technique for content and language development is to have students paraphrase their own thoughts. This helps students develop the skill of condensing ideas, one of the features of academic language described in chapter 2. Model this often by putting up paragraph-length ideas on the overhead and paraphrasing them in one or two sentences. Model the use of nominalization and dependent clauses. Here are a few prompts for getting students to paraphrase:

"How might you say that with fewer sentences?"

"How can we condense what you said?"

"How can we synthesize what you all said?"

"Let's try to get that into one sentence. It can have multiple clauses."

"Can you paraphrase that for us?"

Use Comments to Enrich Classroom Talk

Here are other comments that can support class discussions. Not only can we teachers use these, but students should also use them in their own responses and conversations. Wouldn't it be nice to have students in each group using the comments that follow to maintain and deepen their conversations?

To Prompt More Thinking

"You are on to something important. Keep going."

"I know you may not know, but if you knew, what would you say?"

"You are on the right track. Tell us more."

"I noticed that you mentioned . . . Tell me more about . . ."

"You may have forgotten, but tell me one thing you do remember about . . ."

"Great thinking. Keep going."

"There is no right answer, so what would be your best answer?"

"Wondering is very important for inference. What do you wonder about?"

"What did you notice about . . . ?"

To Fortify or Justify a Response

"That's a good probable answer . . . How did you come to that answer?"

"Why is what you just said so important?"

"Why do you think he did that?"

"Why do you think that?"

"What is your impression [opinion] of . . . ? Why?"

To See Other Points of View

"That's a great start. Keep thinking, and I'll get back to you."

"Why do you think the author wrote this?"

"If you were in that person's shoes, what would you have done?"

"What are the different views of this issue?"

"Would you have done [or said] it like that? Why or why not?"

"If . . . hadn't happened, then how would things have turned out?"

To Consider Ethical Ramifications

"Should she have . . . ?"

"Some people think that . . . is [wrong, right, and so on]. What do you think? Why?"

"How can we apply this to real life?"

"Of what does this remind you from what we studied about . . . ?"

"Let's pull it all together and figure out . . ."

Conduct Metadiscussions

The Common Core State Standards require students to "compare and contrast the varieties of English (e.g., dialects, registers) used in stories, dramas, or poems" (CCSS.ELA-Literacy.L.5.3b), "explain the function of phrases and clauses in general and their function in specific sentences" (CCSS.ELA-Literacy.L.7.1a), and apply knowledge of language "to make effective choices for meaning or style" (CCSS.ELA-Literacy.L.11–12.3). Metadiscussions can help students learn these skills. They are classroom discussions that focus on what the class—teacher and students—should do to improve communication and learning using academic language.

Students can feel respected as they engage in adultlike dialogue about how to best run the class and talk about learning. Metadiscussions can help establish an environment that is focused on learning rather than pleasing the teacher or anyone else. I tell students that I am still learning how to facilitate rich discussions and create interesting learning activities and that I can use their help. Students in all grades can do this. As noted scholar Courtney Cazden (2001) asserts, "The task for both teachers and researchers is to make the usually transparent medium of classroom discourse the object of focal attention" (p. 6).

Metalinguistic awareness is the process of reflecting on the nature and functions of language in a given setting (Pratt & Grieve, 1984). Most students don't think much about improving their language use in content-area classes. Most teachers don't either. Metadiscussion involves talking with students about classroom talk and language development. If we can establish the importance of developing expert language by talking about it at appropriate times, then students tend to buy in to the process. Here are a few starters for talking about language and its acquisition:

"How can we remember this word or term?"

"What can we do to get others to talk in a group?"

"What kinds of questions help us think deeply about science, history, math, or some other subject?"

"How can we use this thinking in the future?"

"How does group work help you develop our language skills?"

"Why does it help to learn academic language?"

"What things do we do in class that make you think?"

We can also metadiscuss our thinking processes. We (teacher and students) engage in metacognition, meaning that we consider how we think about a topic, how we organize our evolving thoughts, and how we might clarify them and use language to describe them. We teachers engage in metacognition quite often and need to pass this skill on to students. Metacognition can introduce students to more abstract uses of language (Hammond, 2006).

One way to build students' metacognition is to analyze thinking and academic language use, as seen in this excerpt from an eighth-grade classroom:

1. *Teacher:*   I think he will declare war. What did I just do?
2. *Students:*   Predict.
3. *Teacher:*   Why do we predict? How does it help?
4. *Student A:*   It makes you interested in what will happen.
5. *Student B:*   It makes you think about all the clues.
6. *Teacher:*   Yes, prediction allows us to use clues and connect them to what we know about those clues in other stories and in our life, then we hypothesize what will happen. Does anyone hypothesize something different?
7. *Student E:*   I hypothesize they will make peace.
8. *Teacher:*   Because?

Notice how in line 6 the teacher built from the two students' responses to create a more academic response that included several clauses, the abstract idea of *connect* and the term *hypothesize*. Student E then used the word *hypothesize* for the first time as a result of the discussion. In line 8 the teacher prompts the student to explain the basis for her hypothesis, even though the teacher did not model this in line 1.

Through metadiscussions, we can give students tips for learning academic language. The more they can teach themselves, the better. For example, we can emphasize the importance of reading a variety of texts, taking chances with the language, repeating what the teacher says at times under one's breath, and connecting ideas to their backgrounds. We can even talk about several of the principles of language acquisition mentioned early in this chapter (input, output, negotiation of meaning). Students are often very interested in the behind-the-scenes work that we do as teachers.

Focus on Deeper Levels of Talk

Not only must we decide on which types of activities will promote talk, we must also focus on ways to enrich and deepen the talk that happens in each discussion. Many group activities in this and other books effectively promote the quantity of talk; it is the quality of talk that we must continue to work on. Students' notions of why we talk in class often differ from ours. We must make it clear to all why we talk during lessons. There will be different purposes at different times, but students should be able to answer the question "Why are we talking about this right now?" Answers to elaborate on as a class might include the following:

- To see how others interpret the text
- To see how others solved the problem
- To get ideas from others for my essay
- For the whole class to know the basics of . . .
- To rationally argue the pros and cons of the issue
- To practice explaining these concepts to others
- To work on turn taking, interrupting, conceding, synthesizing

There are several ways to focus on improving academic talk. First, remind students of the overall purpose of the lesson, the big ideas, and how discussion supports them. Second, put key terms on the wall or on cards for use in discussion. Third, come up with examples that connect to students' lives and are engaging to them. Fourth, use quick-writes to focus students and get discussable thoughts down on paper. Fifth, use smaller groups and pairs at times to promote talking and thinking by more students all at once.

A visual way to scaffold deeper discussions is to brainstorm using figure 3.1. This visual helps challenge students to go deeper than the simple discussion of facts and unsupported opinions. The different "caverns," which highlight many of the standards emphasized in the Common Core, can give us ideas for prompts. We can let students in on our process, too, by putting a diagram like figure 3.1 on the wall.

One way to introduce this visual is to model a shallow conversation for the students. Choose a topic from your class and, in a somewhat exaggerated manner, ask simple fact-based questions. Then model several opinions without giving evidence. Then ask a student to answer a question and model how to *not* acknowledge his or her comment; that is, just blurt out another unrelated thought. I call this *popcorn talk*. Then ask students what was wrong with that type of discussion. They might say that it jumped around, had no direction, no depth. Talk about what they think a good discussion sounds like. Then model a deeper discussion with students (see chapter 5). Remind students that it is acceptable and often necessary to start with facts and simple questions, but these should then lead to questions and comments at deeper levels of thinking.

Figure 3.1 Graphic Organizer for Deeper Discussions

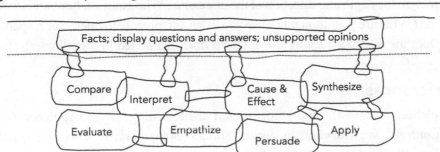

CONCLUSION

In this chapter, we have explored various ways in which teachers can create an environment that is conducive to learning new ways of thinking and communicating in ways that emphasize the new standards. We started with key principles of language acquisition: input, output, and negotiation. Then we looked at ways to model and scaffold academic language and thinking. Important yet underdeveloped teacher habits are those used for responding to students in ways that promote, rather than hinder, their participation in classes. We saw how there is a delicate balance between overscaffolding and undersupporting students' linguistic growth. Finally, we looked at the importance and effectiveness of metadiscussing the complex processes of learning content and language. Metadiscussion allows students to gain some control over their language learning and build abstract language at the same time.

CHAPTER REFLECTIONS

- What motivates students to talk in your class? Why are some students silent?

- Take a passage of text from your content area and do an unrehearsed think-aloud with it. Now plan a think-aloud with a different section of the text. How were they different?

- How do you learn and remember new words in your native language? In another language? In technical language?

- Reflect on the types of visuals, examples, and metaphors you can use with students to help them understand abstract and complex concepts. What language is also needed?

- During a discussion in which you are a participant, take a "metamoment" to analyze the depth and direction of the discussion. Who guides it, how, and to what end? What are your thoughts while you listen and prepare to offer your responses? Does the discussion leader use any behaviors mentioned in this chapter?

References

Applebee, A. (1984). The students and their writing. In A. Applebee (Ed.), *Contexts for learning to write: Studies of secondary school instruction* (pp. 37–54). Norwood, NJ: Ablex.

Bruner, J. (1986). *Actual minds: Possible worlds*. Cambridge, MA: Harvard University Press.

Carroll, M., Tanenhaus, M., & Bever, T. (1978). The perception of functional relations. In W. Levelt & F. d'Arcais (Eds.), *Studies in the perception of language* (pp. 187–218). New York, NY: Wiley.

Cazden, C. (2001). *Classroom discourse: The language of teaching and learning*. Portsmouth, NH: Heinemann.

Chomsky, N. (1965). *Aspects of the theory of syntax*. Cambridge, MA: MIT Press.

Chomsky, N. (1980). *Rules and representations*. New York, NY: St. Martin's Press.

Davey, B. (1983). Think aloud: Modeling the cognitive processes of reading comprehension. *Journal of Reading, 27*(1), 44–47.

Druyan, S. (1997). Effects of the kinesthetic conflict on promoting scientific reasoning. *Journal of Research in Science Teaching, 34*, 1083–1099.

Farr, R. (2001). Think-along/think-alouds and comprehending lead to better comprehension. *California Reader, 34*(2), 29–33.

Hammond, J. (2006). High challenge, high support: Integrating language and content instruction for diverse learners in an English literature classroom. *Journal of English for Specific Purposes, 5*, 269–283.

Hernandez, A. (2003). Making content instruction accessible to English language learners. In G. García (Ed.), *English learners: Reaching the highest level of English literacy* (pp. 125–151). Newark, DE: International Reading Association.

Johnston, P. (2004). *Choice words: How our language affects children's learning*. Portland, ME: Stenhouse.

Johnston, P. (2012). *Opening minds: How classroom talk shapes children's minds and their lives*. Portland, ME: Stenhouse.

Krashen, S. (1985). *The input hypothesis: Issues and implications*. London, UK: Longman.

Long, M. (1983). Linguistic and conversational adjustments to non-native speakers. *Studies in Second Language Acquisition, 5*, 177–194.

Long, M. (1987). Native speaker/non-native speaker conversation in the second language classroom. In M. Long & J. Richards (Eds.), *Methodology in TESOL: A book of readings* (pp. 339–354). Boston, MA: Heinle & Heinle.

Long, M. (1996). The role of the linguistic environment in second language acquisition. In W. Ritchie & T. Bhatia (Eds.), *Handbook of research on language acquisition: Second language acquisition* (pp. 413–468). New York, NY: Academic Press.

Lyster, L., & Ranta, L. (1997). Corrective feedback and learner uptake: Negotiation of form in communicative classrooms. *Studies in Second Language Acquisition, 19*, 37–66.

Marzano, R., Pickering, D., & Pollock, J. (2001). *Classroom instruction that works: Research-based strategies for increasing student achievement.* Alexandria, VA: Association for Supervision and Curriculum Development.

National Governors Association Center for Best Practices. (2010). *Common Core State Standards.* Washington, DC: Council of Chief State School Officers.

O'Conner, M., & Michaels, S. (1996). Shifting participant frameworks: Orchestrating thinking practices in group discussion. In D. Hicks (Ed.), *Discourse, learning, and schooling* (pp. 63–103). Cambridge, UK: Cambridge University Press.

Pratt, C., & Grieve, R. (1984). The development of metalinguistic awareness: An introduction. In W. Tunmer, C. Pratt, & M. Herriman (Eds.), *Metalinguistic awareness in children: Theory, research, and implications* (pp. 2–35). New York, NY: Springer-Verlag.

Rivers, W. (1994). Comprehension and production: The interactive duo. In R. Barasch & J. Vaughn (Eds.), *Beyond the monitor model: Comments and current theory and practice in second language acquisition* (pp. 71–96). Boston, MA: Heinle & Heinle.

Scarcella, R. (2003). *Academic English: A conceptual framework* (Technical Report No. 2003–1). University of California Linguistic Minority Research Institute.

Swain, M. (1995). Three functions of output in second language learning. In G. Cook & B. Seidlhofer (Eds.), *Principle and practice in applied linguistics: Studies in honour of H. G. Widdowson* (pp. 125–144). New York, NY: Oxford University Press.

Vygotsky, L. (1978). *Mind in society: The development of higher psychological processes.* Cambridge, MA: Harvard University Press.

Wong Fillmore, L., & Fillmore, C. (2011). *What does text complexity mean for English learners and language minority students?* Stanford, CA: Understanding Language Initiative.

Zwiers, J. (2005). *Developing academic language in middle school English learners: Practices and perspectives in mainstream classrooms.* Unpublished doctoral dissertation, University of San Francisco.

Zwiers, J. (2006). Integrating academic language, thinking, and content: Learning scaffolds for non-native speakers in the middle grades. *Journal of English for Academic Purposes*, 5(4), 317–332.

Chapter 4

Content-Area Variations of Academic Language

Every teacher is a language teacher.

Different disciplines have different ways of viewing the world, gathering information, interpreting data, and organizing knowledge. Each discipline uses variations (subregisters) of academic language that branch off to accomplish these purposes (as in figure 2.1). This branching begins as students start to learn, for example, that thinking and talking in science differ from thinking and talking in history. These overlapping subregisters then branch off further and become more specialized as they form the highly technical languages of higher education and the professional world. If you have ever heard computer engineers chatting about their work or read a medical research report, you know how specialized such languages can become.

As experts in our content areas, we teachers often have "expert blind spots" (Nathan & Petrosino, 2003) that keep us from realizing that much of our complex and abstract knowledge has become concrete and basic to us. This is like the fish trying to describe water. Our lack of awareness of academic language leads us to skip over information that novices need, because we have lost the sense of being a learner in the early stages of the discipline. Shulman (1987) argues that teachers must develop pedagogical content knowledge. This means knowing how novices think and struggle as they are learning the content. Many students, for example, think about an algebra problem much differently than a math teacher does. We teachers must be able to keenly observe, listen, and predict where glitches in learning might occur, so that we can then use appropriate methods to move students to higher levels of content and discipline-specific language.

Similarly, we need more pedagogical language knowledge (PLK). This is the knowledge about the language in our discipline that is used to describe and advance it. It is the knowledge of how diverse students learn and don't learn the language of the discipline that we teach (for more on PLK, refer to Bunch, 2013). We seldom analyze our communication strategies during class or realize how we are making many grammatical and lexical choices each moment. Similar to the expert blind spots that prevent us from seeing knowledge in new ways, we need to realize our own thinking and language blind spots as they relate to our content area.

Each year of schooling requires students to learn increasingly abundant and challenging concepts in each discipline. Students' language abilities must develop accordingly. Unfortunately, too many schools see language development as the responsibility of the language arts or English teacher. Yet many students don't have as many language-related problems in their English classes as they do in their science, math, and history courses (Zwiers, 2005).

Fortunately, the Common Core anchor literacy standards describe reading and writing standards for students in history, social studies, science, and technical subjects. And a welcome development is having content literacy standards extra focused and aligned with English language arts (ELA) standards. Consequently, language and literacy must be better emphasized in content classes. Science, math, and history teachers, for example, must make extra efforts to be strategic at teaching the many tools and skills of the language that describe the increasingly complex ways of organizing and thinking about knowledge.

The following sections look at academic language in four content-area disciplines: language arts, history, science, and math. I highlight several thinking skills and their language in each content area. The tables contain language that I gathered from discussions and texts in upper-elementary, middle school, and high school classrooms. The dialogues, unless otherwise noted, come from classrooms in which around half the students were English learners and speakers of nonmainstream versions of English. Students A through D are native speakers and students E through H are English learners. The language of each discipline's thinking skill is underlined in these passages.

LANGUAGE OF LANGUAGE ARTS

Language arts classes serve to cultivate the skills of reading, writing, speaking, grammar, and interpreting literature, mostly in the mainstream versions of a language. Early grades (K–3) tend to emphasize getting the main points of the story and understanding literal levels; later grades emphasize more thematic and figurative understandings, which are often displayed through written responses to literature.

The Common Core standards for language arts do not specify particular works of literature to cover each year, but the standards do require many rigorous reading, writing, and literary analysis skills. Typical types of tasks in literary analysis include these:

- Interpreting the events or characters of the story

- Uncovering the author's messages and themes

- Recognizing literary devices

- Analyzing the author's craft

Students of literature use a range of thinking skills and language to accomplish these tasks, such as making inferences, predicting, summarizing, questioning, figuring out unknown words, synthesizing, and seeing multiple perspectives. Three important thinking skills in language arts—interpretation, argumentation, and figuring out causes and effects—are included here.

Interpretation in Language Arts

Literature offers unique views of the human experience through characters and symbolism (Rosenblatt, 1995). Interpretation is the process of understanding messages and underlying meanings from a text, often a story or poem. Through the use of figurative language, character actions, dialogue, and plot, a piece of literature teaches readers about many dimensions of being human.

Teachers and students can often find very different meanings from the same text: what is meaningful for one may be trivial for another, for example. Students and teachers must reach a common ground when it comes to meaning. And as we saw in chapter 1, finding common ground is challenging with many diverse students in a class. Table 4.1 is a partial list of the types of themes that schools tend to consider meaningful. Many language arts departments, in fact, choose pieces of literature based on such themes. Notice the many abstract concepts and academic terms in this list.

Students are still apprentices in the types of thinking needed to read between the lines and interpret deeper meanings in a text. We must be creative at scaffolding the complexity that has by now become automatic to us. In the following excerpt, the

Table 4.1 Selected Discussion Themes That Emerge from Literature

Noble goals and causes are worth extreme sacrifice.	True friendship or love involves deep commitment.
Many stories are based on earlier stories, myths, or legends.	Certain symbols in the story represent the main character and themes in life.
Freedom is everyone's right.	
Do not give in to peer pressure.	People can change.
There is more to life than making money and being comfortable.	Memories are a large part of who we are.
Life is short, and every day is precious.	Cleverness can be more effective than brute force.
True beauty is on the inside.	Envy and jealousy are destructive.
Standing up for what is right is often difficult and even dangerous.	There are many types of heroes.
Teamwork is often necessary.	Helping others is itself a reward.
We should respect nature's power and beauty.	Older people are often wise.
	Losing a loved one is challenging.
There is hope, even when things seem hopeless.	All languages and cultures are valuable.
We must preserve the environment.	People can be both good and bad.

teacher scaffolds, with considerable effort, the moral interpretation of a fable for a sixth-grade, intermediate-level English learner. The student had seldom thought abstractly about how stories with animals could teach lessons about life to people. This story was about a lion that lied to animals, invited them to dinner in his cave, and then ate them. The lion then asked the fox to dinner, who noticed that many animal tracks led into the cave, but not out. The underlined words in this and all other dialogues in this section are expressions in which the teacher elicited or modeled the target skill. In the following dialogue, the teacher models and elicits interpretation.

1. *Teacher:* What did the fox find out about when he looked at the tracks?
2. *Student E:* Tracks went in but did not come out?
3. *Teacher:* <u>What could that mean for people?</u> That the tracks went in but didn't come out. What should we do as people in order to be smart?
4. *Student E:* Not go into caves.
5. *Teacher:* But no longer thinking about caves, we are talking about people; no caves, no lions. <u>What about in real life, like in my life. What can I learn from this?</u>
6. *Student E:* Try your best.
7. *Teacher:* <u>Where did it talk about trying your best?</u>
8. *Student E:* The lion was in there, and you could be like the lion.
9. *Teacher:* But the fox was too smart. <u>How can I be like the fox . . . in life?</u>
10. *Student E:* Oh, the fox.
11. *Teacher:* I don't want to be the lion because he was a liar, right, and he might go hungry because the fox might go tell other people. So in the end, the fox was smarter, right? <u>How can I be like the fox in real life? And the other animals are like people, right?</u>
12. *Student E:* He saw the tracks. He said, "I'd like to, but . . ."
13. *Teacher:* I'd like to, but . . . what did the fox see?
14. *Student E:* The tracks.
15. *Teacher:* Right, he saw what happened to other people, other animals.
16. *Student E:* And then we know what happened.
17. *Teacher:* <u>So how can we do this in life? How can we be smart in our life today, like the fox?</u>

18.	*Student E:*	Watch and learn.
19.	*Teacher:*	<u>From what?</u>
20.	*Student E:*	From others?
21.	*Teacher:*	Watch and learn from others, especially their mistakes.

In this conversation, the teacher is scaffolding not only the thinking skill of interpretation but also its language. The teacher responded to the student patiently and eventually got her to make the leap from the story to real life in line 18. In line 7 she focused the student to use evidence from the text, an important skill required in the Common Core State Standards. Of course, it takes many conversations like this to make the language and thinking processes stick. Therefore, we must try to build constructive, academic ways of communicating into our habit repertoire. In this way, the language in table 4.2 can begin to stick in our students' minds.

An effective way to introduce the language of interpretation is to talk about movies and excerpts from movies. Movies offer a variety of characterizations and dialogues that can provide fodder for literature-like discussions. Such discussions lead us into talking about how movies differ from books, particularly with respect to the figurative descriptions, creating scenes based on reader background knowledge, and looking into characters' thoughts and emotions.

Table 4.2 Academic Expressions for Interpreting in Language Arts

It really means . . . because . . .	For us these days, it could mean that . . .
The . . . is a metaphor for . . .	When . . . shows us that . . .
It wasn't literal; that's the author's way of describing how . . .	If we read between the lines, we see that . . .
The author was trying to teach us that . . .	The author's background helps us figure out . . .
One way to interpret her words is . . .	It's like how people always . . .
The . . . is an important symbol for . . . because . . .	The author used that analogy because . . .
His actions meant that . . .	That is similar to my life in that . . .
It's a figurative way to describe how . . .	The moral of the story is . . .

Argumentation in Language Arts

The Common Core anchor standards for reading and writing place extra emphasis on argumentation. For example, notice the central roles of logical reasoning and evidence in the following standards: "Delineate and evaluate the argument and specific claims in a text, including the validity of the reasoning as well as the relevance and sufficiency of the evidence" (CCSS.ELA-Literacy.CCRA.R.8), and "Write arguments to support claims in an analysis of substantive topics or texts, using valid reasoning and relevant and sufficient evidence" (CCSS.ELA-Literacy.CCRA.W.1). The standards focus on argumentation rather than its relative, persuasion. While these two do overlap, argumentation places extra emphasis on supporting claims with evidence and using logical reasoning as opposed to the unsupported claims, appeals to emotion, and propaganda strategies often used in persuasive messages.

Argumentation consists of logically supporting claims. Often argumentation is done to convince others to take a particular side of an issue. In such cases, you show that the reasoning for your side is more logical and influential than the reasoning that supports the opposing side(s). You provide evidence in support of your position to make it stronger.

The following excerpt is from a seventh-grade small-group discussion based on an article about whether school officials should be able to search students' backpacks:

1. *Student A:*   I <u>don't think we should</u> have backpack searches.
2. *Student B:*   Why?
3. *Student A:*   Because it's our stuff. We have rights.
4. *Teacher:*   What is a right?
5. *Student C:*   Like freedom. Like, they need permits or a reason to search.
6. *Teacher:*   Are there any <u>opposing arguments</u> in the text for having searches?
7. *Student E:*   Well, maybe, like it says, they hear about a gun or something.
8. *Student B:*   Or a knife. I saw this guy last year with one in his bag.
9. *Teacher:*   Those are effective <u>counterarguments</u>. So, like it asks in the text, is safety <u>worth giving up this right</u>? Does safety <u>outweigh</u> our rights?

The teacher responds to students with thinking prompts in lines 4, 6, and 9. She uses the language of persuasion that they might acquire over time. Students E and B understood the idea of opposing arguments. In line 9, the teacher gets abstract and uses *worth* and *outweigh* (with hand motions) to show the process of deciding between two ideas.

The more discussions like this that students have, the more language they can tap when they sit down to write. When students are encouraged to argue their side and back it up with evidence, they show deeper learning and better retention of concepts than when they are asked to regurgitate the answers on tests. The process of preparing for and writing an argumentative essay motivates students to evaluate the evidence, organize their thoughts, and think critically about both sides of an issue. We can also explicitly teach some of the argumentation expressions in the list in table 4.3.

Yet many diverse students struggle to understand argumentation elements due in part to their lack of experience in reading and talking about controversial issues. Indeed, some cultures avoid any type of confrontation in public. Argumentation is not as highly valued in some cultures as in the US mainstream (Brenner & Parks, 2001). In certain collectivist cultures (e.g., Chinese, Lakota, Mexican),

Table 4.3 Academic Expressions for Argumentation in Language Arts

Based on the evidence in the story so far, . . . because . . .	What it seems to come down to is . . . versus . . .
The long-run gains appear to outweigh the short-run losses . . .	I understand what you are saying, but I would like to emphasize . . .
It is a difficult issue, but I feel that the positives of . . . outweigh the negatives of . . .	That is a good point, but I think the evidence shows that . . .
There is a lot of discussion about whether . . . , but the crux of the matter is . . .	These [facts, reasons, data] strongly suggest that . . . Yet some argue strongly that . . .
However, there are several reasons to oppose this point of view.	Although not everybody would agree, our position is . . .
It is also vital to consider . . .	Although some people claim that . . .
The statistics are misleading, however, because they do not show . . .	The issue is not so much a question of . . . but a question of . . .
Well, that is only partly the case. The other side of the story is . . .	They say [claim, maintain, hold] that . . .
The advantages of . . . outweigh the disadvantages of . . .	On the other hand, there are many who disagree with the idea that . . .
Granted, we admit that . . .	Opponents also argue that . . .

argumentation and persuasion are less emphasized because they imply that one person has superior knowledge and that those with opposing views need to change. In particular, public conversations of this nature potentially create disharmony and might not seem appropriate to certain students. In many respects, the products and processes of our individualist schools clash with traits found in more collective-oriented cultures, such as humility, listening, silence, reflective thinking, respect, and holistic thinking (Brenner & Parks, 2001). We must take these differences into account when designing instruction.

Cause and Effect in Language Arts

Cause-and-effect thinking is emphasized in the Common Core ELA and Literacy standards. For instance, in "Describe how a particular story's or drama's plot unfolds in a series of episodes as well as how the characters respond or change" (CCSS.ELA-Literacy.RL.6.3), students must infer causes and effects for understanding both plot and character development. This skill tends to focus on the causes and effects within a piece of literature, often analyzing motives for characters' actions and thoughts. For example, the teacher in the following excerpt focused on events that changed the main character's outlook toward the end of the book *Hatchet*, by Gary Paulsen (1987):

1. *Teacher:* <u>Why</u> did Brian begin to feel more confident about surviving? <u>Because</u> . . .
2. *Student E:* <u>Cuz</u> he caught fish?
3. *Teacher:* Okay, and <u>how did that make</u> him feel about himself?
4. *Student F:* Maybe he felt like he was starting to, like, learn from mistakes and stuff, and <u>so</u> he felt smarter.
5. *Teacher:* So how do you think Brian changed <u>as a result</u> of his time out in the Canadian wilderness?
6. *Student E:* It <u>caused him</u> to lose weight.
7. *Teacher:* Okay, true, but besides physical changes, how did the experience <u>influence</u> his mind and personality?
8. *Student:* He watched things better.
9. *Teacher:* Great, okay, he <u>became</u> more observant <u>because</u> he had to observe things around him <u>to get</u> food and <u>to protect</u> himself. What else? *(pause)*

10. *Student C:*   He learned to try hard even when things were bad.
11. *Teacher:*   Great! What word can we use for trying hard, no matter what? *(no answer)* Persevere. Brian persevered despite many challenges. <u>Why?</u>

Although this conversation was teacher driven, the questions allowed students to think of more abstract changes that resulted from the experiences of the main character. The end of this conversation (line 11) leads directly into interpreting the lessons from the book about being observant and persevering in spite of life's challenges. The teacher then had students write about these topics to connect them to their own lives and what was happening at school.

Other variations of cause-and-effect thinking happen when students look at the events, culture, and context that inspired the author to write a piece of literature. Author studies, for example, often spark this type of thinking and ignite interesting discussions about the deeper foundations and inspirations for a work.

Table 4.4 contains cause-and-effect expressions taken from classroom observations and analysis of instructional materials and texts.

Table 4.4   Academic Expressions for Identifying Cause and Effect in Language Arts

The character likely did that because . . .	It was not a coincidence that . . .
That wasn't caused by . . . because . . .	Even though many people thought the cause was . . . , I believe it was . . .
Just because it happened after . . . doesn't mean it was caused by . . .	Each . . . played a key role. First, . . .
I hypothesize that . . . made them . . .	The purpose of that character was to . . . because . . .
The most likely reason for . . . was . . .	The results of her actions were . . .
	The reason they . . .
	The . . . led to . . . , which led to . . .
	She was motivated by . . .

LANGUAGE OF HISTORY

The language of history is used primarily to describe the past, its interpretations, and its relevance to the present and future. Historical thinking has different layers. The surface layer is composed of facts and events of the story. The second layer then zooms in on particular events or words of the story, and the deepest layer uses abstract ideas to build a thesis and support it with evidence and explanations (Coffin, 1997).

Despite the common images of time lines on the walls, historical analysis is not a linear process. Wineberg (2001) points out that thinking historically means standing back from first impressions, cultivating questions, and letting them point us in new directions of interpretation. Being a historian means suspending judgment about the past, realizing our present-centered biases, and challenging our beliefs about the past in order to learn from it. Expressing our suspensions of judgment, our biases, and our beliefs about the past both requires and develops large amounts of academic language. Many other thinking skills are needed in history as well. Three thinking skills are described in detail here, but other important ones to be developed along the way in history are comparing, synthesizing, persuading, analyzing, and classifying.

Cause and Effect in History

A major problem is that most history textbooks do not rise very far above the first layer of learning history, which is the learning of rote knowledge of facts, dates, people, and events. Yet the Common Core Anchor Literacy standards clearly argue for the need to build students' cause-and-effect skills: "Analyze in detail a series of events described in a text; determine whether earlier events caused later ones or simply preceded them" (CCSS.ELA-Literacy.RH.9–10.3). Apart from a few questions at the end of chapters, many textbooks do not help students delve into deeper thinking about history. The language in history textbooks tends to describe key details and facts, causes and effects in the "stories," and the mental states of people involved, which are usually linked to the key details and the causes and effects. Notice these in this textbook excerpt:

> Most white southerners favored secession. Still, pockets of Union support existed in parts of Tennessee and Virginia. People in the Appalachian region generally opposed secession. In western Virginia

a movement to secede from the state and rejoin the Union grew. In 1861, 48 Virginia counties organized themselves as a separate state called West Virginia. Congress admitted this state to the Union in 1863. (Appleby, Brinkley, Broussard, McPherson, & Ritchie, 2005, 461–462)

Cause-and-effect verbs in the excerpt include *grew, organized,* and *admitted.* Mental states include *favored, support,* and *opposed.* And although there is a lack of explicit "because" connectors between sentences, most sentences are influenced in some way by what happens in the previous sentence; it is up to the reader to infer these connections. This means that we must train our students to make these invisible connections as they read. We do this by modeling our thinking as we read history texts and teaching the less obvious signals for cause and effect.

To understand historical causes and effects, students must have background knowledge of the many ways in which humans influence events and vice versa. In history, most causes fall under one or more categories: fear, racism, religion, compassion, lust for wealth, lust for power, lust for fame, desire for knowledge, desire for freedom, desire for truth, and natural events. Keeping these categories in mind can help students build a framework for understanding cause and effect. For example, in the question "Why did Columbus cross the Atlantic?" under which categories would you say the answers, if they exist, fit?

In the following transcription, the teacher was trying to help Leo, a seventh-grade English learner, to see the causes and effects of the Black Plague, not only relating to the European population but also to their religious beliefs. Notice the scaffolding of language that happens in the interaction:

1. *Teacher:* <u>Why</u> did the Church become weaker after the Plague?
2. *Leo:* <u>Cuz</u> after a lot of monks and they weren't doing their jobs and were being punished and they were in their cages in the castles.
3. *Teacher:* And also the people outside, <u>because</u> they thought God didn't help, <u>what happened later on</u>? To their belief in the Church?
4. *Leo:* They weren't helping anymore.
5. *Teacher:* Yes, they thought <u>if</u> God can't cure this disease, <u>then why</u> should we be religious? The people were mad at us monks <u>because</u> they thought God didn't help. The Church became weaker after the Black Death. You can put "<u>Because of this</u>" or do you want to put "<u>Therefore</u>"? Good word, huh?

6. *Leo:*   Yeah. <u>Therefore</u>, the Church was becoming weak.

7. *Teacher:*   Okay. "<u>Therefore</u>, the Church became weaker <u>because</u> . . ."

8. *Leo:*   There wasn't a lot of monks no more?

The teacher guided the conversation to get Leo to think about the effects of the many deaths from the Plague. He correctly stated that there were not a lot of monks anymore (line 8), but the teacher tried to get him to connect the effects of a weaker Church with the causes of the many deaths and people's subsequent lack of faith. It is likely that Leo had never analyzed or contemplated religious beliefs in such an academic and abstract way before, which is why the conversation was so labored. In line 5 the teacher became a monk, using the first-person-plural forms "we" and "us" to add life to the dialogue. (Personifying is a strategy described in chapter 3.) The teacher provided the cause-and-effect academic term *therefore* twice, and coaxed Leo to use it to begin his answer in line 6. Other common expressions are found in table 4.5.

Interpretation in History

Interpreting in history means extracting and constructing meanings from the past, both remote and recent, of others and ourselves. Yet the interpretation of history is different from that of literature; although a story unfolds, historical accounts and artifacts have very different purposes and focuses from those of

Table 4.5 Academic Expressions for Cause-and-Effect Thinking in History

One reason for their . . . was . . .	There were political, social, and cultural motives for . . .
It wasn't just one cause, though; we need to think about other factors, such as . . .	Even though the textbook says the cause was . . . , I believe it was . . .
That was a result of . . .	
Just because they . . . doesn't mean that . . .	Seeds have been sown.
The most likely reason for . . . was . . .	The ramifications of their actions were far reaching.
The . . . led to . . . , which led to . . .	If they hadn't . . . , what would have happened?
She was motivated by . . .	Had a significant influence on . . .
Each . . . played a key role. First, . . .	The . . . laid a foundation for . . .

novels, shorts stories, and poetry. Moreover, many people have shaped history over time, and for different reasons. Students of history must therefore interpret clues and put pieces together to clarify stories, solve dilemmas, and connect to their own lives (Holt, 1990). And for the Common Core, students need to support analyses of primary and secondary sources, compare primary and secondary sources, and assess how well authors support their claims (National Governors Association Center for Best Practices, 2010). All of this interpretive thinking richly sows and cultivates academic language.

Consider the following eighth-grade discussion about Stephen A. Douglas's argument for state sovereignty in the 1858 Lincoln–Douglas debate. One group discussed the following excerpt:

> The framers of our government never contemplated uniformity in its internal concerns. The fathers of the Revolution and the sages who made the Constitution well understood that the laws and domestic institutions which would suit the granite hills of New Hampshire would be totally unfit for the rice plantations of South Carolina. (Douglas, 1858)

1. *Teacher:* So, what is he arguing?
2. *Student A:* For more state control over their laws, <u>we think. That the fathers didn't mean</u> for so much government control.
3. *Teacher:* How is he arguing?
4. *Student B:* He is <u>using all-or-nothing language</u> like *never* and *totally.* And real long sentences. Could people understand that stuff?
5. *Student C:* And he <u>used extreme examples</u> like the hills and plantations. It was almost <u>like poetry.</u>
6. *Teacher:* So was it effective?
7. *Student A:* I was being convinced. But I still wasn't sure if . . . how much control, like if states would become like new countries.
8. *Student C:* I guess <u>we have to look at</u> the Constitution, right? <u>To see how much control</u> they wanted states to have.
9. *Student B:* And what about the war? Did he want war? <u>It doesn't seem like it</u> in this part here, but then <u>if Lincoln wanted war, was he good?</u>
10. *Teacher:* And we also need to <u>see how</u> slavery <u>fits in</u> to this question.

These students were engaging in important analyses of a text that led to questions and interpretations of Douglas's views. Student B used some meta-linguistic awareness to pick out persuasive language and to notice the complexity of Douglas's sentences (line 4). The students interpreted the text in light of what they knew about the upcoming war and Lincoln's views, but they also realized the need to go back and interpret the Constitution to see how right Douglas was.

An important variation of interpretation is the skill of generalization, which is similar to application. Generalizing means looking at events and interpreting them to come up with a principle or pattern that applies to similar events in the past or future. This implies learning from the past and not repeating our mistakes. For example, if I see patterns in the motivations for spreading religion long ago, I can make generalizations that help me understand religious expansion today. Or in the reverse case, I might see biased views in political speeches today that I can generalize to understand biases in politics many centuries ago.

Table 4.6 lists several expressions that students can use to describe their interpretations of history. With this type of thinking practice over time, students can gradually achieve one of the main purposes of interpreting history: reflecting on who we are, where we came from, and who we might become.

Table 4.6 Academic Expressions for Interpretation in History

Those events can teach us about how to act in the future. For example, . . .	This belongs in history books because it . . .
His actions, though seemingly trivial, likely changed the course of history for . . .	This event was important because . . .
We aren't very different from those people.	It really means . . . because . . .
	I believe that the author did not include . . . because . . .
We can draw several conclusions from our analysis of the documents.	For us in modern times, it could mean that . . .
The evidence strongly suggests that . . .	If we read between the lines, we might make a guess that . . .
We believe that this event shows how humans are generally . . .	
One way to interpret this event is . . .	What did he really mean when he said . . . ?
Back then, . . . had a different meaning.	

Perspective Taking in History

A student's ability to take on different perspectives and empathize fosters in-depth learning because, in order to be able to think in the shoes of another person, one must learn much about that person and his or her circumstances. Perspective also provides a student with a way to participate in the life of others and by doing so, better understand and remember the other's experiences and thoughts. Perspective-based activities and discussions allow students more freedom to be divergent in their thinking, while at the same time allowing them to dig into the content.

As we model perspective taking, we must fight our tendencies to perceive life as we have experienced it. Sam Wineberg (2001) says, "Paradoxically, what allows us to come to know others is our distrust in our capacity to know them, a skepticism about the extraordinary sense-making abilities that allow us to construct the world around us" (p. 24). We must be humble and open-minded when we set out to walk in another person's shoes, whether that person lived three thousand years ago or currently lives down the street.

We must also remember that countless influences have bombarded each of us since the day we were born, including TV shows, school experiences, movies, music, trips, family, and friends, that all work in concert to shape how we might think when we walk in another's shoes. An effective overall goal during the year is to reflect on how present-focused biases shape our thoughts about how people in the past lived and thought. A few expressions to use along the way are provided in table 4.7.

Table 4.7 Academic Expressions for Perspective Taking in History

If I had been . . . , I would have . . . because . . .	Get inside her head for a moment.
Imagine you are . . . Map out your strategy for . . .	One way to interpret this event is . . .
I think that she felt . . .	For us in modern times, it could mean that . . .
There are several clues that show us how they might have felt.	If we read between the lines, we might guess that he . . .
We can draw several conclusions from our analysis of the documents.	I believe that the author did not include . . . about her because . . .
See through her eyes.	From his perspective, I think he was thinking . . .
Walk in their shoes.	
When we try to empathize a bit with . . .	I think that . . . because . . .

Diverse students can face added difficulties when it comes to the new language and thinking of history and social studies. History curricula in the United States tend to assume considerable prior knowledge of US-centric and Eurocentric places, government systems, people, events, and cultures. Moreover, some abstract concepts, such as individualism, democracy, freedom of speech, and privacy, might be less emphasized in students' home cultures. In many of my interviews with diverse students, several said that they feel uncomfortable expressing their opinions during classroom discussions, partly because of language and partly due to how they were raised (Zwiers, 2006).

LANGUAGE OF SCIENCE

Whereas history and language arts registers tend to describe social experiences, science language tends to be more technical, describing what happens in the natural and physical worlds (Martin, 1991). Scientific literacy, moreover, involves more than just text. It requires understanding multimedia genres and making meanings "by integrating the semiotic resources of language, mathematics, and a variety of visual-graphical presentations" (Lemke, 2002, p. 21). Thus, teachers of science must keep in mind that scientific language and literacy can differ significantly from the language and literacy that students use in other classes. The language of science, for example, tends to:

- Describe relationships of taxonomy, comparison, cause and effect, hypothesis, and interpretation. Unlike language arts and history, science texts have few stories or narratives. The text structure is dense and hierarchical (topic, subtopics, details).

- Describe procedures explicitly with procedural language, such as *measure, observe, calculate, graph, record, watch, place, make, seal, hold, predict, remove, examine, pour, prevent, dissolve, attach, connect, mark, insert,* and *align.* These are used mostly in lab directions and lab reports.

- Connect abstract ideas illustrated by various media and models. Photos, diagrams, graphs, charts, math and chemistry symbols, lab experiences, and text all overlap to communicate concepts.

- Use generalized verbs in the present tense to describe phenomena, how something occurs, and why.

- Be highly objective. The author construes message as fact rather than opinion, and there is a lack of first-person perspective and emotion.

- Use large amounts of passive voice construction—for example, "The transformation is carried out in just a few seconds. Then the compound is subjected to intense heat."

- Use many new and big words with new meanings, many of which are nominalizations, such as *condensation, refraction, induction, resonance, reaction, radiation, fusion, erosion,* and most other *-ation* words.

Description of Scientific Inquiry

The scientific community has created and adapted language to meet the needs of the ever-evolving ideas that need to be communicated. Students must be apprenticed into ways of using the language of observing, questioning, hypothesizing, experimenting, interpreting data, and making conclusions.

Table 4.8 demonstrates a way to help students absorb the language of scientific inquiry and practices in the Next Generation Science Standards (Achieve, 2013). This is just a sample; create your own chart along with your students for everyone to use. Be sure to explain difficult terms in the left-hand column, such as *aspect, hypothesis, isolating variables, logically, validity, support,* and *generalize.* Provide plenty of examples of how we and practicing scientists use these steps and their language. Examples might come from published reports, textbooks, newspapers, and the Internet.

Asking good questions is important for each practice. For example, students can ask, Is this worth knowing? Is this knowable? How solid are the results? Could other variables have affected the results? Is there a better way to perform the investigation? Are there alternative hypotheses to the ones proposed so far? Do we need more data and evidence to make our claims? Questions like these allow students to effectively communicate how they think about scientific processes, such as relating evidence to explanations, using models to clarify concepts, or posing alternative explanations.

Science involves a wide range of thinking skills and practices, three of which are highlighted here. Lemke (1990) has identified additional ones worthy of building, such as describing, classifying, analyzing, arguing, justifying, hypothesizing, generalizing, applying, designing experiments, questioning, and theorizing.

Table 4.8 Language Used to Describe Different Steps of Scientific Inquiry

Science Practices	Language for This Step
Ask questions about observations and phenomena (e.g., why it is happening, how).	I wonder why . . . Where does the . . . come from? How does it reproduce? What kind of reaction could cause that? What if we . . . ?
Generate hypotheses that attempt to answer the questions.	If we add . . . , then maybe . . . I hypothesize that . . . because . . . I think that it will because . . . What do you think will happen? Based on . . . , I think that . . . Most likely, it will . . .
Carefully plan and design ways to test hypotheses. Figure out how to isolate variables.	If we isolate the variable . . . , then we can see . . . Several variables come into play. We also need a control group. We need a microscope to see how . . . We need to change the . . . to see how . . . reacts. How can we prove that . . . ? But what about the effects of . . . ?
Use models to represent or describe scientific processes and relationships, collect data (e.g., lab), and predict.	The control group doesn't get treatment. The data should go into a table because . . . We need to measure the . . . As the . . . increases, the . . . decreases. There is a correlation between . . . and . . .
Make conclusions about the validity of experimental data and their support of the hypotheses. Make generalizations based on observations.	The data show that . . . We discovered that . . . Our data were not valid or reliable enough to make solid conclusions about . . . We found a negative correlation between . . . Based on these numbers, it is likely that . . . Our research has demonstrated that . . .

Cause and Effect in Science

A major practice in science is figuring out causes and effects (Thier & Daviss, 2002). This includes hypothesizing possible causes and effects of scientific phenomena and using cause-and-effect thinking to identify variables that bring about changes in experiments. The Common Core Anchor Literacy and Next Generation Science standards abound with references to this practice.

Science has a fascinating range of cause-and-effect linkages across its branches. Physical sciences tend to emphasize causes and effects of geology, gravity, electricity, and light; chemistry emphasizes causes and effects at the molecular level; biology tends to emphasize causes and effects in cells and adaptations of organisms. For example, in the following excerpt from a middle school biology lab in which students dissected squid, the teacher discusses with students the functions of the squid's two long tentacles:

1. *Teacher:* The squid has eight arms and two tentacles. <u>Why</u> do you think two are long and skinny and the others are short and fat? <u>Why</u> the two long ones?
2. *Student:* <u>To</u> feel?
3. *Teacher:* Yes, okay, <u>in order to</u> feel. What else?
4. *Student:* Catching prey.
5. *Teacher:* Yes, to catch prey. They have evolved, or changed over time, <u>in order to</u> catch prey. <u>Therefore</u>, <u>what happens to</u> my squid friends with short tentacles?
6. *Student:* They don't eat <u>because</u> they can't catch fish.
7. *Teacher:* Right, they don't survive. The process is called survival of the fittest, or natural selection. Now tell a partner why the terms *fittest* and *selection* are used.

In line 3, the teacher rephrased the student's response to emphasize the cause-and-effect phrase *in order to*, which she used again in line 5. The teacher used a rolling hand motion when using the term *therefore* to emphasize the term for English learners in the class. Notice how the teacher used the conversation to lead into a bigger idea, that of natural selection. Other language of cause and effect is found in table 4.9.

Table 4.9 Examples of Cause-and-Effect Language in Science

One reason for their . . . was . . .	This process allows . . .
It was due to the reaction between . . .	Since . . .
	Several factors contributed to the . . .
There could be multiple causes.	The purpose of that part is to . . .
The change resulted from . . .	The practical applications of this discovery are . . .
There is a linear relationship between . . .	If we hadn't . . . , what would have occurred?
I hypothesize that . . . because . . .	
If we do that, then . . .	In order to maintain a balance, . . .
It combines with . . . to produce . . .	A force acts on an object.
They transform into new substances.	It is generated by . . .

Interpretation in Science

Interpretation in science classes primarily happens when students analyze data from labs or experiments and when they "compare and contrast findings presented in a text to those from other sources (including their own experiments)" (CCSS.ELA-Literacy.RST.9–10.9) and "translate information expressed visually or mathematically (e.g., in an equation) into words" (CCSS.ELA-Literacy.RST.9–10.7). Students must carefully analyze data and textual claims and then figure out what the information leads them to conclude.

In the following excerpt, the teacher asks students to interpret and synthesize the data gathered for the volume and pressure of a gas. The students put books on a syringe with air in it and recorded the reduced volume each time.

1. *Teacher:* We will see what the increase in pressure from the books does to the volume. Your goal is to figure out the relationship between pressure and volume. You need to analyze the data from the table and turn it into a graph.

2. *Student A:* So how do we use the graph?

3. *Teacher:* You interpret the numbers and then extrapolate, or extend the lines to make educated guesses. For example, you might just use five books, but what if I asked you to predict the pressure for fifty books?

4. *Student E:* But we can't stack fifty books up—it'll break!

5. *Teacher:*   That's why I said *if* and *predict*. It's <u>hypothetical</u>. It can't happen, but we can <u>use our data to predict</u> what would result. Then we look at data from other groups and see if <u>we can come up with general patterns or a rule</u> about volume and pressure.

In this excerpt, the teacher showed how interpretation depended also on the skills of analysis and comparison. Students needed to transfer the data from the table to the graph and then interpret the results when asked to extrapolate the data. Later the teacher asked if they could come up with a formula to help anyone who wants to know the pressure in syringes with books on them but doesn't have the materials or the time to do the measuring. She used the experience, coupled with her words and knowledge of how science works, to apprentice students into interpreting as scientists would in this situation.

Comparison in Science

Comparing helps us understand something because we are forced to analyze it and notice discrete characteristics (e.g., types of cell reproduction, planetary bodies, chemical reactions). Uncovering the similarities and differences helps us better define, understand, and connect to what we are learning. In biology, students often compare the traits of organisms. In chemistry, they compare reactions and the traits of compounds and elements. In physics and earth sciences, they compare physical properties and forces.

In the next excerpt, the teacher is looking at student answers to the question "How are the cells similar?" after students conducted a microscope lab that looked at four different types of cells:

1. *Teacher:*   What's this? *(looking at student's paper)*
2. *Student E:*   They look different.
3. *Teacher:*   And then the next answer you put, "Different looking"? Neither answer is precise enough. How do they look <u>different</u>?
4. *Student E:*   They are small.
5. *Teacher:*   Yes, microscopic. Unicellular. Do you know what *unicellular* means? What does *uni* mean? Do you know what a unicycle is?
6. *Student E:*   No.
7. *Teacher:*   *Uni* means one. Like *uno* in Spanish. So it means . . .
8. *Student E:*   One cell.

9. *Teacher:*   They have <u>different</u> . . .
10. *Student E:* Names?
11. *Teacher:*   No, what you observed. You didn't observe their names. What about movement? How were they <u>different</u>? Were they <u>exactly the same</u>?
12. *Student E:* <u>Different</u> shape? Like bacteria.
13. *Teacher:*   <u>How were they similar</u> to bacteria?
14. *Student E:* Movement.
15. *Teacher:*   Yes, they moved around <u>differently</u>. How?

As you can see, the teacher had to work hard to apprentice this student into being much more detailed in her analysis of differences in the cells. The student was right in saying that they had different names, but she did not yet understand that a major skill in science is to closely observe natural phenomena. (Of course, advanced observation also means advanced language, and some students, despite their noticings, might not want to struggle to communicate them because they lack the language.) The teacher prompted the student to think in these ways by giving her the category of movement to describe and asking, "How were they different?" and "How were they similar?" This type of nudging students into more academic ways of thinking and doing takes a lot of effort and patience, especially when working with students who lack the home experiences with such types of describing.

LANGUAGE OF MATH

"Can I count math as a foreign language for my college entrance requirements?" a high school student once asked me. Math's language (and thinking) can be even more foreign than that of other content areas. It is very abstract, particularly in upper grades. Although some visuals and objects can be used, much of math happens in the brain. The development of mathematical language and literacy can be more challenging than in other subjects for several reasons:

- There is less overlap with concepts, ideas, and terms found in other subjects. Math has many distinct vocabulary terms used only in math.

- Students must learn to decipher and use a wide range of symbols. There is often a range of symbols, numbers, letters, illustrations, and words mixed together in problems.

- A student must read not only left to right but right to left, up and down, and even diagonally when reading graphs and tables, for example.

- Math texts have a denser concentration of abstract concepts than other academic texts (Thomas, 1988). There are more concepts per sentence for a brain to process. Math texts are tightly connected, and each word and phrase is important to process; a student who skims might miss key points.

- Many math concepts are embedded within other math concepts: they depend on prior knowledge and experience. Learning about imaginary numbers depends on other understandings of negative numbers and rational numbers.

- Historically there has been a lack of extended student talk about math in math classes.

In some math classes, I hear much too little math language being used to teach and talk about math concepts. Some teachers simply model how to do math on the screen upfront and then tell students to work on problems. Khisty (1993) also found that teachers avoided using mathematical (academic) terms to explain the concepts and processes. This, unfortunately, is a form of linguistic enabling (see chapter 3) that can be harmful in the long run for many students, although they might succeed on tasks and tests in the short run. Next year's teacher might use math terminology that overwhelms students because they didn't learn the terms this year.

Students often miss out on the foundational concepts because of poor articulation, poor teaching, change of schools, or other lack of extra support. The Common Core math standards emphasize the need to know why something works in math, not just how. The CCSS Standards for Mathematical Practice, for example, focus on teaching students to "make sense of quantities and their relationships," "justify their conclusions," "reason inductively about data," "give carefully formulated explanations to each other," and "examine claims and make explicit use of definitions" (National Governors Association Center for Best Practices, 2010). Knowing and explaining why requires students to use sophisticated language and terminology. In the next dialogue, the algebra teacher builds up the language of balancing equations as the students figure out the following problem: $2(7x - 4) + 3(2x - 1) = 2(9x - 2) - 3(4x - 7)$. I have underlined several of the academic terms that the teacher is modeling:

1. *Teacher:* Why do we balance equations?
2. *Student A:* We want to get the answer in the end and that's how.

3. *Teacher:* Yes, we want to isolate the unknown. So think of a scale—not a bathroom scale but one with the bar across a central point. If you add or subtract from one side, then it tips over, right? So to calculate the variable we use order of operations, right? What's the acronym?

4. *Student E:* PEMDAS.

5. *Teacher:* Which means what?

6. *Student C:* You do parentheses, exponents, multiplication, division, addition, and subtraction.

7. *Teacher:* Okay, so we use the distributive property and multiply the 2 by each term inside the parentheses, right? So we get $14x - 8 + 6x - 3$ on the left side and $18x - 4 - 12x + 21$ on the right. Simplify each side by joining like terms.

8. *Student A:* $20x - 11 = 6x + 17$.

9. *Teacher:* Okay, now we balance. We want to isolate the x on one side, which means to make it all alone. I usually choose to keep it on the side with the largest coefficient. So let's cancel out the constant, negative 11, by adding positive 11 to the left side. Great, it's gone. Now what?

10. *Student D:* You didn't balance it. You gotta add 11 to the other side, right?

As the example shows, math discussions require a lot of concentrated abstract thinking and new language. I zoom in on two types of math thinking next: interpretation and problem solving.

Interpreting in Math

The CCSS math standards strongly emphasize understanding, reasoning, and interpretation. For example, CCSS.Math.Practice.MP4 requires students to "interpret their mathematical results in the context of the situation." "Interpreting in math" means making meaning from words, symbols, data, or visuals. For example, we may need to interpret a graph. All the information is there on the graph, and we need to look at the lines and numbers to find the information we need. Conversely, we may have data that need to go into a graph for us or others to interpret. We figure out how to make the visual (graph) clearly show the differences or changes in the data. We may decide to use a line graph, bar graph, pie chart, or data table. We make the visual as interpretable to others as possible.

Another branch of interpretation is working with mathematical symbols. Each symbol carries a lot of meaning. Students need to quickly decode the symbols into their abstract meanings or quickly encode words and abstract ideas into symbols to solve problems. For example, $25 + a > 35$ means "the sum of 25 and a number placed into variable a is greater than 35." And it gets much more difficult because many formulas contain multiple variables and symbols. For example, the area of any circle is denoted by $A = \pi r^2$. This simple formula assumes a knowledge of what *area* means, the value of the constant, pi ($3.1415 \ldots$), and how to find r, the radius. Students must use symbols to adeptly and fluently read equations as they gradually become experts at math.

Another aspect of interpretation is working with new and challenging terms. New words in this case are *reciprocal, denominator, polynomial, quotient, derivative, numerator, hypotenuse,* and *formula.* These abstract terms tend to be difficult to draw, and they can take on different meanings and values. For example, *denominator* can be any number; a *hypotenuse* can be on the left, right, or bottom as you look at a triangle; and a *formula* can take many forms into which you can put many different numbers.

More common in math are the dual-meaning expressions borrowed from "normal" language for use in math, such as those listed in table 4.10. If you didn't know that this section is about math language, you might just think of the table as a list of daily words. Fortunately, most of these words have some kind of concrete connection in normal life to help students interpret and remember the meanings. For *slope* they can think of a hillside, for *balance*

Table 4.10 Common Terms with Specialized Meanings in Math

balance	interest	difference
coordinate	power	terms
even	similar	radical
imaginary	irrational	improper
plane	axis	chance
product	mixed	expression
round	cube	principal
scale	value	factor
slope	represent	simplify
square	find	function
positive	field	real
tangent	proof	odd

Table 4.11 Math Imperatives, Questions, and Expressions

Math Imperatives	Questions and Expressions
Plot	Which system of equations represents the situation?
Graph	
Interpret	Which ratio represents an approximation of . . . ?
Calculate	What is the measure of . . . ?
Estimate	Average
Construct	Equivalent
Convert	Relevant information
Compare	Descent, ascent, altitude
Substitute	Operations
Find the relationship between x and y	Vary directly
Design it to minimize . . .	Reasonable
Look for a pattern	Dimensions
Work backward	If x equals . . . , then what is . . . ?
Predict	Break the problem down into . . .
Isolate	

they think of a scale, for *factor* they think of parts in a factory, and for *odd* they think of strange.

A third level of interpretation is the most challenging for teachers to teach and for students to learn and use: the set of terms that lack concrete connections to them. These are found throughout texts, tests, and teacher talk, yet we teachers seldom realize their pervasiveness because of our own immersion in them. Some examples are included in table 4.11. We must be on the lookout for these and similar types of less visible terms and explain their meanings in context. We should combine this with as much visual explanation as possible. Many terms are included in our directions and questions. Take a moment to think about how often we assume students know these terms, but also how challenging and abstract the terms can be.

Problem Solving in Math

Much of what students do in math consists of watching the teacher solve problems, working with others to solve problems, and working alone to solve problems. In addition to interpretation, students must use other thinking skills and language to solve complex problems. Students analyze different parts of a problem, hypothesize possible ways to solve it and possible answers, apply previously learned strategies and formulas to the problem, summarize main points and exclude extraneous information, organize the information in a logical way, and compare the problem to previous similar problems. Notice how the teacher scaffolds the language of problem solving in the following excerpt from an algebra class:

1. *Teacher:*   Okay, what do you do first?

2. *Student E:*   We <u>figure out what they want</u>. But I dunno what *"to the nearest foot"* means.

3. *Student F:*   And what's a theodolite?

4. *Teacher:*   A theodolite measures angles, and *"to the nearest foot"* means make an <u>estimate</u>, because you might get a decimal answer that you have to round off. So <u>what are they asking</u>?

5. *Student F:*   They <u>want to know</u> how high the cliff is to bring enough rope.

6. *Student E:*   So we need to use the stuff on tangents or cosines because we talked about it, right?

7. *Teacher:*   Okay, good, <u>you can use</u> trigonometry ratios. But what do you need to know? What information <u>do they give you</u>?

8. *Student E:*   We <u>can draw it</u>, like, a triangle. This is the cliff; <u>we don't know</u> how high.

9. *Student F:*   We <u>can make it be *x*</u>. This angle is twenty degrees from the theo-thing to the top. Then use that plastic thing to get twenty degrees.

10. *Student E:*   And the distance is five hundred feet along the bottom. Now what? We <u>use that formula</u> for tan.

11. *Teacher:*   Why?

12. *Student E:*   We <u>know the angle and the bottom side</u>, and you did some problems on that today. You said <u>we need</u> two out of three things.

13. *Teacher:*   Yes, tangent <u>helps us</u>. Tan A equals opposite side over adjacent. Adjacent is which one?

14. *Student F:*   The one next to the angle, which is A, right?

15. *Student E:*   I guess. <u>Let's try it</u>: tan 20° equals *x* over 500.

16. *Teacher:* So we want <u>to isolate the variable x</u>, *right?*
17. *Student F:* Times the 500 to each side and you get 500 times tan 20° equals x. So x equals 181.985. So like 182. Does <u>that make sense?</u>

In looking at the many underlined phrases for describing problem solving, we see that most terms are common in everyday speech, but in math they are used for complex and abstract purposes when solving problems. The teacher nudged the students along and used some content terms, such as *trigonometry ratios, tangent, opposite, adjacent,* and *isolate the variable.* But the students were in charge of the direction of the problem solving for the most part. Student F even finished with an important step at the end: checking the reasonableness of the calculated answer, which is also a Common Core standard of mathematical practice. Of course, the criteria and components for making sense require much discussion and scaffolding over the years.

Many sets of problem-solving steps exist in books and on posters; I include a basic synthesis of these steps here. I include it as a reminder to analyze the language that we use to teach the steps of problem solving. These steps do little good if students don't understand what they mean. The more we can explain and scaffold this language, the more chances of success they have in future math settings. I have underlined the academic terms in problem-solving steps that might confuse some students if they were to read these on their own:

1. <u>Background</u>: Carefully read the problem and <u>understand</u> exactly what you need to find out. <u>State it in your own words</u>.

2. Underline any <u>key information</u>. <u>Scan</u> the problem for pictures, graphs, or diagrams. What do <u>they tell you?</u>

3. Find clue words that tell you what you <u>need to do</u>. *Area* might mean that you will multiply; *difference* often means you will subtract; *formula* often means you will need <u>to use or derive an expression with variables</u> in it; and so on.

4. <u>Make a plan</u>: Have you seen a similar problem before?

5. <u>What is similar about it</u>? How did you solve it?

6. What <u>previous knowledge and skills</u> do you need in order to solve this problem? Think about sample problems in the text or those solved by the teacher.

Table 4.12 Expressions Used in Problem Solving

We need to figure out exactly what they want.	I bet that . . . because . . .
Let's break it down into parts. First, . . .	This is like the problem we did on . . .
	We need to identify the . . .
Information that I need is . . . because . . .	We don't know . . . , so let's make it a variable.
There are different ways to solve it.	Maybe a data table will work because . . .
The best solution is . . . because . . .	This answer makes sense because . . .
I predict that . . .	
We can draw this part as . . .	I think we need to try another way.
We can check our answer by trying . . .	I think that the answer is . . . because . . .
I don't think this information is important because . . .	This word means that the final units need to be in . . .

7. Think about <u>different strategies</u> for solving this problem (make drawings, guess and check, find a pattern).

8. <u>Solve it</u> using one or more strategies.

9. <u>Reflect</u> on how <u>probable</u> the answer is. Does your answer <u>reasonably</u> answer the question? Do you use the <u>proper</u> language and <u>units</u> of the question?

In the problem-solving steps just described, diverse students often need heavy explanation and modeling of the following: stating something in their own words; noticing key information; interpreting pictures and graphs; finding clue words; comparing the problem to a previous one; making a plan; listing what they need to know; drawing, guessing and checking, and finding patterns; and reflecting on the reasonableness of an answer. Table 4.12 is a list of other expressions that are often used to solve problems and explain their answers.

CONCLUSION

In this chapter, we have looked at the various subregisters (branches) of academic language found in four school disciplines, emphasizing prevalent thinking skills in each discipline and their language. Just as birdwatchers are always on the lookout for important birds, we must be on the lookout for key terms and phrases in our texts, tasks, tests, and talk. Each discipline has its own specialized ways of using language to describe its concepts, and each has its own set of important terms and language strategies that describe certain cognitive processes.

Because information and its uses are changing so rapidly, many "facts" will be out of date in a few years. Indeed, many of the facts that I memorized during my schooling I now do not remember or have never used, but the thinking skills that organized them have remained and served me in a variety of courses, jobs, and life challenges. Mercer (2000) put it well: "Education is not about manipulation of objects. A great deal of it is learning how to use language—to represent ideas, to interpret experiences, to formulate problems and to solve them" (p. 74). The different disciplines in upper grades allow (and require) students to branch out their evolving academic thinking and communication skills. Indeed, a student may never become a scientist, for example, but the cognitive and linguistic skills he or she developed in science classes will be an asset in a wide range of future courses and jobs.

CHAPTER REFLECTIONS

- What are some general academic language expressions that are used across content areas?

- What types of thinking, expressions, and grammar are emphasized in your content area?

- Analyze a challenging article or passage of text on a topic from your content area. What kinds of thinking are required to understand it? What language triggers that thinking?

- What large-scale strategies can your school employ to promote language growth across content areas and grade levels?

- Ask friends in different occupations what types of thinking they do. Take note of the language they use to describe their examples.

- Audiotape a class that you teach, and listen to it for the language of thinking, abstraction, and complexity. Listen also for responses and comments described in chapter 3.

References

Achieve. (2013). *Next Generation Science Standards.* Retrieved from http://www
.nextgenscience.org/search-standards-dci

Appleby, J., Brinkley, A., Broussard, A., McPherson, J., & Ritchie, D. (2005). *The American journey.* Columbus, OH: Glencoe.

Brenner, D., & Parks, S. (2001). Cultural influences on critical thinking and problem solving. In A. L. Costa (Ed.), *Developing minds: A resource book for teaching thinking* (pp. 216–221). Alexandria, VA: Association for Supervision and Curriculum Development.

Bunch, G. (2013). Pedagogical language knowledge: Preparing mainstream teachers for English learners in the new standards era. *Review of Research in Education, 37,* 298–341.

CCSS. (2013). *Standards for mathematical practice.* Retrieved from http://www
.corestandards.org/Math/Practice

Coffin, C. (1997). Constructing and giving value to the past: An investigation into secondary school history. In F. Christie & J. Martin (Eds.), *Genre and institutions: Social processes in the workplace and school* (pp. 196–230). London, UK: Cassell.

Douglas, S. (1858). *Speech of Senator Douglas.* Retrieved from www.bartleby.com
/251/1002.html

Holt, T. (1990). *Thinking historically: Narrative, imagination, and understanding.* New York, NY: College Entrance Examination Board.

Khisty, L. L. (1993). A naturalistic look at language factors in mathematics teaching in bilingual classrooms. *Proceedings of the third National Research Symposium on Limited English Proficient Student Issues: Focus on Middle and High School Issues.* Washington, DC: US Department of Education, Office of Bilingual and Minority Language Affairs. Available: http://www.ncela.gwu.edu
/pubs/symposia/third/khisty.htm

Lemke, J. (1990). *Talking science: Language, learning, and values.* New York, NY: Ablex.

Lemke, J. (2002). Multimedia semiotics: Genres for science education and scientific literacy. In M. J. Schleppegrell & M. Colombi (Eds.), *Developing advanced literacy in first and second languages: Meaning with power* (pp. 21–44). Mahwah, NJ: Erlbaum.

Martin, J. (1991). Nominalization in science and humanities: Distilling knowledge and scaffolding text. In E. Ventola (Ed.), *Functional and systemic linguistics* (pp. 307–337). Berlin, Germany: Mouton de Gruyter.

Mercer, N. (2000). *The guided construction of knowledge: Talk amongst teachers and learners.* Clevedon, UK: Multilingual Matters.

Nathan, M. J., & Petrosino, A. J. (2003). Expert blind spot among preservice teachers. *American Educational Research Journal, 40*(4), 905–928.

National Governors Association Center for Best Practices. (2010). *Common Core State Standards.* Washington, DC: Council of Chief State School Officers.

Paulsen, G. (1987). *Hatchet.* New York, NY: Simon Pulse Paperbacks.

Rosenblatt, L. M. (1995). *Literature as exploration.* New York, NY: Modern Language Association of America.

Shulman, L. S. (1987). Knowledge and teaching: Foundations of the new reform. *Harvard Educational Review, 57*(1), 1–22.

Thier, M., & Daviss, B. (2002). *The new science literacy: Using language skills to help students learn science.* Portsmouth, NH: Heinemann.

Thomas, D. (1988). Reading and reasoning skills for mathematics problem solvers. *Journal of Reading, 32,* 244–249.

Wineberg, S. (2001). *Historical thinking and other unnatural acts: Charting the future of teaching the past.* Philadelphia, PA: Temple University Press.

Zwiers, J. (2005). *Developing academic language in middle school English learners: Practices and perspectives in mainstream classrooms.* Unpublished doctoral dissertation, University of San Francisco.

Zwiers, J. (2006). Integrating academic language, thinking, and content: Learning scaffolds for non-native speakers in the middle grades. *Journal of English for Academic Purposes, 5*(4), 317–332.

Chapter 5

Facilitating Whole-Class Discussions for Content and Language Development

Talk is priceless.

Powerful development of thinking and language can happen when a class engages in effective discussions. Making discussions *effective* is the trick, however. With so many large and diverse classes, challenges abound. This chapter focuses on making whole-class academic listening and speaking more effective for teaching content, thinking, and language. After providing a rationale for using classroom talk in a variety of settings, I include several research-based activities that build academic listening and speaking skills. These activities fit within different categories of question asking, improving whole-class discussions, and using effective whole-class communication activities.

CHALLENGES AND BENEFITS OF CULTIVATING RICH CLASSROOM TALK

Classroom talk is a tool for working with information such that it becomes knowledge and understanding (Mercer, 2000). Unfortunately, talk in many school settings has a linear and static nature. *Linear* implies that if we say something once, we have taught it (or think we have), and *static* means that what students learn is memorizable and testable with fact-based tests. In one study, researchers found that 85 percent of all instructional time in a sample of eighth- and ninth-grade English classrooms was a combination of lecture, recitation, and seatwork (Nystrand & Gamoran, 1991). Yet talk in the real world, such as natural discourse in research and business settings, tends to be circular and exploratory, often digressing and back-tracking, with lots of digging, questioning, disagreeing, and clarifying (Gilles, 1993).

Classroom discussions are unpredictable and sensitive to the slightest nudges. A nudge might be a back channel (*wow, okay, uh-huh*), a question, a period of silence, a smile, a facial expression, or any other comment that changes the course of discussion (see chapter 3). These nudges can send discussions in many different directions. Some have dead ends, some go deep into the fertile valleys of thought, and some just wind along on the surface. One little question at the right time can send a discussion down a powerfully deep road in which students make many connections and reach understandings. The lack of a nudge at the right time, however, can cause the class to miss the chance to go deeper. A consistent lack of good nudges by teachers or students over time can deprive all students of rich thinking and language experiences.

Another challenge is undoing what I call the same-old same-olds—insipid routines or frameworks for communication tasks (Griffin & Smith, 2001). One example is the oral book report. The student summarizes the plot, the teacher asks one or two probing questions, other students ask surface-level questions, and the student sits down. These types of routines unfortunately can start in first grade and continue through high school. The students think that these routines and tasks simply form the script of school, just as they might think that round-robin reading, multiple-choice tests, weekly vocabulary quizzes, and lectures simply *are* school. Yet learning in these ways is not enough for many diverse learners. They need to get involved with new knowledge and work with it under a variety of conditions so that they ultimately own it (Mercer, 2000).

Despite the many challenges, classroom discussions are helpful for several reasons, a few of which are that they:

- Allow for repetition of linguistic terms and thinking processes during the course of conversation (or the course of an entire year), and their eventual acquisition, internalization, and appropriation by students (Bakhtin, 1981; Vygotsky, 1978).

- Push learners to think quickly, respond, organize their thoughts into sentences, negotiate meaning, back claims with evidence, ask for clarification, and construct meaning as the dialogue develops.

- Require students to produce language in order to teach, explain, express, and convince others of the value of their own ideas. This process of teaching others, as we well know, tends to result in deeper thinking about the content.

- Provide a format to make hidden thought processes more public and shared. This allows skilled thinkers and language users to pass on skills and ideas to others.

- Allow students to see how other people think and use language to describe their thinking. They compare their own thinking processes and interpretations to those of others. If their thoughts are way off, they can adjust; if their thoughts are similar, they feel validated. Students can bounce their ideas off peers in a low-stress setting and hear peer feedback on their thoughts.

The Common Core standards add another layer of urgency and focus to the quality of classroom talk. The listening and speaking standards, for example, clarify a range of expectations for student involvement in discussions: engage effectively in a range of collaborative discussions with diverse partners on grade-level topics, texts, and issues, building on others' ideas and expressing their own clearly; refer to evidence; follow rules for collegial discussions; set specific goals; pose and respond to questions with elaboration; review the key ideas expressed; and demonstrate understanding of multiple perspectives (CCSS.ELA-Literacy.LS. 6.1a-d). These are daunting yet possible standards to reach. Thus, it is helpful to move directly to ways in which we can make classroom talking events more academic and engaging.

ASKING QUESTIONS

Questioning is one of the most common ways to start and maintain discussions, as well as check for student learning. Questions are often significant nudges that can shape conversations and push students to use more challenging terms and grammar. It is vital that we reflect on the different types of questions that can be asked and even consider alternatives to questions that might be more effective ways to teach and learn.

Display Questions

Teachers often ask display questions, also known as explicit ("right there") questions, as well as closed questions. Display questions are mainly used to let or make students display their knowledge (What is the square root of x squared? What is an isotope? Where did the boy come from? What did Martin Luther say about that?). Answers to display questions are generally known by the teacher, who is usually trying to get students either to connect to background information or recall recent information that they are supposed to have learned. In my observations of fourth-, seventh-, and ninth-grade classrooms, display questions were used about half the time to connect to background knowledge and half the time to remind students of what they just learned—or to check whether they learned it (Zwiers, 2005).

Both types (connection and reminder check) are used in the dialogue that follows, which is excerpted from a seventh-grade history class. Student E is an intermediate-level English learner from Vietnam. The connection questions the teacher asks are "Do you know what *solved* means?" and "What's a flea?" The reminder-check questions are the others that relate to the current learning about the cause of the Black Plague:

1. *Teacher:*   Look, in 1898, what did they realize the cause was? Read that to me.
2. *Student E:*   In 1898, a French scientist solved a mystery.
3. *Teacher:*   Do you know what *solved* means? *(pause)* To answer the puzzle. What's a flea?
4. *Student E:*   This bug on rats.
5. *Teacher:*   Okay. Where did the rats come from?
6. *Student E:*   The boats?
7. *Teacher:*   Yes. But why did people get diseases?

8. *Student E:*   I don't know.

9. *Teacher:*   Because fleas would come off the rats and bite people because things weren't very clean. They found out that . . . What?

10. *Student E:*   Where the disease come from.

I have observed that teachers in most schools around the world use many more display questions than open-ended questions. This might be due in part to the fact that most standardized tests are made up of right-or-wrong (display) questions that cover discrete pieces of knowledge and low-level skills. It is also likely due to the many years that teachers were immersed in such questioning in their own schooling. Display questioning, despite its apparent interactivity, can dominate class time and take the place of the exploration of deeper issues. One scholar even concluded that "the extent to which a child reveals his or her own ideas and seeks information is inversely proportioned to the frequency of teacher questions" (Wood, 1986, p. 209). Thus, more questions might actually hinder learning!

Even more disconcerting were data that suggested that mainstream students were called on more frequently for responses that involved academic thinking and academic language, whereas English learners were called on more to answer fact-based display questions (Zwiers, 2005). As obviously wrong as this may seem, it is tempting to do. We want our diverse students to participate, so we might give them easier questions to answer. Yet if we do this consistently, we will hinder learning and widen the achievement gaps that already exist.

Display questions nevertheless can serve several purposes. First, they can quickly reveal what students already know before we teach. These questions are often in the form of "Who can tell me . . .," "Who knows . . .," "Does anyone remember why . . .," and, "Let me see a show of hands for those who . . ." Second, they can build up a foundation (or "raw material") with which to build the lesson. They can bring up facts, concepts, and ideas needed for discussion. Third, display questions can help us quickly find out what students have learned. Fourth, although this practice is often overused, display questions can get students to learn something. For example, I might ask, "How many planets are there?" This may ignite a short discussion, as some may not know there are nine (more or less), and some may know about the controversies surrounding other planet-like bodies out there.

Another advantage of display questions is their potential to model language in the questions and in the feedback, as seen in the following examples:

"What feature evolved to help it survive in the dark parts of the ocean?"

"Which events incited the protest movement?"

"What evidence did he use to convict her?"

"How does the reciprocal of this fraction help me?"

Notice the academic terms in these questions. Notice other terms in the following feedback samples:

"Excellent hypothesis. We'll see if it holds true."

"Almost. Think about the context at the time—all that was happening and how people felt."

"Okay, Silvia thinks that the man's testimony is false because he had ulterior motives."

"Yes, a reciprocal changes the operation from division to multiplication. Why?"

A slight variation of the display question is what Edwards and Mercer (1993) call a *cued elicitation*. This is the practice of drawing information from students by using verbal hints and visual clues, which allows students to play a small role in what would normally be a teacher-dominated lecture. One common example is unfinished sentences. Here are a few examples:

"The family ventured west because they . . ."

"She said that the experience was similar to . . ."

"We use the quadratic formula because . . ."

"The politician was motivated primarily by . . ."

Cued elicitations like these have advantages and disadvantages. When overused, they are just another way for the teacher to control the scene and establish dominance and dependence. (This happens in a scene from the movie *Ferris Bueller's Day Off*, in which the teacher does this in a history class, following his elicitation with "Anyone? Anyone?" droning on in monotone.)

Display questions and cued elicitations tend to be easier to generate quickly than open questions, partly because we must first have in mind the answer that we hope to hear as we make up the question. Our cognitive energy is already stretched to the limit as we teach. A good way to avoid the overuse of surface-level questions is to put open-ended questions into our lesson plans beforehand (and perhaps up on the board), which gives us additional time to think about the more involved answers that we hope to hear.

Open-Ended Questions

Open-ended questions allow students to come up with lengthier and more personalized responses. Teachers ask open-ended questions that usually fall into four categories: (1) personalizing (e.g., thoughts, feelings, opinions, and interpretations), (2) justifying, (3) clarifying, and (4) elaborating (Zwiers, 2005).

In the next dialogue, the history teacher used personal questions ("What do you . . .?" and "Why do you . . .?") with an emphasis on the word *you* in order to make sure that the student, a shy intermediate-level speaker, felt safe to answer. The teacher used many questions to help him prepare an oral presentation in which he needed to describe life as a medieval monk in the first person:

1. *Teacher:* What do you want to say?
2. *Student F:* I'm a monk, and my name is Javier.
3. *Teacher:* What do people want to know about being a monk?
4. *Student F:* We wake up at 2:00 a.m. and then at 3:00 a.m. We go back asleep for three hours.
5. *Teacher:* Why do you do that? Why wake up at 2:00 a.m.?
6. *Student F:* It says right here.
7. *Teacher:* It doesn't say why, though. You have to tell them, because that's interesting. So do you know why you would wake up so early? I wonder why you have a church service at 2:00 a.m. Do you have a guess?
8. *Student F:* Maybe to be, like, extra holy?

In line 7, a variation of open questions that we teachers can use is showing perplexity about something (see the related discussion in chapter 3). This leads to prompting the student to think beyond the text and guess. We might say, "I still wonder why the Mayan civilization declined a thousand years ago." Or, "I am confused. Why does ice float when most precipitates sink?" Or, "I wonder why this critic thought the novel was about revenge." After all these, we might follow up with "What do you think?" Or, "Are you still perplexed about anything?" These types of open questions show students that we teachers still ask good questions and that experts in a content area still seek deeper knowledge about a subject.

Several examples of open questions that I have heard in classrooms are these: "How did you solve this problem without a calculator?" "Why do you think this statue is important?" "Why would someone say that a virus is alive?" and "How would you have acted differently from the main character?" Many of the best open questions prompt students to use such higher-order thinking skills as analysis, synthesis, evaluation, application, interpretation, and perspective.

PROMPT POSTERS

An effective scaffold for open questions is a poster with question starters and prompts on it. When anyone, including the teacher, gets stuck, the prompt poster offers ideas for deeper thinking. Select from the following ideas (adapted from Robb, 2003):

- Use hindsight to explain how this problem or event could have been avoided.
- Explain how what we learn from this can help future generations.
- Explain different solutions or sides to the issue.
- How does the author try to persuade you? Are you convinced? Why? Do you have any more questions now than before reading?
- Can you find any strong words or statements in the text? Why are they there?
- Have your thoughts about this topic changed? Why or why not?
- Connect this topic or issue to another text or situation in the world.
- Persuade us to take a side of an issue.
- Use data, examples, or other evidence to suggest a change.

Questions in Response to Student Responses

We also ask a range of questions as we respond to what students say. We usually ask for more information. Here are a few of the more academic types of questions that elicit more information from students, usually challenging them to think more deeply about their initial answer and to use more sophisticated language.

Justification Questions

Justification questions are used to prompt students to logically support their answers. We might ask such questions as these:

"Why do you think that?"

"What evidence do you have?"

"Do you have a good reason for thinking that . . .?"

"For example?"

Such questions are important builders of thinking, especially for the thinking required by the writing assignments in middle and high school. Most assignments in upper grades tend to require justification and evidence. Unfortunately, a problem is the lack of modeling of justification by teachers. We often ask many questions that relate to justifying thoughts and opinions and providing good reasons, but we do not sufficiently model good justifying. We must make an effort to model the justification of our own thoughts and then discuss what makes reasons and evidence strong or weak.

Clarification Questions

Clarification questions require students to explain their responses. These can be genuine (we truly don't know what they mean) or instructional (we want them to clarify their own thoughts for themselves or to benefit the class). The most common questions tend to be these:

"What do you mean by . . .?"

"Can you explain?"

"How do you define . . .?"

"I think we should clarify the meaning of . . ."

The main reason that teachers ask these questions is that students rely too much on shared background knowledge. They assume that their short answer is enough or that others know the rest of their thoughts. In many cases, they are right. If a topic has been discussed in class, students may rightly feel that they don't need to clarify because the others who are involved know the details.

Elaboration Questions

Elaboration questions are a form of open-ended questioning that teachers commonly use. In many cases, such questions prompt students to think more deeply about a concept or to define their understanding of it further. Elaboration questions should be clear. For example, a student may answer "because he was greedy," and the teacher might respond, "Okay, he was greedy. What else?" Was this student right? Wrong? Not right enough? In this instance, the teacher repeated or rephrased a student response, which the student considered to be an acceptance of a correct response. But the teacher followed up with another question ("What else?"), suggesting that the response may not have been adequate after all and that another, even better, answer was desired. Such teacher responses, common in many classrooms, may confuse students because they send both positive and negative evaluation feedback in reaction to their answers.

Rethinking the Use of Questions

I believe that questions are overused in school. Students see them on the board, in the book, and on quizzes and tests, and they hear them from the teacher day after day, year after year. Students have been bombarded by questions in all forms from their first day in school. They are tired of questions, especially other people's questions. Even "good" questions that require extra thinking may not be the best way to teach and learn. We should entertain the possibility that questions, despite their widespread use in school for generations, are not always the most effective tools for learning. We should question our questioning practices: What kinds of questions are we asking, and why? How often? Can students learn in other ways? Here are a few suggestions to lighten the question load while increasing learning:

- Ask fewer questions, and give more time for thoughtful answers.

- Make the questions that you do ask more interesting and relevant to real-world applications (more open and implicit-level questions).

- Ask questions of students that you would ask of yourself.

- Train students to ask their own questions (that get them to learn what they need to learn). Questions can be based on charts, pictures, texts, current issues, and so on.

- Invite students to elaborate on their answers and reword their own responses.

- Create learning tasks and assessments that are not so dependent on questions.

This last point is especially important. The real world doesn't have as many lists of questions as we hear in school and see on tests. Real-world people are asked to produce or perform, asking their own questions along the way, and are not being stopped every few minutes to answer less important questions. Questions should be a means to learning, not the end.

Pseudo-Discussions

Sinclair and Coulthard (1975) analyzed elementary classroom language and found that teacher–student interactions often followed a predictable structure: the teacher initiated with a display question (I), a student responded (R), and the teacher provided positive or negative feedback (F). This traditional format of school talk has been passed down for generations and still permeates most lessons. Even in higher education, business, religious, and technical classes, the teacher talks a lot, asks quick questions, waits for answers, and responds to them, often praising the answers or rewording them to lead into another topic. Yet IRF is in fact a pseudo-discussion format that remains on a shallow level of stimulus and response.

The following example from a middle school science class has several IRFs:

1. *Teacher:*   What is happening in the diagram?
2. *Student E:*   An object is being thrown into the air straight up.
3. *Teacher:*   Good, and what happens when gravity acts on this object?
4. *Student F:*   It slows down.
5. *Teacher:*   Okay, it slows down, right. Does it ever stop?

6. *Student G:* Yes, at the top.

7. *Teacher:* Great, so its velocity is what up here?

8. *Student G:* Zero, I think.

9. *Teacher:* Great, zero.

In an IRF ambience, students often complain about playing the old "try to please the teacher with the right answer" game. Those who don't or can't play along end up watching most of the time. IRF has a number of negative aspects:

- The teacher maintains too much control over the content and direction of classroom discussions.

- Questions are usually fact based and do not encourage higher-level thinking.

- IRF allows one student to talk briefly, thus establishing unequal status in the classroom (usually the same students always answer the questions).

- Students begin to expect teacher initiation of talk about topics all the time.

- IRF is used to transmit knowledge passively, which means that little construction of meaning happens.

- IRF can place extra stress on students who feel that they have to answer correctly in front of the entire class, which causes many students to seldom raise their hands.

So rather than using IRF, we can try other tactics that may be more effective for cultivating thinking and language. First, set up a classroom environment in which pleasing the teacher is not the focus. Answering questions should not be motivated mainly by positive feedback from the teacher. We teachers have to emphasize that we are not know-it-alls and that together we can all learn new things about the discipline.

Some other ideas are these:

- *Hmmmm.* Avoid always responding to student answers with evaluative responses, such as *Great; Excellent; Yes; Right; Perfect* (or *No; Not exactly; Not quite; There's a better answer; I don't think so*). These can limit student thinking. Foster an air of questioning, thoughtfulness, openness, even wonder. Try responding with *Okay; Interesting; Hmmm; All right.* You can follow these responses with *Why do you say that? Are there other thoughts about what so-and-so said or other answers? Does anyone else have anything to add?* Let the class know that you are not going to tell them they are right or wrong right away and that you want a variety of answers and questions to emerge during each class. Let them know that it is okay to guess and be wrong. They will learn more from wrong answers than from no answers.

- *Did-who.* Ask a display or open question, but rather than having a student answer it out loud, have the whole class just think, share their thoughts with a partner, or write down what they thought. Then offer the answer by asking, "Did anyone think of [the answer]?" or, "Who has in mind [the answer]?" "How many of you got the answer . . .?" You can use formative assessment such as putting fingers up, closing one eye, and so on. This allows everyone to nod their heads or raise their hands, and it avoids giving status to a student who answers the question and avoids embarrassing a student who might answer it incorrectly. An important goal of questioning is to get students to think.

- *I also ask.* Ask questions to which students know that you don't know the answer, so that they can grapple with it without fear of being wrong. They can form their own opinions and answers. Some starters are, *What do you think about . . . How might . . . Why might . . . I often ask . . . I still wonder why . . .*

CRAFTING WHOLE-CLASS DISCUSSIONS

Whole-class discussions give students a chance to see how ideas grow and are built by a group of people. Students are challenged to think about their own ideas, articulate them, defend them, and modify them in real time. This tends to mirror what often happens in the real world in businesses, institutions, and politics. Participants in any discussion need to be ready to think and talk on their feet, or their ideas and voices will never be heard.

Effective discussions seldom just happen. It takes talent and planning to make them worth the time and energy. We teachers play vital roles in guiding the academic nature and depth of a discussion. As Northedge (quoted in Mercer, 2000) writes,

Without a teacher a group discussion tends to gravitate towards a common denominator in terms of an "everyday" discourse that everyone can understand and use effectively. Whereas, a teacher can, without necessarily dominating the discussion, help to translate some of what is said into terms of the "academic" discourse, so that the group members can see how the ideas they already hold can be made to work within that discourse. (p. 82)

We must function as translators, or guides, who help our students shape their new ideas into the language of the discipline. At the same time, we must cultivate in our students the norms and rules for academic talk in the field. I have often compared classroom discussion to the act of balancing on a round log on water. It is easy to fall off on either side: one being too much teacher talk and control, the other being too much unrelated, misdirected, or erroneous student talk. It is challenging to get the right balance of teacher modeling, student talk, focus, and depth.

Leading Classroom Discussions

Early on we need to cultivate a positive, receptive classroom environment where effective discussions can happen. Discussions may take the form of instructional conversations, which are classroom situations in which talk is used to explore ideas rather than regurgitate answers (Tharp & Gallimore, 1991). Instructional conversations should be engaging and relevant, maintain a discernible topic throughout, not be dominated by any one student or teacher, and have all students engaged in extended conversations (Goldenberg, 1991).

Each response should build on, challenge, or extend a previous utterance. This means creating new ideas, not just parroting back answers (as in IRF formats) or "spraying the room" with unconnected ideas. Students (and adults) are sometimes sitting there focused so much on their own ideas that they cannot listen. When this happens, students should temporarily "park their thoughts" in order to build on the current idea being discussed (Nichols, 2006). Students can write their thoughts down and return to them when appropriate. This joint building of ideas is hard work and requires the academic skill of mental multitasking; that is, a student must keep track of the ideas from other students, adding his or her own thoughts to the overall idea being constructed throughout the discussion.

Effective discussion thrives in a nonthreatening but challenging atmosphere (Spiegel, 2005). Participants should support claims using texts, examples, experiences, and other reasoning (e.g., "What makes you say that . . .?"). But everyone must do this in positive ways ("I am interested in your idea but need some clarification") rather than in a combative manner ("ha-ha, you're wrong" or "that's a weak idea"). In the United States, in particular, we must try to undo the overly competitive and stubborn *I must win and stick to my way of thinking* mentality that often prevails. For idea building to truly succeed, students (and teacher) must be humble, flexible, and willing to modify or even abandon ideas when good reasons arise.

We need to plan for effective discussion. The discussion should directly relate to helping students succeed on ongoing and summative assessments. Plan what you want students to talk about. This may not happen, but at least there is a possible direction that is based on learning standards. I have even put an outline or web of this plan (as in figure 5.1) on a poster to help students and me stay on topic. Predict and plan for possible tangents, elaborations, and connections to student lives. You can add or modify the main categories.

Think about the cultural and knowledge demands of the lesson. What types of background knowledge do you assume students will have to build on? If they lack it, do a quick background-building session. Students need to come to the discussion with something to say. They should be allowed to write in response journals before the discussion to get some thoughts down and self-assess their understanding. You can come up with different visual organizers that students can fill in before the discussion to prompt their thinking and provide a tool for

Figure 5.1 Visual for Planning Effective Discussions

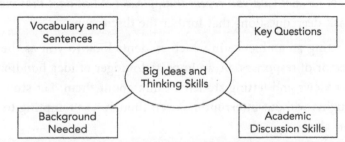

the less verbal, less spontaneous students to use. These might be webs, Venn diagrams, and charts with different columns for opinions and reasons.

Here are eight other suggestions for improving your discussion-leading abilities:

1. Motivate students with discrepancies, teacher errors, case studies, current issues, controversies, problems, big questions, mysteries, and so on.

2. Set up ways to get all students to talk to each other without being put on the spot. For example, they could share what a partner said in a think-pair-share or small group. The talk should go around and among students, not back and forth from students to teacher.

3. Teach nonverbal responses and facial expressions that are appropriate for school and professional settings, such as nodding one's head, smiling, and leaning forward. Teach how to avoid insensitive and hurtful behaviors, such as looking away, staring, or leaning away with arms folded.

4. Strategically redirect tangential comments back to the main point. Find a way to synthesize what a student says to make it fit into the main direction of the discussion (*Excellent point, but we must continue on the topic of . . . Good thinking, yet we must remember the importance of . . . Okay, hold that thought as we focus on . . .*).

5. Use pairs and groups at times during the discussion to zoom in on topics and reflect on them. For example, give one side of the room a point of view to discuss and the opposing view to the other side. Do a quick pair activity to spark thinking and participation of those who seldom share in the large group.

6. Train students to ask questions when they misunderstand: *Excuse me, but I didn't understand that question. Can you give an example? Can you draw that concept for me? Can you repeat that, please? What does that mean?* Train them to ask deep questions that further the discussion.

7. Avoid creating an ambience in which students look to you as the validator and corrector of responses. Be an impartial nudger of idea building, inviting a range of views and letting students think about them. Let students finish their thoughts without interrupting, even though it is tempting to move the discussion along.

8. With the help of your students, create a list of norms for classroom discussion—for example: wait until a person is done talking; respectfully disagree; speak loudly and clearly; back up assertions with evidence; stay on topic; do not yell; be open to all ideas; refer to the previous person's comments and provide a transition into what you want to say.

Building Classroom Discussion Language

Classroom discussion language consists of words, phrases, and behaviors that keep a group or whole-class discussion going on a purposeful and productive level. In table 5.1, the terms in the right column serve various discussion functions on the left. I gathered these terms during my observations of classrooms from grades 4 through 10 in science, history, math, and language arts.

Many of these expressions are not quite "academic enough" for writing, but they are appropriate in oral discussions (e.g., *piggyback, build on, along those same lines, let's backtrack*). We must point out these differences to students, especially to English learners, because if we don't, they will overuse the expressions in their writing.

Students often use colloquial and figurative terms to serve academic purposes. These include such expressions as "Kinda like what he said," "That's true, I guess, but what about . . .?" "Your evidence is wacked, dude!" In fact, one scholar, George Bunch (2004), argues that students can skillfully use a host of what many teachers consider to be nonacademic terms for academic purposes. If, after all, the language is used for academic purposes, then is it not academic? In such cases it is imperative that we validate students' ways of describing academic concepts as we concurrently provide additional ways to describe the concepts as the discipline's experts might.

Lecturing

When we talk most of the time about a topic and expect students to listen and take notes, it is more of a lecture than a discussion. The word *lecture* has become negative in recent years (and many lectures are), but let us start with a few advantages of traditional lectures: they are efficient ways to introduce a body of information in an organized way, they provide academic language input, they develop oral comprehension abilities (which can also help with reading

Table 5.1 Classroom Discussion Functions and Starters

Discussion Function	Discussion Starters
Add to what a peer has said.	Let's build on Juan's idea. I want to piggyback off of what . . . My idea is related to Laura's idea. Along those same lines, . . . I would like to add that . . . I have two points that relate to what you said. First, . . .
Contradict or disagree.	On the other hand, . . . I disagree with what Ana said. That's a good point, but I think . . . It is not a case of . . . but rather . . . We have all heard that . . ., but I propose a new way of looking at . . . True, but I would like to point out that . . . I understand the idea of . . ., but we believe that . . . That's a valid point, but I feel . . . Then again, we shouldn't forget . . . And yet, we need to remember that . . .
Shift the focus to clarify.	I think it is more helpful to look at . . . This isn't that relevant because . . . We must dig deeper into the idea of . . . Let's consider not only . . . but also . . . One aspect of this that is particularly important is . . . because . . .
Analyze.	Okay, let's backtrack. Another aspect is . . . We ought to distinguish between . . . Let's see how the pieces fit together to make . . . There is a pattern that emerges when we look at . . .
State an opinion.	What struck me was . . . I hadn't thought about that. Along those same lines, I feel that . . .
Support a point with evidence.	For example, . . . Based on what? It is analogous to . . . Evidence includes when . . .

comprehension), and they prepare students for lecture-based learning and note taking in future years of schooling, especially when they move into higher education.

The disadvantages, of course, are many: the all-too-common tendencies of students (and adults) to lose concentration, "zoning out" for periods of time; many students might not know all of the words, and they get the information only once, passing them by (e.g., PowerPoints are pretty, but the slides go away quickly); and the information is passively transmitted, interspersed with a few display questions. This relates to what Paolo Freire (1970) aptly called "banking education," the process of depositing inert information into what are considered to be empty heads. So to maximize the advantages and minimize the disadvantages, take a look at appendix C for some suggestions for before, during, and after the lecture. (My top suggestion, though, is to use minilectures, that is, keep "lectures" to about a minute per year of your students' ages.)

Whether or not we lecture a lot, we can help students acquire language typically used to organize ideas in lectures and presentations. The four columns in table 5.2 contain a few of the terms that we can use to help students better understand and remember the ideas they hear in lecture-based settings. We must build our own lists for our content needs. We can then have students create similar columns in their notebooks for these terms and highlight them when they come up in class. We can also metadiscuss the importance of the four categories in organizing information in school. I have noticed students using these terms in their writings, discussions, and presentations.

Improving Academic Listening

The Common Core provides a progressively challenging set of listening standards from one grade level to the next. The standards tend to move from paraphrasing, to explaining how information contributes to a topic to analyzing main ideas, to evaluating supporting evidence (National Governors Association Center for Best Practices, 2010). Similar to the comprehension of complex texts, students need to become increasingly skilled at listening to complex messages and thinking to comprehend them.

Much of our academic language is acquired through listening. Thus, beyond the more obvious goal of helping students understand content better, improving

Table 5.2 Academic Language Categories for Comprehending Lectures

Main Idea, Introductions, Conclusions	Comparing and Contrasting Ideas	Supporting with Evidence, Examples, Analogies	Connecting Ideas, Transitions, Cause and Effect
Today's topic is important because . . .	Similarly	For example	Main causes of . . .
Previously, we talked about . . .	Likewise	For instance	First, . . . second, . . .
Now today we will discuss . . .	Also	This is a little like when you . . .	Another reason . . .
This argument has four main parts [points, elements]. First, . . .	Compared with	Can you think of any examples of this?	We must also consider . . .
So, what have we discussed so far? First, . . .	In the same way	A good analogy for this is . . .	Now let's think about . . .
In conclusion, we must continue to think about . . .	On the contrary	It is similar to when . . .	We need to look at . . .
Let's quickly review what we discussed.	However	An illustration of this is . . .	Therefore
Last but not least, . . .	On the other hand	Such as	As a result
	Nevertheless	More specifically	Thus
	Yet	Let's say that . . .	Because of these . . .
	Unlike the . . .	Let's look at the case of . . .	This leads us to think that . . .
	Differs		Moreover
	Conversely		Reasons for . . .
	Regardless		Ramifications of . . .
	Whereas		

listening can improve their development of academic language and thinking. Two challenges exist for teachers when it comes to improving listening: (1) we are seldom trained to teach listening (few of us were ever directly taught listening skills), and (2) listening is much more complex than we realize. We already know too well that it is not enough for students to sit there quietly with eye contact and nodding heads. Listening, aptly described by Lundsteen (1979, p. 1), is "the process by which spoken language is converted to meaning in the mind." It requires thinking, not just hearing. Students need to pay attention, organize what they think, and remember the main points. Listening can be even more difficult than reading, especially if what we listen to is highly academic. A listener can seldom go back over confusing parts multiple times to understand it, as a reader can do with pages in a book.

One of the core strategies for making meaning during listening is chunking information into levels of importance (Lund, 1990). This is what most good listeners do when they take notes. They focus on the key ideas, which the speaker often signals. Yet diverse students typically have more trouble interpreting the intonation and nonverbal signals of emphasis on key points and topic changes. Effective listening also depends on a student's background knowledge and vocabulary. If the student knows enough of the content and direction to provide a foundation for comprehension, then he or she can successfully construct new learning on that foundation. For example, if a student already knows that animals adapt in various ways and that viruses are not quite alive, then listening to detailed talk on viral adaptations becomes easier.

I have included a listening activity, as well as some suggestions for procedures, that can help students acquire academic language as they listen.

DICTATION DISCUSSIONS

Pick a vocabulary-rich and concept-rich text. Students listen as you read the academic text out loud. They listen the first time and jot down key words and phrases. The second time you read the passage, they pick two or three of the most important sentences and write them down word for word. You might need to repeat the text for longer and denser sentences. Students in a group or pairs get together to negotiate what might be missing or incorrect in what they have written. Students can read their results aloud or present results on a poster, overhead transparency, or whiteboard. Students compare results with those of other groups and share back to the teacher.

Source: Adapted from Wajnryb (1990).

The process of taking notes can develop listening, synthesizing abilities, and overall language proficiency. But if we just assume that students instinctively know how to take notes, we often get a hodgepodge of words and ideas scattered between doodles and scratched-out notes to neighbors. We must train students to take high-quality notes that have thinking and language aspects built into them. Students can take notes during lectures, discussions, group work, videos, and student presentations. Have them refer back to their notes and use academic language to synthesize them or prepare other products of learning.

One format for taking notes is three-column notes, a variation of Cornell note taking, which involves taking notes in two columns (Pauk, 1989). In the three-column format, listeners put details on the far right; main ideas in the middle; and personal opinions, applications, and questions in the far left column. Some teachers may have students merge the middle and left columns or make other adaptations to the page.

You can have different types of notes for different columns: problems, solutions, predictions, evidence, hypotheses, theories, new words, and so on. Lots of modeling on the overhead or on posters is needed. But it is worth the time because it trains students not only to chunk information into main ideas but also to think actively while listening to fill in the left-hand column.

Providing Silence and Time to Think

In our rush to cram thousands of standards into student minds, we cut out time for core thinking that would strengthen language and content understanding. Students need extra seconds and minutes to mentally work with complex language as they piece together new concepts.

We seldom pause due to the fact that we know our content front, back, and sideways from studying it in college and teaching it over and over. But many of our students see it for the first time and need time to process it. We can slow down the conversation, but we must be disciplined, diligent, and deliberate, especially at first. I have seen too many lessons where the conversation flies along at the pace of the teacher and the top four students in the class. The others try to keep up but seldom get enough of a mental break to put things together. The bell rings, and the students are off to another fast-paced lesson in a different content area. Providing thinking time shows respect for the student, conveying the message that we are confident that the student can think and accomplish the task. Not waiting, by contrast, can convey the message that we do not expect the student to succeed independently (Johnston, 2004).

Silence can be golden thinking time for students. Unfortunately, in most of my observations of classrooms, the average wait time after a question is around one second. But if we give a little more time to think, good things can happen:

- Student responses tend to be more thorough (more academic).

- Students use more precise language related to the topic.

- More students get the answer right.

- Students gain a more genuine sense that the teacher cares about their answers, not just about being an interrogator.

- Teachers tend to ask fewer—and, ideally, more important—questions.

- More lower-achieving students participate (Rowe, 2003).

All of these advantages come from a few more moments of silence.

USING ACTIVITIES TO IMPROVE DISCUSSIONS

Although whole-class activities are often in the form of discussions, other activities can be engaging and effective at building thinking and communication skills in our discipline. I have included several here that you can use in most subjects in most grade levels. Many of the activities can be used along with checklists and rubrics to help students see and focus on different academic skills in the process.

The first five activities involve lots of movement and interaction between students but do not require a lot of preparation. Many are ideas from language teaching that we can borrow and adapt for use in content-area classes. Try them before you write them off as too chaotic. It takes some time for students to get used to what they must do and how to talk to others in these contexts. The activities can even become part of your weekly routine. The remaining activities are more involved and also very effective.

⇒ **Conversation Circles and Lines**

These two strategies, often found in world language classrooms, promote talk among students who might not typically interact in class (adapted from Duffala, 1987). They also allow students to practice new language patterns as they respond to the same prompts with different partners. Students get needed repetition of terms and grammar as they bridge information gaps with other students. Finally, they offer a break from sitting in the same spot all period.

Before the activity, you choose several academic prompts, controversial topics, or thought-provoking questions—for example:

- Why did the Southern states secede?
- Describe the differences between viruses and bacteria.
- What are gravitational waves?
- How do you graph a linear equation?
- How would you change the ending of the story? Why?

Students then form two circles, one inside the other, with equal numbers of students in each circle. (They can also form two or more facing lines.) Give the prompt and have students discuss the topic with the partner facing them. They can take notes, if needed. After a short time, tell the inner circle to move two people to the right to talk with a new partner. You can give the same prompt or a new one. Encourage students to use academic language posted on the walls and their notes. At the end, the class as a whole can synthesize the information that the individual student pairs discussed.

⇒ **Interview Grids and Mixers**

In grids and mixers, the students move around and talk to one another (adapted from Gibbons, 2002). Students use question tables, treasure hunts, matching cards, and other activities to exchange information. An example of an interview grid used in a middle school science class is shown in table 5.3. The teacher tells students to pair up with their first partner and ask the questions. They each do so, then switch to a second partner, and so on. In this way, they practice their oral language and fortify their answers each time they talk.

As students take notes, they synthesize what their peers have said, and they hear similar answers multiple times. To make this activity more academic, encourage students to listen for and use target terms such as *nucleus, nutrients, venom, adapt, differ, developed, traits, senses, chloroplast,* and so on. At the end, you can also have

Table 5.3 Interview Grid for a Middle School Science Class

Name	Compare plant and animal cells	Explain how sharks have adapted	Argue that a virus is a living organism
Julia	Plant cells have chloroplasts	Keen senses for smell and electric impulses	It reproduces, but not on own
Ben		Tough skin, fast	Yes, nucleic acids
Simranjit	Plants have long shapes		Can be killed by our antibodies

them tell their partners an answer and reflect on how this last answer differed from the student's first attempt at answering at the beginning of the activity.

In language arts, to introduce the play *A Raisin in the Sun* by Lorraine Hansberry, for example, you can have students fill in an interview grid with questions about dreams and justice. Students then interview four other classmates and summarize their answers on the grid. Model for students how they can dig deeper by asking follow-up questions when the partner's answer is insufficient, too vague, or too colloquial. A possible grid could look like this:

Name	What are your dreams?	What might prevent you from reaching them?	How should a family make big decisions?

Students then briefly share what they heard from others. They might say, "Clara thought that not having money might prevent her from going to school and reaching her dream of becoming a lawyer."

Card matching can also be used to get students to interact (adapted from Gibbons, 2002). Each student has a card with information that matches the card of one or two other students in the room. They walk around asking for matching people. In the example that follows, there are three questions, so three students need to find each other with the same card and then figure out the problem using the information that each has on the card:

Need to figure out the total cost of plastic to buy to make 4,000 plastic balls with diameter 20 cm and thickness 0.5 cm.	Volume of a sphere = $\frac{4\pi r^3}{3}$	Plastic for making balls costs $36 per cubic meter.

Another variation is having all students move around and put themselves in a sequence, such as in chronological order or in order of importance (Thornbury, 2005). On their cards they might have events from a historical period (without dates) that they must talk about in order to sequence themselves. They might have several quotations from a person that they put in order of importance or a list of current issues in politics that they need to rank. The goal is to get students to listen well, negotiate meaning, and move around as a result of their conversations.

⇒ **Take a Side**

In this activity, students choose a side of an issue and get up and go to different sides of the room (adapted from Wilhelm, 2002). It supports many of the Common Core standards that focus on supporting ideas with reasons and evidence. You can give students the option of placing themselves more in the middle of a continuum line, but they must have valid reasons and supporting evidence on both sides to remain there. And they must be on one side of the center point and be able to explain why they chose that side. Students then tell those near them why they chose that side of the room (or spot on the continuum). Next, tell students to move to the other side and argue the opposite points with their peers.

This activity is predominantly oral and gets students moving around the room. This can be done before or after group discussions. Prompts might be *Are you in favor of gene therapy? Do you think you should always forgive those who have wronged you? Should the United States have entered the Vietnam War?* Academic language for this activity is mostly persuasive and evaluative, including the terms *negative influence, long-term effects, short-term advantages, drawbacks, outweighs, evidence, risks, because,* and *ramifications.* You can then have students share what the person next to them shared.

⇒ Prediction Café

This activity, adapted from what is called a Tea Party (Beers, 2006), is an engaging prereading mixer activity that gives students a chance to predict, infer, synthesize, and interpret. This thinking, of course, requires certain academic terms for giving one's rationale for predictions and inferences (*makes me think that, I believe that, because of a quote I heard from, if we consider the title and this line here, therefore, we can assume, we will likely learn about*).

First, pick out important headings or quotations from a complex text that students will read. Put them on separate strips or note cards, enough for the whole class (I often use six to eight different quotations), and put the title of the text up where all can see it. You can also read a portion of the text aloud, distribute verses of a poem, hand out lists of key words from a text, put up an image, or show just part of an image.

Tell students that the goal of the activity is to form an idea of what the text will be about. Hand out different quotations to students, who then read them to other students as they circulate around the room (this can also be done in groups of three to five). You can give quotations from the same person or section of text to a group so that they discuss their piece in depth when they return from mingling. Pairs or groups then analyze the lines and make inferences about their importance in the upcoming text or lesson.

Student predictions and inferences should improve as they hear more and more quotations and predictions from other students. They can then jigsaw with other groups to share what they have discussed and guessed. Students can even become the quoted person and share their thoughts from a first-person point of view. Optionally, at the end, ask students to guess the sequence of their pieces in the text. Lead a brief discussion on what students predict the text is about. This can be effective in any content area.

⇒ Voting

Having students think about something and vote on it can become an effective low-prep teaching activity. Voting makes all students think about a question for a moment and then respond in a low-pressure way. A teacher can then get a good idea of how students are thinking and learning. A raised hand can show thinking, and you can then ask someone with his or her hand raised further questions, such as, *Why?* This will get them thinking and keep them honest in case they just look around and follow the crowd. You can also have them share with a partner why they voted a certain way. You can even have pairs discuss the topic and cast one vote. A variation is having students hold up a certain number of fingers to indicate how much they agree or disagree, five fingers meaning "much" and one finger meaning "a little."

A simple starter, "How many of you . . .?" can get students into the voting mode. Ask such questions as "How many of you would like to be the main character?" "How many of you think this story is true?" "How many of you think this material will conduct electricity?" "How many of you can say why we use proofs in geometry?" "How many of you think the history book is wrong on this issue?" Make sure to wait a few seconds to let everyone think; warn them that you might ask them to back up their vote with a good reason or two. Students can quickly justify their votes to a partner or on paper and use such language as *believe that, makes the most sense because, logical choice,* and *long-term advantages.*

⇒ Simulations

Simulations allow students to experience what they learn. Students become a part of recreating events in history or a story or representing processes in science or math. Simulations and reenactments can be valuable ways to build up background knowledge (and feelings) about a topic, inspire research about a topic, and assess learning.

Simulations are effective because they create teachable moments, provide a referent for the entire unit, and let students actively experience complex and abstract concepts (Bower & Lobdell, 1999). They also allow students to take in and use new language in low-stress ways. Some simulations offer students chances to deal with real-world issues that do not have clear-cut solutions. These, in a sense, are case studies that put students in engaging situations where they develop communication strategies (Huckin, 1988).

Students role-play characters or characterizations of persons, animals, or even scientific and mathematical concepts and processes. Simulations can be done with the whole class or in groups and pairs. Topics can range from portraying the food chain, to playing a scene from Shakespeare, to acting out the final events of World War II.

To design a simulation, try the following steps. First, think about the scenario that you want students to experience. Think about the big ideas, concepts, and feelings that they should understand. Consider a scenario where thirty people can be involved in some way, or smaller groups can do the same simulation. Try to think of a parallel scenario that will not use the real names and places. This will give the situation its own life. Think about what will happen during the simulation and how students will react. Try to set up situations in which the students might react in ways similar to what really occurred. Think of props that can be used to make things more realistic. And think of ways in which you can intervene and support the students. Jot down the types of language strategies and terms (tools and skills) that they will need during and after the simulation.

One successful simulation taught the change from agricultural to urban life. All students started off as farmers who made paper symbols of farm products. They then made small squares of needs, some changed jobs to trade with the farmers, and more jobs were added over time as needs arose and technology advanced. Other simulation ideas are westward expansion in the United States, designing a building and figuring its costs, balancing equations, the birth and growth of our planet, a turn-of-the-20th-century assembly line, the start of World War I, a trial of war criminals, scenes from a novel, scenes from the future, plate tectonic movement, covalent bonding, and nuclear fusion or fission.

Another teacher opened a unit by simulating Japanese American internment by "kicking out" four students (who were informed of the role-play beforehand) from the class based on what they were wearing. The teacher told the class that this happened because students who had worn similar clothes had caused a big problem the day before. The teacher announced that the governor was about to sign an order that all students with light-colored hair needed to leave the school and move to a different part of the state where they would live in camps. Students then responded to the prompt "How would you feel if this really happened tomorrow?" This quick simulation provided a foundation for later discussion about similar events during World War II.

SAMPLE SIMULATION: STATES' RIGHTS AND THE AMERICAN CIVIL WAR

This preunit simulation helps students gain an understanding of the rights that Southern states believed they had leading into the American Civil War. The activity refers to an abridged Declaration of Independence ("abridged" in that it includes the parts most relevant to the activity).

1. Have an equal number of blue and gray cards that students pick out of a hat to determine where they will be. Blue cards say, "You are at a Blue table and must make shirts to earn money." Gray cards say, "You are at a Gray table, and you get your goods [cotton balls] from the teacher or teaching assistant [who represents slavery] for you to sell for money." A student acts as a merchant and buys the cotton balls from the Gray tables, then sells them to the Blue tables so they can make shirts.

2. Let Gray students be comfortable, put their feet on desks, eat and drink, and so on. You can model the language and behavior of the comfort, fun, relaxation, and wealth of Southerners; they can play cards, listen to music, eat candy, and so on. Blue tables trace and cut out shirt patterns and then paste ten cotton balls onto them.

3. Give Gray tables a dollar for ten cotton balls; sell five cotton balls for a dollar to Blue tables; pay three dollars for a shirt.

4. Have a vote with Blue and Gray tables on whether to make Gray table people pay for the cotton that they then sell. (There is likely to be a tie: three tables to three tables.)

5. Announce that a new Blue table is going to be added; it will be a "pay table." Now the vote will be 4 to 3. Ask Gray tables what they will do. Hand out an abridged version of the Declaration of Independence; help them discuss the part about an abusive government and setting up their own government.

6. The Gray tables will likely decide to secede.

7. Have tables discuss these questions in groups (both groups can refer to the Declaration and Constitution):
   Gray: "Why do you want to secede?"
   Blue: "Why should the Gray tables not secede?"

8. The teacher then acts as president: "But I am the president of these United Tables, and I say you cannot secede! What will you do? What will I do?"

(continued)

9. Follow-up: Journal and then share about what happened and how students felt.
10. Make a T-chart to compare the simulation with what students think happened before the Civil War. Have students predict what they will learn in the unit.

A variation in biology is to have groups do a cell division simulation after their reading. Give students yarn, twine, and an assortment of different-colored blocks (they can decide how much of what). Each group manipulates the blocks and string to form a cell. They decide how to move the blocks to mimic the movement of the chromosomes in the cell. This activity requires students to be creative with the materials they are given and to work as a group to show a demonstration of meiosis in action. Students narrate the phases as they act out the process (they can use their books). For groups that move faster, ask them to narrate the process without their books to make it a bit more challenging (Krasnow, 2004).

⇒ **Radio Talk Show**

A mock radio talk show (adapted from Wilhelm, 2002) is a low-prep way to add some drama and structure to a discussion. A radio talk show host (you model this at first) introduces an issue, problem, or case study and responds to audience members (students) who "call in" and offer comments. Beforehand, allow time for students in groups or pairs to read about and discuss the issues that will be brought up in the talk show. In addition to calling in as themselves, students can take on a variety of relevant roles, such as farmworkers, politicians, doctors, presidents, actors, authors, or any other relevant person. Then the talk show host may start with, "Today on Rad Talk, we are talking about the electoral college system. Many people think it is not effective. Others do. Let's open the phone lines and hear what people say." The host may add some dramatic flair to his or her talk.

The teacher encourages callers to use argumentative language and thinking, and models the host's abilities to paraphrase and develop the discussion. For example, the host might say, "So what you are pointing out is that democracy is a government decided by elections. And yet a presidential candidate can win an election without receiving the majority of the votes. Is that what you are saying? Therefore, what needs to happen?" The host must be able to stir things up a bit, quickly taking in caller responses, creating some healthy academic tension, and probing issues. The host must get students to articulate the importance of their claims, as well as support their points of view with evidence (National Governors Association Center for Best Practices, 2010). Along the way, you can highlight key language terms that emerge and put them on the wall so that they stick in students' minds to be used later on. Once students get the gist of being a host, they can act as the host for the whole class or in small groups.

⇒ **Structured Academic Controversy**

Controversy can fuel some great discussions and cultivate rich thinking and language. Developed by David Johnson and Roger Johnson (1995), structured academic controversies (SACs) emphasize communication, perspective taking, and problem solving. And unlike debates, they lead students to work together to collaborate on a resolution to the controversy after they have taken both sides of the issue. SACs also are easier to put together and facilitate in one class period, and they are less competitive—there is no "winner" or "loser." SACs are effective ways to give students practice in the Common Core standards related to synthesizing information from different sources, supporting ideas with evidence, and evaluating evidence in speaking and listening contexts.

The basic steps are as follows:

1. Students form groups of four and pick an interesting real-world case or issue to analyze—for example: Are tobacco companies to blame for deaths of smokers? Was the American Civil War needed to end slavery? Should medically assisted suicide be legal? Does television promote violence and other crimes in young people? Was it just for Juliet's father to insist that she marry Paris? Most two-sided issues that arise in the unit of study will work.

2. Students split up into pairs and take sides of the issue. They research a side of the issue and develop logical, compelling, well-reasoned arguments.

3. Groups of four form again and present their arguments. As one pair presents, the other pair listens, analyzing the strengths and weaknesses of the arguments.

4. Both sides discuss their positions and try to challenge the other positions respectfully and academically.

5. Pairs switch sides of the issue, splitting apart briefly to discuss and look for the most persuasive arguments to defend the side that they had previously argued against.

6. Students get back into groups to defend their new sides.

7. Groups select the best reasoning from both sides and synthesize it into a new position to which all can agree. Because both pairs take both sides, it is more likely that they will not compete as they draft a synthesis. The group writes a short report that explains their discussion and conclusions.

One of the most important things to do when using controversies in classrooms is to help students develop appropriate argumentation and communication skills. These are effectively outlined by the following SAC rules (adapted from Johnson and Johnson, 1995):

- I can tactfully criticize ideas, but I don't criticize people.
- I remember that we are all in this together, sink or swim. I help the group focus on coming to the best decision possible, not on winning any argument.
- I encourage everyone to participate and to master all the relevant information.
- I listen to everyone's ideas, even if I don't agree.
- I appropriately ask for clarity.
- I try to understand all sides of the issue.
- I change my mind when evidence clearly indicates that I should do so.

CONCLUSION

At every level and in every subject, we need to immerse students in rich academic language experiences. We design experiences in which students interact with more proficient others to gain familiarity with new language forms, hear other ways of describing academic concepts, and hear themselves produce academic messages. James Gee (1998) points out the importance of talk when he writes,

It is, by the way, very rare, indeed, that people understand this sort of language if all they have ever done is read books. Without having had the opportunity to engage in discussion with people who use this sort of language and without having experienced some of what such people do, where they do it, and why they do it, it is very hard, indeed, to gain real understanding—just as hard as it is to learn French only by reading French books. (p. xi)

Whole-class interactions can be powerful opportunities for students to build their thinking and language skills. Most teacher preparation programs lack the time to adequately cover the complex topic of leading effective discussions. For example, it is important to reflect on the types and quantity of questions that we use in classroom discussions. We must be extra careful to avoid overcontrolling conversations with the initiation-response-feedback format. This often results in what Perkins (1992) calls the Trivial Pursuit model of education: the view that education is just an accumulation of facts. Students who are only looking for right answers often find them quickly on shallow levels of thought and neglect to dig beneath. The digging abilities that we desire can be developed in whole-class discussions, the topic of this chapter, and also through group and pair activities, the topic of chapter 6.

CHAPTER REFLECTIONS

- What are the prompts and contexts that get experts in your discipline talking about interesting issues? How can you scaffold and simulate similar prompts?

- How do you help students organize their thoughts as they listen during discussions?

- Create a mock transcript of an effective (ideal) classroom discussion in your setting. What are the key terms and transitions that students use? How do you participate?

- What questions do you still have about leading effective discussions in your class?

- Design a simulation that involves all students in your class in some way. Come up with a few discussion prompts to process the experience afterward.

References

Bakhtin, M. (1981). *The dialogic imagination*. Austin: University of Texas Press.

Beers, K. (2006). *Tea party*. Retrieved from www.mcte.org/resources/beers.html

Bower, B., & Lobdell, J. (1999). *History alive: Engaging all learners in the diverse classroom*. Rancho Cordova, CA: Teachers' Curriculum Institute.

Bunch, G. (2004). *"But how do we say that?": Reconceptualizing academic language in linguistically diverse mainstream classrooms*. Unpublished doctoral dissertation, Stanford University.

Duffala, J. (1987). *The teacher as artist*. Santa Rosa, CA: Author.

Edwards, D., & Mercer, N. (1993). *Common knowledge: The development of understanding in the classroom*. London, UK: Routledge.

Freire, P. (1970). *Pedagogy of the oppressed*. New York, NY: Herder & Herder.

Gee, J. (1998). Foreword. In L. Bartolomé, *The misteaching of academic discourses: The politics of language in the classroom* (pp. ix–xvi). Boulder, CO: Westview Press.

Gibbons, P. (2002). *Scaffolding language, scaffolding learning*. Portsmouth, NH: Heinemann.

Gilles, C. (1993). We make an idea: Cycles of meaning in literature discussion groups. In K. Pierce & C. Gilles (Eds.), *Cycles of meaning* (pp. 199–217). Portsmouth, NH: Heinemann.

Goldenberg, C. (1991). *Instructional conversations and their classroom application* (Educational Practice Report 2). Santa Cruz, CA: National Center for Research on Cultural Diversity and Second Language Learning.

Griffin, P., & Smith, P. (2001). Assessing student language growth: Kirsten's profile. In P. Smith (Ed.), *Talking classrooms: Shaping children's learning through oral language instruction* (pp. 121–140). Newark, DE: International Reading Association.

Huckin, T. N. (1988). Achieving professional communicative relevance in a generalized ESP classroom. In D. Chamberlain & R. J. Baumgardner (Eds.), *ESP in the classroom: Practice and evaluation*. Hong Kong: Modern English Publications and the British Council.

Johnson, D., & Johnson, R. (1995). *Creative controversy: Intellectual challenge in the classroom* (3rd ed.). Edina, MN: Interaction Book Company.

Johnston, P. (2004). *Choice words: How our language affects children's learning*. Portland, ME: Stenhouse.

Krasnow, K. (2004). *Meiosis lesson plan.* Unpublished lesson plan.

Lund, R. (1990). A taxonomy for teaching second language listening. *Foreign Language Annals, 23,* 105–115.

Lundsteen, S. (1979). *Listening: Its impact on reading and the other language arts.* Urbana, IL: National Council of Teachers of English.

Mercer, N. (2000). *The guided construction of knowledge: Talk amongst teachers and learners.* Clevedon, UK: Multilingual Matters.

National Governors Association Center for Best Practices. (2010). *Common Core State Standards.* Washington, DC: Council of Chief State School Officers.

Nichols, M. (2006). *Comprehension through conversation: The power of purposeful talk in the reading workshop.* Portsmouth, NH: Heinemann.

Nystrand, M., & Gamoran, A. (1991). Instructional discourse, student engagement, and literature achievement. *Research in the Teaching of English, 25,* 261–290.

Pauk, W. (1989). *How to study in college.* Boston, MA: Houghton Mifflin.

Perkins, D. (1992). *Smart schools.* New York, NY: Simon & Schuster.

Robb, L. (2003). *Teaching reading in social studies, science, and math: Practical ways to weave comprehension strategies into your content area teaching.* New York, NY: Scholastic.

Rowe, M. B. (2003). Wait-time and rewards as instructional variables, their influence on language. Logic and fate control. Part 1: Wait time. *Journal of Research in Science Teaching, 40*(3), 19–32.

Sinclair, J. M., & Coulthard, R. M. (1975). *Towards an analysis of discourse: The English used by teachers and pupils.* Oxford, UK: Oxford University Press.

Spiegel, D. (2005). *Classroom discussion: Strategies for engaging all students, building higher-level thinking skills, and strengthening reading and writing across the curriculum.* New York, NY: Scholastic.

Tharp, R., & Gallimore, R. (1991). *The instructional conversation: Teaching and learning in social activity* (Research Report 2). Santa Cruz: National Center for Research on Cultural Diversity and Second Language Learning, University of California.

Thornbury, S. (2005). *How to teach speaking.* Essex, UK: Pearson.

Vygotsky, L. (1978). *Mind in society: The development of higher psychological processes.* Cambridge, MA: Harvard University Press.

Wajnryb, R. (1990). *Grammar dictation.* Oxford, UK: Oxford University Press.

Wilhelm, J. (2002). *Action strategies for deepening comprehension*. New York, NY: Scholastic.

Wood, D. (1986). Aspects of teaching and learning. In M. Richards & P. Light (Eds.), *Children of social worlds* (pp. 191–212). Cambridge, UK: Polity Press.

Zwiers, J. (2005). *Developing academic language in middle school English learners: Practices and perspectives in mainstream classrooms*. Unpublished doctoral dissertation, University of San Francisco.

Chapter **6**

Academic Listening and Speaking in Small Groups and Pairs

Talk and understanding walk hand in hand.

No matter how well we might engage the whole class in discussion, many students—often our diverse students—miss out on chances to talk. Many are shy and feel intimidated by the thought of sharing in front of a large group. And yet the benefits of academic talk in class are too powerful to ignore. Fortunately, we can use small groups and pairs. These smaller-scale discussions, when properly supported, can be very effective for building thinking, language, and content understanding in all students (Cohen, 1994; Johns, 1992; Johnson & Johnson, 1994). In this chapter, I focus on the dimensions of group work that relate to academic language development, such as the design and support of group tasks, scaffolds for conversations, drama activities, jigsaw activities, and pair interactions.

Using groups has several advantages. Smaller discussion settings give students chances to find their own way through ideas, construct opinions and defend them, challenge their preconceived ideas of the field, and try on new perspectives (Mercer, 2000). Students hear responses to their ideas, which spark more thinking, and they hear different ways of communicating ideas (Gilles, 1993). Students in smaller groups are more likely to ask their own questions and genuinely seek new information. In addition, group tasks offer more purposeful reasons to use language, chances for students to work independently from the teacher for a while, low-stress opportunities to practice language, and much-needed repetition of words and ideas (Faltis, 2001). This redundancy helps the content and language to stick better. And for teachers, group and pair activities offer chances to (1) model, scaffold, monitor, and assess student learning and (2) work with smaller groups of students to build relationships with them.

The Common Core State Standards emphasize that students be able to interact in small groups and pairs. For example, several standards include the following elements: engage effectively in a range of one-on-one and group discussions, build on others' ideas, and express their own ideas clearly (National Governors Association Center for Best Practices, 2010). There are other related elements, but these are plenty to work on for now. This chapter provides ideas for developing these elements during lessons and activities across content areas.

CHALLENGES OF USING GROUPS

Despite the many advantages of small groups, scores of teachers give up on them. They cite such challenges as behavior problems, high decibel levels, and inefficient use of time. Many teachers consider groups to be more of a depth strategy, not useful for breadth. Therefore, the trends and pushes to cover long lists of standards can unfortunately squeeze out some of the most effective group strategies that develop deep learning. To the teachers who say that there isn't enough time to put students into groups or have them share in pairs, I answer with a simple analogy: you rush into a fast food place, order a hamburger, and tell the server you are in a hurry. He says it will be quicker if you get it without the meat. You laugh and answer that it's the meat that makes the burger a burger. The server says, "Okay, but cooking it will take some time." Thinking and talking take time, but they are essential for deep, lasting, and authentic learning.

Another challenge is that groups do not automatically produce academic talk. Research has shown that surprisingly little academic talk happens during class (Nystrand, 1997). In many of my own observations of group tasks, the student conversations and their products were focused on learning facts or simply filling in the requirements of the assignment (Zwiers, 2005). And in many classrooms where academic talk is needed the most, it occurs the least. Often the more diverse a class is, the more teacher centered it is. In one diverse eighth-grade history class, for example, students were asked to do a range of tasks at different stations, such as listening to a tape, reading a paragraph, or performing some action. Students did not have to talk in most instances, and when they did, the talk didn't need to be academic in order to accomplish the task. In science classes, I have seen group work focused mainly on completing observational tasks and then silently writing up labs on these observations. Students were merely sharing equipment or space at the time.

Just because an activity is engaging or hands-on doesn't mean it will automatically cultivate academic talk. It is rare to see activities that require students to process the experience with other students, share opinions, disagree with each other, construct meaning, create a product, or solve complex problems together.

In some cases, activities provide too much context, such that the students can simply point to an object or visual rather than attempt to describe it in an academic manner as if to a distant audience (Zwiers, 2006). This seems to be most evident in science labs, history simulations, and drama-based activities. Although these experiential exercises are important, we must also know how to use them as foundations for building higher-order thinking and academic communication that supports content learning. Consider what one middle school science teacher says about labs:

> In order to do the hands-on labs, they need the knowledge and concepts in order to get something out of it, because you can just come into the room and play around with a bunch of stuff, but what did you learn? That part of science is fun, but that's it. You didn't grasp that connection or understand what it was supposed to show you and demonstrate to you.

FORMS OF GROUP DISCUSSION

Two main forms of group discussion are seminars and deliberations (Parker, 2006). In a seminar, groups discuss in order to come to a deeper understanding of a topic. Participants speak and listen to learn. Topics tend to include the issues, ideas, and values that emerge from a text. Opening questions might be "What does it mean?" and "What is happening?" Literature discussion circles and book clubs are examples of seminar discussions. In deliberations, by contrast, learning is not the goal; rather, students address a problem and decide which course of action to take. Learning happens, of course, but the goal of the talking is to make a decision. Students must generate and weigh alternative solutions to come to their decision. This process cultivates such thinking skills as evaluating, comparing, inferring cause and effect, and persuading, along with the language of these skills. Opening questions might be "What should be done? What is the best alternative?" Academic controversies (chapter 5) and problem-based projects (chapter 9) are examples of deliberations.

Both types of discussion need to be practiced in school. They embody two important elements of education—reflection and action—that prepare students for life beyond school and for democratic participation in society (Parker, 2006). Of course, many discussions have aspects of both types, just as in the real world. For example, a literature group may enlarge their understanding of a character in a novel and then decide how to best communicate it to another group. Before they begin, students should know what form of discussion they are expected to have. Too many group-work minutes can be wasted because the type of discussion is too vague. I even encourage students to ask me directly what type of discussion they need to have when I forget to make it clear.

Once we have a better idea of the type of group (seminar, deliberation, or a combination of the two), then we can create a clearer idea of what should happen in groups. We can ask, "What does an ideal group discussion on this topic sound like in my class? What types of talk bring about the most learning? What do we want to hear that shows evidence of deep thinking and learning?" As we develop a clearer idea of what we want to hear and see, we can teach them to students, listen for them as they work, and provide ongoing feedback. Here are several levels to keep in mind when developing group-work abilities:

- *The cognitive level.* Consider the types of thinking that students should engage in as they talk. What types of visual or verbal prompts will get them to think?

- *The linguistic level.* There are many academic phrases and content words that we would like to hear students use, such that they sound like content-area experts. Some terms are found throughout this book, and others arise in texts and class discussions. You can make a list, model them to students, and include them in rubrics.

- *The sociolinguistic level.* This level includes what students say to show respect, disagree, connect thoughts, maintain the conversation, and stay on topic.

- *The knowledge and skills level.* Students need to be taught how to build on their prior knowledge and how to communicate that knowledge in a group in a democratic manner.

PROCESS OVER PRODUCT: THINKING TOGETHER

Although it is tempting to focus on the more visible products of group work, we must keep in mind the power of the process. The learning that happens on the way to the final product is usually a rich array of exchanges that have a cumulative impact on student language. Along the way, we must help students build what I call *academic collaboration skills:* elaborating and probing meaning, reasoning together, analyzing problems together, comparing possible solutions and ideas together, and making decisions together. In a sense, students use talk to "think together" (Mercer, 2000). When I observe students thinking together, they focus on coming to a shared understanding of a topic or final product through reasoning and constructively criticizing ideas. They strive for clarity and justification of ideas that push them to think about the quality and nature of abstract ideas. Ultimately students construct new knowledge and new academic skills.

This type of talk is evident in the following middle school (advanced and intermediate English learners) discussion about John Brown near the end of the unit:

1. *Student E:* I don't think he was a hero.
2. *Student F:* Why?
3. *Student E:* Because he killed five people.
4. *Student G:* But he also got antislave stuff going.

5. *Student F:* And he talked against slavery, like saying slavery was a crime right before they kill him.

6. *Student H:* But you can say that and not kill people.

7. *Student G:* I guess, but maybe no one listened if all he did was talk.

8. *Student E:* So, maybe there's different types of heroes. Maybe he got people thinking about—

9. *Student H:* Maybe he killed those people but more slaves were saved cuz of what he did.

10. *Student F:* Okay, so, we can say that he was, like, part hero.

11. *Student G:* Can we say that?

Notice several key elements of effective discussions: disagreeing and challenging (lines 4, 6, 7), requesting justification (line 2), building off another's point (line 5), conceding a point (line 7), and synthesizing and problem solving (lines 8–10). This discussion also shows the importance of learning content knowledge in order to talk about it. The teacher would not have been able to say at the beginning of the unit, "Now discuss whether John Brown was a hero or not." No student at that point knew who Brown was or what he had done. A considerable amount of previous teaching of content and thinking allowed this conversation to happen. There were many minilessons on the events surrounding John Brown, as well as basic academic discussion processes. As this excerpt shows, students can successfully think together when we equip them with content knowledge and thinking skills both before and during conversations.

DESIGNING AND SUPPORTING ACADEMIC GROUPS

Rather than relying on fact-based charts, fill-in-the-blank worksheets, chapter questions, and formulaic essays, we should create scenarios where students think about the facts, using key cognitive skills of our discipline, to accomplish complex tasks in real-world ways. Groups must be given effective tasks that help them own the content and language, not just memorize it. Indeed, this focus on collaboratively using information in authentic ways to learn is a key feature underlying the Common Core standards.

I have therefore synthesized a list of key considerations for designing groups (Cohen, 1994; Gibbons, 2002; Robinson, 2000). Group tasks should:

- Be content-based (based on the course's content standards) and integrated with a broader curriculum topic.

- Have a clear outcome and an authentic and engaging purpose.

- Challenge students to use higher-order thinking skills.

- Involve all learners in the group to share in the task and its language.

- Encourage cooperation, rather than competition, between partners and groups.

- Recycle academic terms and grammatical ways of connecting ideas.

- Generate ways in which low-academic-status students can contribute.

- Require students to bridge information gaps in order to accomplish a task.

Needing to talk, rather than just being allowed to talk, develops language and thinking abilities (Gibbons, 2002; Light & Glachan, 1985). Doughty and Pica (1986) found that tasks needing genuine exchange of information helped students generate such conversational modifications as confirmation checks and clarification. (Examples of gap tasks are found later in this chapter.) Work by Long (1981) also showed that two-way tasks produced more interactional modifications (repetitions, confirmation checks, and elaborations) than one-way tasks in conversations between native speakers and English learners. Lasting learning happens when students negotiate meaning, pooling their knowledge to establish a shared understanding that was not there before.

A well-designed task is not enough, however. Students must be trained to work well in groups. This is easier said than done: few teachers sufficiently scaffold group skills, but we can improve. Students can watch us model effective group behaviors and then practice the behaviors with a variety of topics. The following list offers tips for working in groups that we can model. During group work, students should:

- Share assumptions about what the task involves, what the final product is, and what information the others hold.

- Appropriately (academically) disagree, interrupt, question, critique, and compare; challenge and reconcile conflicting ideas in mature and respectful ways.

- Make their thinking visible to others; justify interpretations, hypotheses, and opinions; give reasons and evidence for suggestions.

- Actively listen to one another and respond to others' comments; consider others to be sources of information.
- Work as a team, work toward agreement, and finish as a team without depending on the teacher.
- Play the roles agreed to at the beginning of the task. This is especially important because certain students can dominate group discussions, essentially becoming miniteachers, which takes away the intended feeling of independence from the other members.

These behaviors take years to develop, and the responsibility to improve them each year should be discussed at the school and district levels. Think of the potential impact if teachers in all content areas focus on them and build them in every class.

A responsibility that both students and teachers share is monitoring the effectiveness of the group work. Metadiscuss with students the questions "Why do we talk in class?" and "What happens in good group discussions?" Try it in pairs or groups, and then discuss the topic as a class. The answers will be very insightful. I have kept a list of answers on a poster that evolves over the year. Other good processing questions that can guide metadiscussions about group work and the creation of rubrics are the following (Gordon, 2001):

- How can listeners show they are listening?
- How can listeners show they accept and respect what speakers say?
- How can we encourage shy people to participate?
- How can we reach agreement when we have different ideas?
- How can we make sure everyone gets to speak without putting pressure on anyone?
- How can we keep talkative people from talking too much?
- How do we make sure that we stay on task and not waste time?
- How do we come to an agreement (e.g., without voting)?
- How can we agree on what is relevant for the task?
- How can we talk more as experts (e.g., historians, authors, scientists, mathematicians) might talk about this topic?

LANGUAGE FOR WORKING IN GROUPS

"Respect, connect, build, and support" is a motto that helps students use appropriate language while working in groups. To *respect* means to acknowledge what others say without criticizing the person talking, responding instead to the idea. Even if an idea is wrong, silly, or way off topic, students need to respond academically with such responses as "I don't think it says that in the text," "That might be a bit off topic for now," or, "That's one idea, but let's make sure to stick to the topic of . . ." To respect also means to listen actively and put one's own thoughts aside.

To *connect* means to acknowledge how a peer's response is useful and how it relates to what one is about to say. A student then explains how his or her thoughts *build* into a shared idea that is bigger than the individual ideas. A student also must *support* any points with evidence from the text or experience.

"Respect, connect, build, and support" tends to give the discussion more depth and meaning, and keeps the activity from being just four people tossing their unrelated ideas around the circle. They also tend to keep one student from dominating the discussion with his or her ideas without using the ideas of the others.

To improve discussions, we can teach students to listen and use connective phrases such as these:

"That's a good point, but I disagree because . . ."

"I would like to build on what [name] said about . . ."

"True, but what about . . .?"

"We need to write that down and use it in our final . . ."

"Similar to what [name] said, I think that . . ."

"Although I already knew that . . ."

"However, one question I still have is . . ."

In what is called *collaborative reasoning* (Anderson, 2006), students can use a variety of argument phrases that serve as social functions or help develop the argumentation process. You can work with students to generate a list of possible stratagems for discussions—for example:

"What do you think, Samuel?"

"I am interested in what Delia has to say."

"We have been focusing a lot on . . . , but we also need to talk about . . ."

"But in the story, it says that . . ."

"What kind of evidence is there for that?"

"What else should we consider?"

TECHNIQUES FOR REPORTING OUT

One of the most important yet underdeveloped stages of group work is the reporting out of what was learned or decided. Reporting out provides some focus to the group discussion, allowing students to mold the knowledge as they synthesize it and put it into their own words (ideally more academic ones). Students hear recurring themes from other students to reinforce or challenge their own ideas, while the teacher assesses learning and fills in gaps if needed.

Unfortunately, much of the reporting out that I have observed is weak. Often the person who dominated the group discussion or did much of the work is "nominated" by the group to quickly talk about what the group did. Other groups don't pay attention because they are worried about their own reports or they have the same information. In addition, good reporting is rarely modeled by the teacher, and students rarely have a rubric to use to prepare the report. These weaknesses can be reduced, however. Besides increasing teacher modeling and using rubrics, here are a few suggestions:

- Make sure students have enough time to prepare; then require that they stop preparing when a group reports out.

- Have a different topic for each group.

- Have listeners fill in a form based on the information reported out.

- Structure a way to have audience members ask genuine questions.

- Have group members rotate such that reports are repeated and given in smaller settings than the large class.

One reporting-out option is to have groups create posters that teach different topics and put them up around the room. One person from each group stays with his or her poster for two or three turns—not the whole time. This person answers questions and describes the poster to others. Groups move around the room at five-minute intervals, looking at other posters, asking questions, and taking notes. They can also add thoughts to a separate piece of poster paper, combining their thoughts with those of previous groups. They can use different colors for different types of information on posters, such as summaries, questions, opinions, and suggestions. You circulate and take notes on thinking skills evidenced and key linguistic terms used in the process. The last group at each poster briefly synthesizes and relates it to the main topic of the lesson. Other related ideas are found in chapter 9.

GROUP ACTIVITIES

You are likely familiar with many of the following activities. But take a moment to see how this chapter modifies them to get more language and thinking mileage out of them. I have divided this chapter's group activities into four categories: (1) conversation scaffolds, (2) drama-based group activities, (3) jigsaw-like group activities, and (4) pair activities. Additional group-based reading and writing activities are found in chapters 7 and 8.

Conversation Scaffolds

Academic conversation is a constructive process in which participants build from one another's ideas with a joint purpose in mind. Each participant's understanding of a topic becomes stronger and broader during an effective conversation. But good academic conversations don't just happen. They usually require a hefty amount of modeling and scaffolding. Here are a few activities that provide this needed support, especially for diverse learners.

⇒ Make Conversations More Academic
Model for students how to turn an informal conversation into a more formal, academic one. Start with an informal nonacademic transcript of a dialogue about a topic in your discipline. You may need to create it. (You can use this to teach or review content concepts as well.) Model how you would change the first half, as shown in the sample in table 6.1. Then have pairs upgrade ("academify") the second half of it. Finally, have pairs share their changes and justify them. Types of corrections and changes include increasing the length of turns; being more explicit

Table 6.1 Example of Making Conversations More Academic

Before	After
A: They couldn't vote. It wasn't fair.	A: African Americans didn't have the right to vote. This wasn't fair.
B: Yeah, but they couldn't read.	B: Yet they couldn't read. You need to read in order to vote.
A: They were kept from it. No schools.	A: They weren't allowed to read because they weren't allowed to go to school.
B: I guess. But some could read.	B: True, but some African Americans could read—Frederick Douglass, for example.
A: So without voting, they couldn't change stuff, like to get education.	A: Yes, but he was one of a small percentage. It was a vicious circle in which you needed to vote to get an education, and you needed an education to vote.

for a more distant audience; using organizational markers like *in order to, however,* and *in addition*; using more hedging and modality (*some, could, might*); and using evidence. Have students rehearse the new dialogue in pairs and monitor their progress.

⇒ **Discussion Cards**

Discussion-starter cards (adapted from Thornbury, 2005) are an effective way to put manageable chunks of language into student hands during a discussion. Gather academic discussion phrases that are used in a particular unit of study and are also applicable to other topics in the discipline. These can go on a poster or word wall. Choose five or six, and put them on different-colored cards that students will use to generate and facilitate discussions about the topic. Challenge students to use the phrases as they work, discuss, and argue. If the topic is genetic engineering, for example, you might use the following phrases:

- "People will always . . ."
- "Only when . . ."

- "We must bear in mind that . . ."
- "In the long run, . . ."
- "When we tamper with . . ."
- "On the other hand, . . ."
- "It's not known whether . . ."
- "I still wonder . . ."

Put one to three phrases on each card. Have a whole-class discussion at the end to see how many terms were used and how they helped the discussions or hindered them.

Discussion feature cards (see figure 6.1) are a more "meta" variation: put key features of effective discussion on cards. These cards can remind and challenge students to use a variety of discussion-deepening strategies and thinking skills (see figure 7.2 in the next chapter for ideas on what your students might need to work on). Give each group or pair two to four cards for use in a conversation. Of course, the cards will need to be clarified and modeled beforehand. And remember to talk about why these are important components to any discussion they will have in the future.

Figure 6.1 Feature Cards That Scaffold and Enrich Academic Discussions

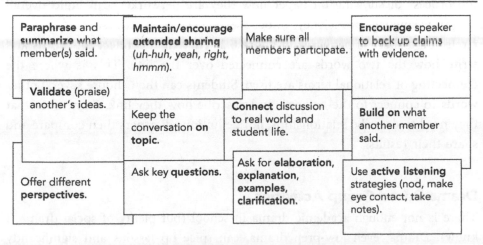

⇒ Academic Term Cards

Put five index cards in an envelope with key words and academic expressions on them, give the envelope to a group, and have students organize the cards in whatever ways they see fit (semantic web, categories, sequence, scene, and so on). As they organize and discuss, help them use such terms as *categorization, main idea, connects to, cause and effect,* and *as a result of.* This can be a prelesson, prereading, or postreading activity.

You can also put several blank cards in the envelope for students to add terms during the reading or lesson. Another variation is to give students additional cards of another color for connecting terms and text organization strategies. Students can then make up key sentences with both sets of cards. For example, students might create such sentences as these:

• "Cooling caused the vapor to condense and become precipitation."

• "The feather symbolized the grief lifted from his heart when they found his son."

• "People should have the universal right to have as many children as they want."

• "We can use calculus to calculate the areas beneath curves."

Creating a word network, a visual organizer that shows how content words are related to each other (adapted from Allen, 1999), is a variation on the idea of academic term cards. Because "words of a feather often flock together," the process of showing on paper how they are networked can build overall academic language proficiency. Choose several key words that students put into circles on a sheet of paper, as in figure 6.2. They then connect the words and write how the two words are connected over the line. This is where the connecting or relational terms are used. Students can then choose several other words to connect to the network and describe how they link. Remember that they need to describe relationships, not definitions. Partners then compare and share their results.

Drama-Based Group Activities

There is not enough academic drama in school (but plenty of social drama, I know). Drama, even low-prep drama, can spice up lessons and significantly

Figure 6.2 Sample Word Network

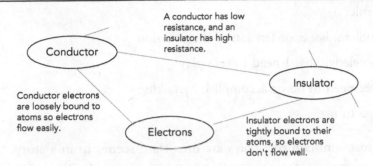

improve long-term learning of language and literacy (Ferree, 2001; McMaster, 1998). Before you begin using drama activities, though, have students brainstorm what is needed to be a good actor, such as empathy, focus, confidence, interpretation, translation of verbal to nonverbal, passion, connection with the audience, creativity, risk taking, being able to give and receive critique, negotiation, intonation, immersion, versatility, exaggeration, improvisation, humor, energy, perseverance, imitation, and observation. Drama not only requires these qualities but also builds them.

⇒ Role Plays

Role plays tend to increase the level of interest and engagement in a topic (Wilhelm, 2002). In role plays, students play the role of someone or something. I include them here because they can be effective at building literacy, language, and thinking skills—if we design them to do so. This means heavy scaffolding of the process before the final performance; the bulk of the work, after all, is done in small groups.

I find it useful to have three types of purposes when planning to use role playing: (1) an overarching purpose that relates to essential understandings and bigger life questions, (2) content-specific purposes that teach key aspects of the content standards, and (3) language, literacy, and thinking purposes.

Role plays require several elements: some knowledge of context, a situation to represent, roles to play, and assessment criteria. Students can use the MOPKAL acronym to plan the role play.

M my role

O other role(s)

P the problem, issue, or tension of the situation

K the knowledge that I need to role-play

A what we need to do or accomplish by talking

L language to use

The most common role plays are important scenes from a story, historical accounts, current issues, or scientific processes. Some effective role plays that I have used are what I call untold scenes and silenced voices. With the Common Core anchor literacy standard "Identify aspects of a text that reveal an author's point of view or purpose (e.g., loaded language, inclusion or avoidance of particular facts)" (CCSS.ELA-Literacy.RH.6–8.6), I might have students act out scenes of minor characters or other underrepresented people from a historical period or event. They logically fill in the missing pieces of history or a narrative. In doing so, they interpret and infer together, which they must do with advanced language.

In most role plays and discussion activities, you must provide considerable support to keep the learning happening, the talk flowing, and the thinking going. This means that you must help students take on multiple perspectives, consider different solutions, use the text as a basis for playing a role, confront misconceptions, ask provocative questions, use appropriate language and expressiveness, connect the role play to real life, and stay in the role and not diverge from the role play's situation. At times you will need to complicate the task, question students' shallow answers, and challenge them to learn from the experience (Heathcote, 1978).

I tend to be more interested in the learning that comes from the process than from the product. The negotiation of meaning and thinking together that happens while students create their role plays are rich opportunities for learning. Students must use the language of interpretation, synthesis, application, abstraction, empathy, perspective, and creativity (e.g., *symbolizes, stands for, means, captures, teaches us, relates to how, author's purpose, was similar to today in that, in her shoes*). Students must refer to the text and connect it to life while considering how the audience will interpret the drama. Notice the thinking in the following dialogue from a ninth-grade world history class as they prepared a role play:

1. *Student A:* Moctezuma thought Cortés was that god Quetzal-whatever.
2. *Student F:* Why?
3. *Student B:* Because he had light skin and rode on horses.
4. *Student F:* So how can we act that out? We need something to symbolize horses.
5. *Student H:* Did they really believe that? I know the book says it, but I don't know.
6. *Student B:* Think about it. If you never saw horses or cannons or a white face, . . . and you remember that legend about the Quetzal-god returning, . . . and they came that same year, what would you think?
7. *Student F:* Okay, maybe we can have Moctezuma talk about that with someone. Maybe they can argue.

A variation in science is to have each student act as a system in the human body. Students can talk about their system's functions and create movements for them. For example, the circulatory system actor might open her arms wide and talk about going through arteries, then get much smaller when squeezing in between two desks and describing capillaries. Then a system interacts with other systems. For example, the circulatory system returns from the desks and shouts to the respiratory system, "I need some oxygen!" The respiratory system replies, "Okay, squeeze back into a capillary next to one of my alveoli, and I will trade you some oxygen for that extra carbon dioxide that you are carrying." Students can come up with props, if needed.

Students can present to the whole class, but it is more time efficient to have groups present to one another. Afterward, have students reflect on and express their conclusions about what happened in the role play and what they learned. For example, in a lesson on Columbus, we discussed several feature films that were "based on real events" but drastically distorted the truth. We then discussed why lies about history mattered and still might matter.

⇒ Expert Panel

An effective way to get students to use academic language to which they are not accustomed (or even resist using in front of peers) is to have them act as real-world experts. An expert panel (adapted from Heathcote and Bolton, 1995) allows students to use the target language to talk about content concepts as they play another person.

The basic process is as follows: describe the issue or topic from the lesson or text; generate with the students a list of possible experts needed to discuss the topic; ask students why the experts would discuss the topic and who would benefit from the discussion; divide students into groups, with each group member choosing to play an appropriate expert role that relates to the text, issue, or lesson. Roles might include museum exhibit designer, reporter, psychologist, historian, archeologist, professor, senator, president, principal, doctor, astronomer, biologist, lawyer, judge, statistician, forensics expert, detective, engineer, art historian, author, and so on. Each student becomes an expert, and there can be more than one of a given expert.

Provide research time so students can become even more prepared. Then ask them to write a short reflection from the expert's point of view on the topic. This quick-write gets them better situated into the perspective of the expert. It is also a chance for you to lend students the language and thinking of experts in that field. After they read their points of view aloud, the audience asks questions of the panel. The audience—another group or the whole class—can be themselves or play roles as well. At the end, panel students are given time to discuss their final report as students in the audience write their reflection summaries.

The panel can also be a review board that hears and discusses issues that arise. For example, it may be a school safety review board, election review board, fiscal oversight committee, energy use board, judicial review board, anticorruption board, historical truth committee, food and drug approval board, morals and ethics review board, or technological advances committee. As in the real world, you can make up a decision-making committee for almost anything. Any students not playing board members can write short letters to raise issues and concerns. Then, before making decisions, the board must rank the importance of the issues raised. This process requires a considerable amount of evaluation language, such as *ramifications, long-term impacts, environmental costs, risks, outweigh, human rights, justify,* and *responsibility.*

Another option is a press conference, where a person or group is asked multiple questions from reporters. Model for students the types of questions that are academic and appropriate. Students can be authors, book characters, real-life people, an idea (communism), a science concept (gravity), and so on. After the activity, a student volunteers to summarize what happened, and then all students can write a reflection or report in their logbooks.

⇒ News Program

A technique for training students to practice the more mainstream types of language found in the media and politics is to have them put on a news program presentation (adapted from Wilhelm, 2002). Most students have seen news programs and know the types of language and mannerisms that newscasters use to communicate the news. Tell a group of students that they are to put on a news program on the highlights of a story, historical event, person, scientific issue, opinion, or other topic. They then write up an interesting summary and use the language of news reporters. They can even refer to "on-site" reporters (in other corners of the room or on video) for exclusive looks at a topic. Each member of a group can do a different feature: top story, related story, interview, opinions, book reviews, environment, consumer tips, and so on. One or two can be producers who organize the program. Use a rubric that you generate with students for ongoing and final assessment.

Model for students the types of language and intonation that newscasters use as they report. You can also watch and analyze video recordings of actual news shows to pick out language and presentation styles. Language to encourage includes such terms as *results of this, this led to, significant because, unlikely turn of events, dramatic unfolding, considered by many to be, violence erupted, what happened next was shocking,* and so forth. Have students listen to news programs at home for ideas and language.

Jigsaw-Like Group Activities

In a typical jigsaw activity, each group reads, views, or listens to a different "text," becomes an expert on that text, and then shares it with others who haven't studied the same text or topic (Coelho, 2004). This activity can be effective, especially in science and history classes, when it is properly scaffolded. However, some teachers (and workshop presenters) often default to what I call the poster time filler (PTF), in which groups are asked to make a poster about a topic and then share it with the whole class. This "activity" often lacks clarity, modeling, guidance, depth, and authentic discussion. Alternatives to the PTF are offered next.

⇒ Jigsaw Labs

In science class, instead of having students do the same lab, have half the pairs or groups in the class do one lab and half do a different one. For example, I had students create a graph of data of the distance of a wheel going down inclines. One group changed the height of the incline, and the other group changed the diameter of the wheel. When they finished, each pair shared with another pair that did the other experiment. They discussed initial observations, hypotheses, choices about data and variables, and conclusions.

Even before they began to work, I modeled the use of scientific method terms and encouraged them to use these terms as they worked and shared their results. In my lab example, I changed the weight of the wheel. Scientific method language that I previewed and asked students to use as they worked included these terms: *observe, constant, hypothesize, independent variable, dependent variable, control, gather data, graph,* and *extrapolate.* Other language that sometimes emerges from student work includes *procedure, increment, adjust, factor, inaccurate, guarantee, inertia, reduce that effect,* and *found that.* Academic grammar might emerge; for example, *If we had put tape on all sides, then it would have made it roll more evenly.* I also encourage students to ask questions of each other as they work: *What do you think will happen if . . . ? Why do you think that would happen? What about if we . . .? So you think it did that because . . .?*

Finally, I find it helpful to have a student in each group record academic talk and then share it later with the other group and the entire class.

⇒ Jigsaw with the Teacher

In this activity, students who might not normally talk in groups get to be the experts, while also giving them close access to teacher language and attention. Choose one student from each group of four or five to work with you for five to ten minutes on a topic that other groups are not working on. You facilitate a group discussion (there may be eight to ten students with you) about the text such that students become "experts" on the topic. Guide them in building their ideas from their interpretations of the text. Encourage the experts to use and teach certain academic phrases when they return to teach their groups. During this time, the other three or four students in each group work on individual tasks or discuss a different part of the text that they then share with the missing student. The now-expert student then leaves the teacher-led group and teaches the other students in his or her original group what she or he learned, as they do the same for him or her.

⇒ Discussion-Focused Split Groups

Unlike many other group activities, the goal for this one is just great discussion. All its parts and tasks are meant to support a high-quality academic discussion. First, students need a sufficient amount of content knowledge in order to talk about the topic in academic ways. As students build this knowledge through listening, reading, or viewing, they must develop a sense of how they will use the information when they discuss it. A Common Core standard in each grade level, for example, focuses on teaching students to prepare for discussions by reading required materials, explicitly drawing on material that they have studied, referring to its evidence, and stimulating a thoughtful, well-reasoned exchange of ideas (National Governors Association Center for Best Practices, 2010).

Students can have some autonomy in deciding what they will discuss, and you can guide them if needed. For example, in science, the groups might choose to discuss one of several environmental issues: acid rain, global warming, renewable energy, or vanishing rain forests. In history, they might want to talk about why Europeans were colonizers rather than colonized or the effects of desegregation laws in the United States.

As groups of four build their content knowledge, they prepare a visual or some product that organizes their learning of a topic. They discuss the topic for a while before two of the group members rotate to another group. The remaining two briefly lead another discussion on their topic with the two new visitors. Rotation happens several times, and each time the visitors' ideas and the resulting conversations add to the product. Original members can return for a final discussion that uses some of the insights from other discussions of other topics. Try to make this an additive idea-building activity rather than a controversy-based argument one. Students might even start each rotation chat with "We need your help with the following topic."

Pair Activities

Pair activities tend to maximize the amount of language that students use because, theoretically, half the students talk at the same time. Although we might see them talk a lot, students need more training in holding good conversations than we

Table 6.2 Sample Chart of Good Speaker and Listener Behaviors

A Good Academic Speaker	A Good Academic Listener
Maintains eye contact	Maintains eye contact
Uses gestures and facial expressions to emphasize points	Nods head and uses facial expressions to support speaker
Varies voice tones and volume to emphasize points	Responds with conversation continuers, such as *wow* or *interesting*
Pauses to let the listener process information	Waits for appropriate pauses to talk
Pauses to let the listener respond	Asks probing questions to clarify and have speaker elaborate, give examples, and provide evidence
Checks to see if the listener understands (*You see? Understand?*)	Paraphrases what speaker is saying to show understanding and to clarify
Stays on topic	

often think. Some areas to improve are listening with empathy, asking for help, taking turns, validating others' responses, helping others without giving answers, disagreeing politely, staying on topic, sharing feelings, paraphrasing, keeping silent to allow others to think, and asking guiding questions. Other ideas are listed in table 6.2.

Table 6.2 can remind us and our students of how to be a good speaker and listener in a conversation. It is best to start with student ideas for this chart to give them ownership of it. You can add ideas from here if students don't generate them early on.

You can use a fishbowl activity to model these behaviors to students. Have other students gather around you and another student to watch you model the behaviors and skills. And, of course, take some time to discuss why it is important to use these skills and behaviors in conversations.

⇒ Think-Pair-Share

An effective and low-prep activity is the think-pair-share (TPS) (Lyman, 1981). It is a quick exchange between two students who process an important piece of learning. During activities and teacher presentations, TPSs provide "breaks to think" that push students to organize their thoughts well enough to communicate them. The listener gets to hear how another person is processing the learning, which further builds language and knowledge. Several CCSS listening and speaking standards focus on building on the ideas of others.

TPSs can be used in a variety of ways and have a variety of prompts. Perhaps the biggest challenges of this simple procedure are (1) realizing that it is worth the loudness and time used in class and (2) remembering to stop and use it during a busy day, which is, of course, every day. TPS should happen several times a day. It can be used spontaneously, too, when you prompt discussion and there are too few responses or, conversely, when you prompt the class and too many students want to answer all at once. Table 6.3 contains a few tips for creating prompts.

Table 6.3 Tips and Examples for Generating Think-Pair-Share Prompts

Tip	Example
Create questions or prompts that focus students on key content concepts in the text, the author's purpose, essential meanings, and ways to connect to previous learning and background knowledge.	What was the Declaration of Independence, and why was it important? Why do authors use foreshadowing to enhance a story? Give examples from our last book. Draw and explain how the respiratory system interacts with the circulatory system. Explain to your partner how to divide fractions.
Create open-ended questions or prompts that connect to students' lives and allow personalized, divergent responses. These questions are less threatening or boring than many fact-based questions in textbooks, yet they still get students to think about the content in complex ways. They also show that you care about what students think—not just what they know or don't know.	If you were a colonist, would you have . . .? Why? Describe how acids and bases are used at your house. If you saw bullying going on at school, what would you do? Would you have done what the main character did? How would you like to be a whale? What was it like being a monk in the simulation yesterday? How would you use geometry to build a house?

(continued)

Table 6.3 *continued*

Tip	Example
Create prompts for academic skills that you want to emphasize, such as synthesizing, predicting, inferring, classifying, persuading, evaluating, analyzing, comparing, and applying. Use academic language in the prompts that students will likely integrate into their responses. Show them how to do this.	How might this war be similar to the Revolutionary War? What were the causes and effects of the war? Tell your partner why we would use the quadratic formula. What can you infer about the character's feelings from his actions? How does this relate to current events?
Prompt an opinion about a topic. Each shares for a minute. They get to share their thoughts, they must put them together quickly with support, there are no wrong answers, and the activity is quick.	What is your opinion of Hamlet? What is your opinion of global warming? What do you think about Lincoln's words and actions? What is your opinion of the recent war? Should the main character have done that?
Other ideas for prompts: give vocabulary definitions, prepare a dialogue, compare two ideas or concepts, make predictions or hypotheses, connect to big ideas, share homework, brainstorm.	What does *sacred* mean? Play the roles of two brothers arguing for different sides of the war. Compare ionic to covalent bonding. Predict the answer to this equation. How does the ending of this novel relate to the big idea? Come up with ideas for how they survived.

To start the TPS, have students think in silence for thirty to sixty seconds to mentally organize what they will say. They can write notes or draw as they think. Then prompt them to build an idea rather than just tell each other what they are thinking. (For additional suggestions for building ideas in conversations, see chapter 5.) Let them talk for one to five minutes, and encourage them to use language from the charts or posters on the walls. You can also model how a person might start to respond to your prompt if pairs are having trouble starting. When you stop them, ask them to share with the class (or with another pair) a synopsis of the ideas that they built. You can preselect as you go around and listen for interesting conversations, and ask students to share: "I heard Alex and Priya talking about the ethics of genetic tests. Would either of you share your thinking with the class?" You can also ask a student to share what the partner said, which publicly validates what the partner said—and encourages genuine listening.

A variation of TPS is a double-prompt-pair-share, in which you create two different questions, one for each student, so that they can't say things like "ditto" or "I agree." Ideally the two questions connect and can form a foundation for a short conversation (*How are acids and bases different? How are they used?*). I have even done triple-prompt-pair-shares, in which each student first answers a background question that generates information to jointly answer a more open third question (*What are the benefits of globalization? What are the drawbacks? Can technology solve major world problems?*).

More time-consuming variations integrate various reading and writing components: think-write (quick-write)-pair-share (TWPS); think-pair-write-share (TPWS); think-pair-think-share (TPTS); read-pair-share (RPS); RWPS; TWRPS; TRWPWS; TWRWPSW; and so on. The ongoing goal is to get students to fortify language, thinking, and literacy in low-stress, short bursts throughout the day.

⇒ Think-Pair-Square

Instead of whole-class sharing after students talk in pairs, each pair turns to another pair to share and create a synthesis of the two pairs (Millis & Cottell, 1998). This step offers each student a chance to talk with three other people instead of in front of the entire class. (You can add another share session of four-by-four as well for even more practice in a larger group of eight.) This offers a chance to say and hear the same words again and put the ideas under the scrutiny of a larger group. Of course, it is important to share with students how to be positive and constructively "scrutinous." That is, you should model how to take another person's idea and mold it, preserving the strong or right parts and gently changing the weak or wrong parts. Consider the following fourth-grade example (A and B were a pair, as were E and F).

1. *Student A:* We need to say, like, that the magnet picks up metal things.
2. *Student E:* Okay, but it doesn't pick up *all* metals. Look (*showing that the magnet doesn't pick up aluminum*).
3. *Student B:* Well, most metal things.
4. *Student F:* We can't say "most." It has something to do with iron. Look here in the book.
5. *Student E:* Yeah, but we should also say why.
6. *Student A:* Okay, we'll say it picks up metals with iron because iron is magnetic.
7. *Student B:* But why is iron magnetic?

Notice how the two groups negotiated what they were going to say to the whole class. Also notice the more profound *why* question at the end. This student might not have asked this question had it not been for the discussion.

⇒ A-B Information Gap Activity

Most conversations are basic examples of how language is used to fill gaps. A gap is filled when a speaker, writer, or artist provides information that the listener, reader, or viewer wants or needs. Information gap activities allow students to authentically communicate with other students and provide needed practice in checking for clarification and elaborating (Long, 1981; Pica & Doughty, 1985). Information gap activities also satisfy Ur's criteria (1991) for a successful speaking activity: learners talk a lot, participation is even and fairly distributed, motivation is high, and the language is at an appropriate level. As far as developing academic language is concerned, gap activities tend to provide redundancy of terms and content, challenge students to use new language to accomplish a task, and offer fun practice with academic language in small settings.

In a gap activity, each student, A and B, has different information that the other person needs, somewhat like a jigsaw puzzle (and like the jigsaw activity described earlier). The teacher provides new information to each, or students research it themselves. Each student is also given some kind of need for the other's information, such as a diagram to fill in, problem to solve, or project to design. Examples include a scientist and a reporter talking about stem cell research, a contractor and a home owner talking about costs for remodeling a house, two characters in a novel talking about their motives, and a Spanish conquistador and an Aztec leader discussing religious rights in the sixteenth century. Remember to

Figure 6.3 Organizer for Designing Information Gap Activities

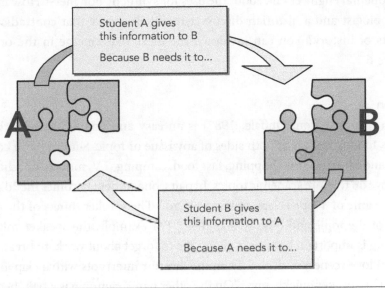

Student A gives this information to B

Because B needs it to...

A

B

Student B gives this information to A

Because A needs it to...

Topic/Content/Information to be learned and exchanged

How do students learn content so that they can talk about it? (text, cards, video, picture, research, interviews)

Task/Performance/Product What do students do or produce as a result of talking? Examples: Solve a problem, exchange opinions, make a decision, comprehend a text, create a project or product (information grid, completed map or diagram, article, poster)

Academic language to be used: _____

Situation: _____

Roles: A is a _____   B is a _____

---

set it up so that students have to talk; they shouldn't merely look at another student's information. Figure 6.3 is a graphic organizer that I sometimes use to help me design information gap activities.

Information gap activities are not just for language classes. All you have to do is imagine two people in your discipline who need to talk about the discipline in some way or two types of information that two experts need to exchange in the real world. Think about how the target information might be talked about in the real world and who might talk about it. For example, how might a scientist and an environmental engineer talk about the uses for synthetic polymers? How might an anthropologist and a historian discuss a recent discovery that contradicts most accounts of history? You can jot down the ideas that emerge in the organizer in figure 6.3.

⇒ Pro-Con

Pro-con (adapted from Duffala, 1987) is an easy and popular activity that gets students to look quickly at both sides of any issue or topic. Start off with common actions and ideas, such as shopping, fast food, camping, TV, movies, or school, and then move on to more academic topics. In pairs, one student becomes the "director," says the name of a topic, claps, and says, "Pro." The speaker thinks of the positive aspects of the topic and quickly lists them. For example, the speaker might say, "Camping is important because it allows me to forget about work, to breathe fresh air, and I love scenery and . . ." Then the director interrupts with a clap and says, "Con!" The speaker quickly says, "On the other hand, camping is a pain because of the insects and the hard ground. My back often hurts in the morning and . . ." "Pro!" and so on. The intervals get smaller and become more rapid. The speaker uses transitions, such as *however, on the other hand, on the contrary, then again, of course, nevertheless,* to smooth out the changes. (I don't let them use *but* because it is already used plenty in oral discourse.) Finally, this activity can be an engaging way to build students' abilities to support oral arguments (which can help with their written arguments), as described in many Common Core standards on using evidence.

Adaptations include clapping between saying *cause* and *effect* or between *compare* and *contrast.* You can probably come up with other adaptations for your setting.

CONCLUSION

I have seen many quiet and passive learning environments that produce short-term results in which students "cram and then flush" their knowledge at regular intervals during the school year. Yet students who talk through knowledge and manipulate it in social settings tend to construct meaning that is more transferable and enduring. In this chapter, we looked at ideas for getting students to build academic language and think in small-group settings. Research has shown that students can learn a great deal from interactions with peers (Johnson & Johnson, 1989), yet such interactions are challenging for teachers to manage in large classes. We must be creative and tactful in order to make each minute of each activity worth the time and energy.

This chapter also highlighted the need to model and scaffold a variety of group and pair communication skills. Students need considerable training to learn how to interact in academic ways with others. This is especially important in grades 5 through 12, when students are expected to engage in meaningful discussions about a wider range of topics and concepts based on complex texts across disciplines (National Governors Association Center for Best Practices, 2010). The language of academic reading, conveniently enough, is the topic of the next chapter.

CHAPTER REFLECTIONS

- What would you like to hear in a group or pair conversation in your class?

- How do you help students maximize their on-task talk in each group?

- How can you get students to self-monitor their talk and seek to improve their construction of meaning as they talk in groups and pairs?

- What types of information gaps in your discipline are bridged in the world every day? What types of thinking happen in these interactions?

- Choose a topic that you teach and come up with several effective prompts for think-pair-shares in your class. What ideas, terms, and grammar would you like to hear in student responses?

References

Allen, J. (1999). *Words, words, words: Teaching vocabulary in grades 4–12.* Portland, ME: Stenhouse.

Anderson, R. (2006). *Collaborative reasoning: An approach to literature discussion that promotes children's social and intellectual development.* Retrieved from www.reading.org/downloads/annual_handouts/r_anderson_comprehension.doc

Coelho, E. (2004). *Adding English: A guide to teaching multilingual classrooms.* Toronto, Canada: Pippin.

Cohen, E. G. (1994). *Designing groupwork: Strategies for heterogeneous classrooms* (2nd ed.). New York, NY: Teachers College Press.

Doughty, C., & Pica, T. (1986). "Information gap" tasks: Do they facilitate second language acquisition? *TESOL Quarterly, 20*, 305–325.

Duffala, J. (1987). *The teacher as artist.* Santa Rosa, CA: Author.

Faltis, C. (2001). *Joinfostering.* Upper Saddle River, NJ: Prentice Hall.

Ferree, A. M. (2001). Soaps and suspicious activities: Dramatic experiences in British classroom. *Journal of Adolescent and Adult Literacy, 45*(1), 16–23.

Gibbons, P. (2002). *Scaffolding language, scaffolding learning.* Portsmouth, NH: Heinemann.

Gilles, C. (1993). We make an idea: Cycles of meaning in literature discussion groups. In K. Pierce & C. Gilles (Eds.), *Cycles of meaning* (pp. 199–217). Portsmouth, NH: Heinemann.

Gordon, D. (2001). Practical suggestions for supporting speaking and listening in classrooms. In P. Smith (Ed.), *Talking classrooms: Shaping children's learning through oral language instruction* (pp. 57–73). Newark, DE: International Reading Association.

Heathcote, D. (1978). Of these seeds becoming: Drama in education. In R. Shuman (Ed.), *Educational drama for today's schools* (pp. 1–40). London, UK: Scarecrow Press.

Heathcote, D., & Bolton, G. (1995). *Drama for learning: Dorothy Heathcote's mantle of the expert approach to education.* Portsmouth, NH: Heinemann.

Johns, K. (1992). Mainstreaming language minority students through cooperative grouping. *Journal of Educational Issues of Language Minority Students, 11*, 221–231.

Johnson, D., & Johnson, R. (1989). *Cooperation and competition: Theory and research.* Edina, MN: Interaction Book Company.

Johnson, D., & Johnson, R. (1994). Cooperative learning in second language classes. *Language Teacher, 18*, 4–7.

Light, P., & Glachan, M. (1985). Facilitation of problem-solving through peer interaction. *Educational Psychology, 5*, 217–225.

Long, M. (1981). Input, interaction and second language acquisition. In H. Winitz (Ed.), *Native language and foreign language acquisition* (pp. 259–278). New York, NY: Annals of the New York Academy of Science.

Lyman, F. T. (1981). The responsive classroom discussion: The inclusion of all students. In A. Anderson (Ed.), *Mainstreaming digest* (pp. 109–113). College Park: University of Maryland Press.

McMaster, J. C. (1998). "Doing" literature: Using drama to build literacy. *Reading Teacher, 51,* 574–584.

Mercer, N. (2000). *The guided construction of knowledge: Talk amongst teachers and learners.* Clevedon, UK: Multilingual Matters.

Millis, B. J., & Cottell, P. G., Jr. (1998). *Cooperative learning for higher education faculty.* Phoenix, AZ: Oryx Press.

National Governors Association Center for Best Practices. (2010). *Common Core State Standards.* Washington, DC: Council of Chief State School Officers.

Nystrand, M. (1997). *Opening dialogue: Understanding the dynamics of language and learning in the English classroom.* New York, NY: Teachers College Press.

Parker, W. (2006). Public discourses in schools: Purposes, problems, possibilities. *Educational Researcher, 35*(8), 11–18.

Pica, T., & Doughty, C. (1985). Input and interaction in the communicative language classroom: A comparison of teacher-fronted and group activities. In S. Gass & C. Madden (Eds.), *Input in second language acquisition* (pp. 115–132). Rowley, MA: Newbury House.

Robinson, P. (2000). Task complexity, cognitive resources, and second language syllabus design. In P. Robinson (Ed.), *Cognition and second language instruction* (pp. 287–318). Cambridge, UK: Cambridge University Press.

Thornbury, S. (2005). *How to teach speaking.* Essex, UK: Pearson.

Ur, P. (1991). *A course in language teaching: Practice and theory.* Cambridge, UK: Cambridge University Press.

Wilhelm, J. (2002). *Action strategies for deepening comprehension.* New York, NY: Scholastic.

Zwiers, J. (2005). *Developing academic language in middle school English learners: Practices and perspectives in mainstream classrooms.* Unpublished doctoral dissertation, University of San Francisco.

Zwiers, J. (2006). Integrating academic language, thinking, and content: Learning scaffolds for non-native speakers in the middle grades. *Journal of English for Academic Purposes, 5,* 317–332.

Chapter 7

Language for Reading Complex Texts

I read, therefore I am.

This chapter describes how we can develop both the language of academic reading and the reading of academic language. It points out ways to help students acquire the terms and grammar of the varying complex texts across content areas. After fourth grade, texts become much denser, and their thinking demands increase (Wong Fillmore, 2004). One of the key shifts of the Common Core reading standards is the increased emphasis on building all students' abilities to comprehend grade-level complex texts (EngageNY, 2013). In this chapter, we look at how authors of complex texts in upper grades expect readers to think about and organize ideas in different ways. As we saw in chapter 4, a math text differs greatly from a novel, which differs from a science textbook chapter, which differs from a historical primary source document.

Many high-quality resources are available on teaching reading strategies to students (see Harvey & Goudvis, 2000; Tovani, 2000; appendix A, this book). Most of them describe how to develop cognitive strategies, such as making inferences, predicting, summarizing, questioning, and monitoring comprehension. This chapter assumes that you and your students are already weaving these core reading strategies into reading and that students need more training in comprehending challenging texts, many of which are complex expository pieces (e.g., textbooks, articles, tests). Providing the tools of academic language and building the skills of using it can help.

BENEFITS OF ACADEMIC READING

Besides the learning of content concepts, students benefit from reading challenging academic texts in several ways. Perhaps most important is that they can learn a large amount of academic language from reading (Shefelbine, 1998; Wallace, 1992). Reading introduces new terms and grammar at the student's pace, and it provides multiple exposures to academic vocabulary that is rare in oral contexts (Elley, 1991). Students also see a variety of academic text structures that they are unlikely to hear in spoken exchanges (Wong Fillmore & Fillmore, 2011).

Another language-building feature of reading is redundancy. Unlike when they are in listening situations, readers can reread confusing parts of the text, such as those with words that are new to them, complex syntax, or referential problems (e.g., "I have no idea what *this* refers back to"). This is a good problem, though, because students realize that they are confused and pause, and the repeated processing of challenging language forms and functions aids their language growth (Hafiz & Tudor, 1989).

Academic reading builds students' capacities to use multiple thinking skills in combination. To comprehend most texts, a reader must use such comprehension strategies as predicting, summarizing, inferring, questioning, connecting to background knowledge, and figuring out words (Keene & Zimmerman, 1997). Yet authors expect readers of their academic texts to use these strategies along with other thinking skills, such as classifying, synthesizing, inferring cause and effect, predicting, evaluating, interpreting, applying, analyzing, and comparing. For example, you might be mentally summarizing this paragraph right now, questioning how you can teach this to students, and thinking about how to apply it to the texts in your content area. This is another example of mental multitasking that typifies academic reading.

KEY COMPREHENSION STRATEGIES FOR ACADEMIC READING

Readers are expected to figure out implicit links in complex texts (Rose, 1997). If they do not, the logic of the text is lost on them. For example, a text might say, "Supplies were minimal since several bridges had been destroyed. The general wondered if the men would remain to fight." Students must link the destroyed bridges to the lack of supplies, which might cause the soldiers to complain and leave. To make these connections, students must be able to quickly learn new words and continually organize and condense information. In many cases, long nominalized subjects at the beginning of a sentence require a reader to quickly pack a lot of information into the subject position as they look for the main verb. Other clauses add information to the mix but often lack explicit and concrete links.

Readers need to infer these many links and be able to work with the abstract ideas in the text. They must "translate" the abstract and complex messages into more concrete and understandable terms. This is an especially challenging task when students read an academic text in which the author has condensed, semantically and grammatically, ideas from previous texts or has assumed that readers can figure out the condensed clause. I often see this thinking when a teacher reads a highly academic passage aloud and then translates it to students. For example, the following academic passage is taken from a resource on history teaching:

> Understanding how students deal with such complexity, and how teachers aid them in doing so, would not only provide a knowledge base for improving school history but would also inform theories of reading comprehension, which are surprisingly mute about the processes used to form interpretations of complex written texts. (Wineberg, 2001, p. 51)

A more understandable translation of this academic sentence that a teacher might offer is this:

> We could teach history better and help students to read it better if we knew how students think about complex ideas and how teachers help them.

We can train students to do similar types of translation when they come across difficult spots in the text, but as is true in learning a new language, we don't want students to rely on translation. We want the text as it is written to make sense more and more automatically over time. This means we must avoid overtranslating for them, which enables students to avoid digging into complex texts, exercising their mental muscles, and getting used to complex language.

Let's now look at a few strategies that good readers use to understand academic texts. These, of course, are the strategies that we must scaffold.

To understand any sentence or paragraph, a reader must know and do several things, usually all at once. First, the reader must sufficiently align his or her word meanings with the author's meanings for those words. This can require mental flexibility and creativity. For example, often there are many abstract and figurative expressions that a reader must adapt in order to figure out the text in question, such as *deal with, a knowledge base, inform theories,* and *mute.* This cognitive flexibility to quickly adapt an expression from the concrete to the abstract is vital in the upper grades and beyond. (See CCSS.ELA-Literacy.RL.4–12.4 standards, which focus on figurative language.)

Second, a reader needs to understand and condense (chunk) what came before in the text. This ability is necessary because authors condense the ideas of previous sentences into complex nominal groups, which become subjects of the sentence. I did this three sentences ago, when I used, *This cognitive flexibility to quickly adapt an expression from the concrete to the abstract* as the subject of the sentence. Proficient readers, like teachers, quickly process that sentence without a problem. But many students haven't built up the cognitive muscles to do that much chunking yet.

Third, a reader must be able to determine the important information in a sentence by analyzing its clauses to understand the main participants, processes, and circumstances (Schleppegrell & de Oliveira, 2006). Many academic sentences begin and end with subordinate clauses that are used to add information and detail but do not carry the main subject or verb of the sentence. When speaking or reading aloud (and even as we read silently), we often deal with these clauses with a lower tone, slightly quicker pace, and less emphasis. For example, "Driven by a constant hunger for power, the king depleted the country's resources in military campaigns, the last of which cost him his throne." If you read this aloud, you hear yourself stress and slow down the middle clause. The first and third clauses provide circumstance information, and the middle clause carries the main participant and processes.

Fourth, the abstractness of academic texts often requires readers to connect to existing knowledge and come up with their own examples. I was reading a journal article in which the authors did not use any concrete examples to illustrate their theories. I kept on saying out loud to the text, "For example . . .?" and "How does this apply?" Then I realized that *I* was supposed to do the work of coming up with applications and examples. These authors did not want to limit themselves to a few examples when they were trying to describe general ideas to a broad range of distant audiences. You have probably done this at times while reading this book.

Similarly, we must train students to make their own connections, examples, and applications when they read abstract and general texts. Most have had practice connecting literature to their own lives in language arts classes, yet they must move to another level to read an abstract scientific or social theory and connect it to academic examples that are not so personal. For example (I am saving you the work here), in reading an article about historical bias, a student might need to quickly recall the two conflicting accounts of the Cuban missile crisis that she read last year to help her understand the ideas about bias in the article.

Finally, readers must recognize the author's purposes, structure, and commitment in a text. This means being in a constant state of metareading—thinking at a deeper level than just getting information. Most students see reading mainly as a conduit for transferring basic information from those who know much to those who know less. But when we equip students to metaread, look for the underlying themes, and analyze and critique the writing, they gain important insights into how writers use language in academic ways. It helps to tell students to "read as a writer."

The Common Core reading standards in each grade level also provide a helpful outline for the skills that students need to learn to read grade-level texts. These standards can help us design and fortify reading activities in each lesson. The rest of this chapter offers ideas for building students' abilities to organize the thinking that needs to happen as they comprehend complex academic texts.

ORAL SCAFFOLDS FOR ACADEMIC READING

Many of the students who struggle to read at grade level lack the many hours of being read to that proficient readers have had. Oral scaffolds are ways to build, strengthen, and diversify language into forms that readers will see in complex texts.

⇒ Read-Aloud

Reading aloud does more than just get content into students' heads when they can't or don't want to read the text. It is an effective way for students to acquire academic language, mostly because school texts are more academic than the typical talk of teachers and other students (Elley, 1991). If you have ever noticed how academic (and mentally taxing) a speech becomes when a speaker starts reading aloud, you have experienced this. Reading aloud builds language and thinking in these ways:

- Building students' interest in a text so that they will read it, even though it contains challenging language

- Developing academic listening skills, such as discriminating important from unimportant information, often through hearing differences in tone and emphasis

- Providing multiple exposures to academic vocabulary and figurative language

- Developing abilities to handle longer and more complex sentences (chunking)

- Exposing students to text and concepts that are above their current independent comprehension levels

- Building up the knowledge needed for class and group discussions

We must not deprive students of chances to hear good modeling of complex texts. When we read aloud, students get to hear how we, experts in our content area, use punctuation, pauses, and intonation to separate clauses, stress key points, and subordinate information. They also get to hear how we stop and struggle to actively process the text.

We should read aloud in all classes, from kindergarten through graduate school, from math to language arts. And we should use many kinds of materials that have a variety of language features, such as articles, editorials, children's books, newspapers, textbook chapters, novels, short stories, poems, math problems, and math-based articles. I usually read the first part of any assigned text to hook students into the text and to get their language processes rolling in the right direction.

Echo reading is a simple strategy for building academic intonation and punctuation. It sounds a bit juvenile to have everybody repeating the teacher at once, but it is effective. Remember that many students have not been immersed in such language growing up or heard proficient readers read academic texts with appropriate pauses, expression, and prosody.

⇛ Comprehend-Aloud

A lot happens in the mind of proficient readers while reading. Less proficient students need to see these thoughts, processes, and strategies. The more we make these thoughts visible, the more our students can appropriate our thinking and our language for their own uses. An activity that offers students this opportunity is called a *comprehend-aloud*, which is really a think-aloud (Davey, 1983) that is used when reading to students. But again, rather than just focusing on reading strategies and content learning, here we seek to emphasize the language and thinking of a complex text.

Armed with a fortified knowledge of a text's academic thinking skills such as perspective taking, evaluating, comparing, and problem solving (see chapters 2 and 4), we can show students how authors structure texts and use certain terms and grammar to show what they are thinking. For example, I might stop reading to say, "The author began the sentence with the clause *Because of this.* Because of what? Now I look back and see that the clause refers to the part about the Egyptian farmers wanting to be ready to plant their seeds." (Notice, too, the use of the academic terms *clause* and *refers to the part* in my statement.)

We must be explicit and descriptive as we describe our thinking, because much of the subject and its language has become second nature to us through our studying it or teaching it multiple times a day over many years. A few comprehend-aloud categories to model are shown in table 7.1.

Table 7.1 Comprehend-Aloud Categories and Sample Sentence Starters

Comprehension Processes	Examples of What to Say
Noticing academic language and thinking	Here the author is comparing . . . *Ramifications* means effects. Why would it cause that to happen? If I substitute the word . . . , does it make sense enough to move on? *If they had seen* means they never saw it and a guess of what would have happened
Identifying confusing parts and clarifying them by rereading; monitoring comprehension	I didn't catch whether she escaped or was set free. I need to check back to see why the revolution began. I don't understand why they thought that. I'll read ahead a few lines to see if it becomes clearer.
Figuring out long sentences and breaking them down into chunks	This basically means that light is a wave. So it was greed that caused the war.
Making predictions and inferences; seeing if they are answered or confirmed	Because of the subheading, I predict that the next section will be about how women helped war efforts. Oh, interesting; my prediction was wrong. Now . . .
Connecting text to one's own life, other texts, world issues	This reminds me of the movie I saw about JFK. I have a picture in my mind of a star collapsing. This is similar to when my mom was sick and we . . .
Asking questions	Why does the author want me to care about sharks? How did they know how old the bones were? Who really fired the first shot? I wonder why light goes at just one speed.

Table 7.1 (*continued*)

Comprehension Processes	Examples of What to Say
Monitoring your understanding of what the author of a text wants readers to get out of the text	So far, I think the author wants me to see them as symbols of hope and freedom. The authors want me to understand that mass is conserved when . . .
Describing how each part of the text supports its main theme or purpose	The author used this quotation to show how the government brainwashed people. She made this character persevere to teach us a lesson.

As you read aloud, pause to make comments about what you are thinking and how you are organizing your thoughts in order to comprehend the text. You can even come up with randomly triggered thoughts and point out how they don't help you understand the main points of the text. Emphasize how you monitor comprehension, sculpt the main idea, prune unhelpful thoughts, use fix-up strategies (looking back, reading on), paraphrase, and connect pieces of text. Show students that it takes loads of thinking to comprehend and that you must stop often to think.

After a short while (roughly one-third of the way through text to be read), you can ask students to think aloud to each other in pairs, to the whole class, or both. When students start to comprehend aloud, this activity becomes shared reading (Holdaway, 1979) in which you and the students think through a text together. When you stop reading, you give students a chance to share their thoughts about the text to that point. You might prompt them to analyze, synthesize, summarize, question, predict, compare, figure out causes and effects, evaluate, interpret, and so on. This is a good opportunity to formatively assess whole-class thinking. Similarly, for more talking time, try having students do comprehend-alouds in pairs or small groups with other students. Partners can listen along and record comments.

⇒ **Improv Read-Aloud**

To make the reading of a challenging text more active, let students act. In this activity, students become parts of the text, either animate or inanimate, while you read aloud. Students might play nobles, serfs, kings, cells, planets, atoms, story characters, and so on. You have them move and say certain lines at different points in the text. For example, a teacher might stop reading and tell a student to be a king, who announces, "I will spare your lives if you render total allegiance to me and pay tribute to our cause." Or a teacher might say to a bacteria cell, "The antibiotic is weakening your cell wall because . . ." Thus, students get more interested in understanding the text, and we get chances to introduce and fortify the language as we give them their improv lines. If students lack proper emotion, be like a director who models it and has them do it again, thereby repeating language and further helping them and the rest of the class.

Try this out with almost any text; you will be surprised at how many texts can be acted out. But you must plan how this will work. Preread the text and think of places where students can do some improv.

⇒ Lyric Summaries

In most effective teaching activities, both process and product are important for developing language that describes abstract and complex ideas. In this engaging and creative activity (adapted from McLaughlin, 2006), pairs or groups read a text and then create a summary that goes to a common tune. It works best to choose the tune and build the summary from there.

An effective way to start is with a semantic web. Begin with core ideas, and surround them with branches of important information. Then students must build sentences that become verses. Remind students that they should include only important information and in a concentrated manner. Tunes might include "Row, Row, Row Your Boat," "Twinkle, Twinkle, Little Star," "Happy Birthday to You," TV show theme songs, and other popular songs that students agree on.

Language that students use as they work with one another can include such terms as *this is important because . . . , we can leave that out because . . . , this word is clearer, it should be in this order,* and so on. Model this process and the language that you use to think about the summary.

Two lyric summaries are shown here. Notice content-specific terms in the first song such as *perfect square, polynomial, x-intercepts,* and *square root.* Notice the general academic terms in the "Cell Mitosis Chant" (adapted from Krasnow, 2004), such as *continue the trend, underestimate, bound nicely together, pass on traits, on their way to make,* and *most commonly seen.* Optional hand motions are also described for different parts.

Quadratic Formula Reggae Song

When $ax^2 + bx + c$
is not a perfect square, I do not leave
I use the Quadratic Formula to find x
The polynomial's x-intercepts
X equals negative b like in "boot"
Plus or minus the square root
Of b that's squared minus $4ac$
All divided by $2a$, how easy!

Cell Mitosis Chant

Now here's a simple story I like to tell
Of the reproduction skills of a cell
Before the little cell's life comes to an end
It's got to procreate to continue the trend.
In the very middle there's a ring, let's say *(fingers make a circle)*
It's called a nucleus and houses DNA
DNA is stuff we mustn't underestimate
It makes up genes that pass on the cell's traits
The DNA coils up good and tight,
To make a chromosome; it's quite a spiral sight *(hands in fists together)*
Yet the chromosome doesn't have just one side
It's made of two chromatids that just can't hide *(hold fists separately)*
The chromatids are bound nicely together
By a centromere through good and bad weather *(one fist grabs other thumb)*
Then it's time for the chromatids to say goodbye
Spindle fibers separate them, but they don't cry *(fists pulled apart)*
For they are on their way to make a brand new cell
That has all the parts and pieces to turn out well
With a pinch around the center, the cell splits in two
Now you can't tell which is which and who is who.
Most commonly seen under a microscope, it's
The making of twin cells by the process of mitosis.

TEXT DISCUSSION ACTIVITIES

Plenty of research supports the position that students should talk about what they read (Alvermann, Dillon, & O'Brien, 1987; Gambrell, 1996). Students' comprehension increases when they discuss texts (Gallagher & Pearson, 1989), and discussion offers students the chance to process the ideas, opinions, and questions that emerge from texts. Students also get to hear teacher and peer responses that fill in their knowledge gaps and provide redundancy of language. (Also refer to chapters 5 and 7 for other discussion activities that involve reading.)

⇒ **Anticipation Chats**

An anticipation chat, inspired by the anticipation guide (Herber, 1978), is a prereading, prepresentation, or prevideo activity. Give students a topic from the text that has a continuum of opposing answers (e.g., yes-no, right-wrong, moral-immoral, just-unjust). You can have students mark on a continuum where they believe themselves to be, using a graphic organizer like the one in figure 7.1. For example, they may respond to this statement: *People have equal opportunities in this country.* They write their thoughts and then, in groups or pairs, briefly discuss their positions (D, d, a, A), along with reasons and evidence for them (in the *Why?* box). They can discuss what they think the text, lesson, or video will cover and what they expect to learn in the unit or lesson. (A more kinesthetic adaptation is to have students get up and place themselves on a continuum line in the middle of the room and discuss with those next to them.) It is helpful to put up terms and expressions for students to use as they discuss their points of views and predictions. Language might include *I believe that, I somewhat agree that, it depends on your definition of, rights, education, discrimination, percentages, poverty, factors, consider the source,* and *look at.*

The example in figure 7.1 is from science in a table format (two or three more anticipation statements can be used as well). Notice how the format does not allow

Figure 7.1 Sample Organizer for Anticipation Chats

D = Disagree   d = somewhat disagree   a = somewhat agree   A = Agree

Cloning should be banned.			
Before Reading		After Reading	
A	Why?	d	Why?
	It's not natural and we are unique.		Perhaps it can benefit sick people. For example,... But I also think...

a student to take the easy middle route. The student must consider the reasons closely and take one side of the issue:

A = strongly agree   a = somewhat agree
d = somewhat disagree   D = strongly disagree

Then they finish and discuss their answers.

Often students can learn more from making errors in their answers and predictions than from predicting correctly early on. When the text or presentation clashes with what a student anticipated, there is cognitive dissonance, or what I call "learning energy," as the student tries to sort things out and change original ideas. As long as the environment is safe to make such guesses and errors, this kind of learning can flourish. And along the way, students should use academic (persuasive, analytical, and comparative) language to organize and describe their conceptual changes.

⇛ Role-Based Discussion Groups

In role-based discussion groups, students take on various roles to accomplish tasks as a group. Popular variations include reciprocal teaching (Palinscar & Brown, 1984), complex instruction (Cohen, 1994), and literature circles (Daniels, 1994). Group members take on a variety of interdependent roles in order to jointly accomplish a task and develop cognitive and academic skills along the way. Substantial modeling and minilessons are often required for the different roles before students can successfully perform them in independent groups. Possible roles include those listed in table 7.2, but we can work with students to come up with other roles, depending on the task.

Student roles can be on a pocket chart or other visual, to be assigned by you or chosen by them. Add-on roles, which are less academic, can be tacked on to students' main roles. Students can emphasize the responsibilities of their role but should not be limited to their own role. For example, a questioner should share predictions, a facilitator should share comparisons, and so on. The roles should be considered as scaffolds, to be reduced and eliminated at some point to allow students to independently engage in discussion using the skills of all the roles as soon as possible.

After prereading activities, students form groups, and the group facilitator tells members the next place to stop their silent reading. Fast readers can jot

Table 7.2 Ideas for Academic Discussion Roles and Add-On Roles

Academic Discussion Roles		Add-On Roles
Facilitator	Synthesizer	Materials manager
Observer, group assessor	Comparer	Encourager
Main idea sculptor	Summarizer	Presenter
Word expert, word detective	Opinion generator	Liaison
Predictor	Clarifier	Note taker
Inferer	Categorizer or classifier	Graphic designer
Cause-and-effect finder	Empathizer	Timekeeper
Problem finder	Controversy finder	
Prior knowledge connecter	Quote searcher	
Connector	Questioner	

down thoughts to share after they finish. When all stop, the facilitator asks students to emphasize the duties of their roles. The questioner should prompt for and pose questions about the text; the connector should offer text-text, text-world, and text-self connections and ask others to do the same. The main idea sculptor should help the group establish a possible main idea and clarify the author's message to readers. The alternative view finder can offer and prompt for controversies or other perspectives. Students can use some of the language starters from the cards shown in figure 7.2. (Also see chapter 6 for group discussion ideas.)

The group then creates a final product or shares notes with other groups (as in a jigsaw). The members can switch roles or assume all roles to read another portion of the text. Optionally they can use a study guide or "expert sheet" that helps them learn the information and language that they need to become experts on their text's topic. The sheet may have questions (open-ended or under-the-surface), a task to perform, or a graphic to fill in. Experts can also create a questionnaire for other expert groups to answer in a group of eight (e.g., four experts on one subject and four experts on another). This allows students to generate their own questions and speak in larger groups.

Figure 7.2 Cards with Language for Scaffolding Oral Responses

Main Idea Sculptor	Questioner
Can someone give a quick summary of the last section? What are the most important points? I think the main idea could be that... I think the author is trying to teach us...	Why do you think the author wrote this part? How did the author describe...? Why is that part important to the text? Did you find any interesting or puzzling parts?
Connector	**Alternative View Finder**
How does this relate to other books? How does this teach us about life? What would you have done in this situation? I think that the author wants us to think about...	I don't exactly agree with that because... We should also look at it another way... On the other hand,... What about seeing it from the perspective of...?

⇒ **Partner Problem Solving**

In this math or science activity (adapted from Lochhead and Whimbey, 1987), partners switch roles as listener and problem solver as they read through several problems. The problem solver reads the problem aloud, and then thinks aloud to describe his or her thoughts about solving the problem. The listener may ask for clarification and offer subtle suggestions. Problem solvers should go through the following steps: figuring out what is asked, identifying skills and knowledge needed, generating possible solutions, deciding on the best solution, and checking the answer. You will have modeled this many times and put language up on the wall for students to use. Remind students that the emphasis is on the process and on being extra clear about the problem-solving process. Here is a sample conversation from algebra:

1. *Solver:* This problem asks us to find the distance from the house it takes the car to catch up to the bike. The bike leaves 3 hours before. I think we need to know how to make two equations, one for each thing, then do what the teacher said about substituting variables. So it should have two equations, one for each thing. Let's see, maybe one equation is for the bike. Like, it goes 15 miles per hour and starts at distance 0.

2. *Listener:* Yes, they both start at 0, I think.

3. *Solver:* Okay, if t equals time, which we don't know, the distance the bike goes is t times 15. So after 3 hours, for example, the bike has gone 45 miles.

4. *Listener:*	But the bike doesn't stop.
5. *Solver:*	Yeah, so the car goes 30 miles an hour, which would make it go t times 30, but it left three hours later, so . . . Hmmm, t minus 3 or t plus 3?
6. *Listener:*	We can try both and see what works best.
7. *Solver:*	Okay, so we get $30(t3)$ for the car and $15t$ for the bike. Since the distance is the same, we can set them equal to each other. Okay, so $30t - 90 = 15t$. Subtract 90 and $15t$ from each side and we get $15t = 90$, so t equals 6 hours. But that's not the distance!
8. *Listener:*	We can use one of the equations.
9. *Solver:*	Oh yeah. So 15 times 6 equals 90 miles. And 30 times $(6 - 3)$ equals 90 miles, too. I guess it worked.

A variation of this activity is to have the pair solve the problem in the first column or row of blank space on a piece of paper, cover it up or fold over it, then send the solved problem on to another pair who also attempt to solve it. When they are done, they look at the previous pair's work to compare their work and results. This happens one more time with a third pair. The three pairs can then briefly gather and share how they solved it.

⇒ Figuring Out the Figuratives

In this activity, adapted from an analogical study guide (Bean, Singer, & Cowen, 1985), students get much-needed practice in interpreting the many figurative and double-meaning expressions that permeate academic texts and talk. They often get this practice while reading, but it can be done any time a rich expression emerges during a lesson (or outside school, too). Students find a figurative expression, determine out why the author used it, and consider its origin (see table 7.3). They make a chart in their notebooks and then explain the figuratives to one another. As a class you can discuss the most important expressions and put them on a large chart up on the wall.

This is a fairly quick way to build students' figurative and abstract language abilities when comprehending expository texts. It encourages students to be on the lookout for figurative expressions, even—and especially—in science, math, and history classes. These disciplines are filled to the brim with such expressions, many of which we tend to take for granted.

Table 7.3 Sample Chart for Figuring Out Figuratives

Figurative Expression	How the Two Are Similar; Why I Think They Relate	What It Describes
He didn't want to burn all of his bridges yet.	In war, armies would burn bridges so they couldn't be followed, but later they might want to use them. His bridges are his friends.	He wanted to show how the character broke off relationships that could later help him.
Sow the seeds of revolution.	Seeds are small, but they grow into large trees. Seeds were secret actions; trees were the revolution.	The people were doing many little things that would get others to rise up against the government.
Not even light can escape gravity's powerful grip in a black hole.	A person or animal cannot escape from the powerful grip of someone or something that is stronger, like the gravity of a black hole.	She wanted to show how strong the gravity is in a black hole.
A root can sometimes be irrational.	*Rational* means logical, and *irrational* means illogical, without a pattern or repetition.	The term is used to show that a number can go on forever without ending or repeating.

ACTIVITIES FOR UNDERSTANDING TEXT ORGANIZATION

The Common Core standards clearly emphasize the need for students to see and use text structure. For example, CCSS.ELA-Literacy.RI.7.5 requires students to "analyze the structure an author uses to organize a text, including how the major sections contribute to the whole and to the development of the ideas." Students who identify text structures tend to remember what they read better than students who lack a strong sense of text organization (Taylor, 1982). They also learn more academic language and strategies for organizing their own academic texts.

Authors use a variety of academic terms to create different text structures, such as narratives, sequences, research reports, and persuasive articles. The more quickly a student recognizes the language and structure of a text and can create a mental framework, the faster and better the student can process the text and hang its information on the "frame." The following activities help students organize the complex ideas that they read.

⇒ Dissection of Textbook Thinking and Language

Most teachers see textbooks only as content delivery systems. Yet students can learn a lot of academic language, thinking, and idea organization from textbooks. We teachers tend to take expository organization of ideas for granted. As we read textbook chapters and articles, we automatically categorize information and organize its importance into a hierarchy. We create mental headings, subheadings, and details that fall under them, determining the importance of each chunk of information as we read. But many students do not do this. They might simply make a list of facts in their minds or try to think of the nonfiction text as a story.

We can use textbook chapters and expository articles as opportunities to show students the common academic terms and grammar that content experts use to signal how they organize their content understandings. For example, the following paragraph on neurons has several key language and thinking points that we could teach, many of which are academic terms and thinking skills that are used in a variety of texts across different disciplines:

> When nothing much is happening, a neuron usually sends impulses down the axon at a relatively slow, irregular rate. When a neuron is stimulated (receives excitatory signals from another neuron), however, the sodium channels in the membrane open and the positively charged sodium ions enter the cell. This makes the potential difference temporarily more positive inside than outside. As soon as this occurs, however, positively charged potassium ions leave the cell, changing the voltage to more negative than normal. (Zirbel, 2004, p. 5)

Which academic features would you highlight in this paragraph? There are several embedded clauses, two *howevers*, a causal *This makes* sentence, an *As soon as this occurs*, and a participial clause that starts with *changing*. These academic terms and grammar moves are quite common in science texts. Going over the common terms and grammar that are used in a discipline, along with how authors organize the ideas in paragraphs, can significantly help students comprehend difficult texts like this one.

One effective way to dissect texts is by color coding. Students can identify the linking of ideas, for example, by underlining terms with different colors. Terms to mark contradictions (*however*) might be in red, causal links (*this makes, as a result*) are in green, and so on. In math texts, for example, I have found many cases where authors use *to* and *if*. One might see "To determine . . . ," "To find whether . . . ," "To calculate . . . ," "If the coefficient is 2," "If the value does not exceed . . . ," "If the radicals are different . . . ," "If x equals 0," and so on. When students see *to*, they color it and look for something to do. When they see *if*, they color it and look for the condition that connects to it. Symbols may also be used to mark the different ideas and moves in a text. Students then discuss their text analyses with peers.

⇒ Historical Source Analysis Table

Creating a table like the one shown in table 7.4 helps students think critically about what they read in history books and other sources that describe events and people. This can be done in groups, pairs, or individually, but it should have some whole-class discussion at the end to synthesize student answers. Students can use the table for the same text and then compare their responses in groups, which can be effective for starting academic conversations. Remind students that they aren't expected to come up with clear-cut right and wrong answers in the columns. It's up to them in their discussions to decide the quality and validity of their answers. This activity gives much-needed oral practice in the skill of supporting ideas with evidence. Several terms that they might need for this activity are *hypothesize, purpose, significant, bias, turning point, perspective, in their shoes, empathize, conflicting accounts,* and *offers insight into.*

⇒ Brain Folders

The idea behind brain folders is to use ordinary manila folders to mimic reading processes that happen in the brain (adapted from Reinken, 2006). The front of the folder is used for background knowledge pertaining to the topic of the text; the back is for student questions about the topic. You have students create pockets on the inside for different thinking processes, such as summarizing, predicting, comparing, evaluating, identifying the author's purpose, inferring, figuring out new words, and asking questions.

Table 7.4 Sample Historical Source Analysis Table

Event, person, source	French Revolution	Napoleon	
My questions	Why did it start? Why is it important?	Did he do more good or bad?	
Hypothesized answers	People were mad. People were freed.	More bad because he caused wars	
Purpose and importance	Got people thinking about freedom and rights	Spread revolutionary ideas around	
Empathy notes	I would have fought if treated like that.	I would like all that power, but not abuse it.	
Possible biases	Lots of people not talked about in text	What did Napoleon write about himself?	
Application and lessons	Ideas still around; church and state separation?	Many modern leaders are like him	

Figure 7.3 Contents of Brain Folders

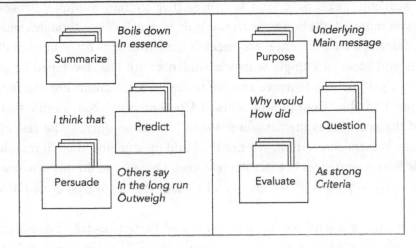

Around the pockets, students write down language that they can use to describe their thinking, such as common terms that might come from walls, discussions, and texts. This academic language starts to overlap and look a little messy after awhile—which is exactly how it should look. Figure 7.3 offers a graphic representation of brain folders.

READING ACTIVITIES THAT BUILD ACADEMIC GRAMMAR

Text understanding improves when readers learn to pay attention to language forms and features (Scarcella, 2002; Snow, Burns, & Griffin, 1998). Rather than simply reading for the gist, looking for discrete pieces of information, or guessing meanings based on titles and visuals, students must dig into a text to understand the logical and often implied relationships. Earlier chapters reminded us that even (and I would argue *especially*) in science, math, and history, we must teach key academic grammar and metalinguistic knowledge in order to help students decipher the complex texts that we ask them to read (see chapters 2 and 4). We must teach grammar in the context of real reading and writing, not with isolated worksheets and follow-the-rule activities (Weaver, 1996). Here are a few activities that help students learn the most common tricks and tactics that authors in our disciplines expect readers to use in order to comprehend the material.

⇒ Marking Up Long Sentences

Most academic texts have long sentences that contain multiple clauses. At any given moment, the brain can handle only so much of one thought, which is often described by a sentence. But because academic texts often have multiple clauses and ideas in a single sentence, students with less developed language skills can get lost in a sentence and fail to see its main point. For instance, in example 1 in the "Examples of Marked-Up Sentences" box, notice that the gist of the sentence is the first four words: "It was so quiet." The rest of the sentence is extra description. We need to build up students' mental muscles to handle longer sentences in every content area. One way to do this is to analyze and identify key parts of sentences and clauses (Schleppegrell & de Oliveira, 2006).

Every part of a sentence has a purpose, and there is usually a hierarchy of importance for what the writer wants to communicate. There is a main subject and main action or condition, and the rest of the sentence supports these or connects the sentence to other sentences. (In passive constructions, the main subject can be implied.) The key parts of a sentence often include

- Main participant/subject/actor
- Main process/verb phrase and its object/receiver

In other words, much of the time readers are asking, *What is doing what* to *what?* or *What is what and why?* To improve the ability to answer these questions quickly with long sentences, readers can use different types of underlines, fonts, or circles to mark the parts they want to emphasize. Fonts and underlines are used in the four examples in the box. You can also assign a color to each part of the sentence if you have colored pencils. For marking up textbooks, I make photocopies of textbook pages we will read.

You can choose other types of parts to mark—for example, opposing thoughts, cause-and-effect phrases, and additional adjective or adverb or conditional phrases. But remember that we aren't seeking to teach the many terms and twists of grammar; what we are training students to do is to focus on meaning. We want them to seek out the main participants and processes in each long sentence and emphasize them in their minds as they use the other information to shape the entire message that the author intended. The box shows several examples that have been marked to show their parts: bold words are the main subject, underlined words are the main verb phrase, italicized words are contradictory ideas, and bracketed words are cause-and-effect phrases.

EXAMPLES OF MARKED-UP SENTENCES

Example 1

It <u>was so quiet</u> [that she could hear the creak of buggy wheels receding far down the lane toward the road], and the voices of the girls surprisingly clear and close-seeming, *though they must have been almost a half mile away.* (Stegner, 1971, p. 498)

Example 2

[To decide whether the graph of an equation is a function, perform the vertical line test]—if a vertical line crosses the graph more than once, **the graph** <u>is not a function</u> [because the x-value of the vertical line is associated with more than one y-value.] (Haenisch, 1998, p. 246)

Example 3

We the people of the United States, [in order to form a more perfect union, establish justice, insure domestic tranquility, provide for the common defense, promote the general welfare, and secure the blessings of liberty to ourselves and our posterity], <u>do ordain and establish this Constitution</u> for the United States of America.

Example 4

Even though classical mechanics does not supply us with a sufficiently broad basis for the theoretical presentation of all physical phenomena, still **we** <u>must grant it a considerable measure of "truth"</u> [since it supplies us with the actual motions of the heavenly bodies with a delicacy of detail little short of wonderful]. (Einstein, 1920)

It is helpful to read such sentences aloud to students with proper intonation (prosody), which lets them listen to how supporting clauses are less emphasized. They can echo-read as well. I sometimes start with a monotone reading to show students how lifeless and confusing it is without intonation and pacing. The purpose is to add some attention to longer sentences, how they work, and ways to break them down.

Another way to teach long sentences is with hand motions. As you say a long sentence out loud, put one hand up for the main subject, link it to the other one for the main verb clause, and for subordinate clauses move hands underneath at a lower level. To emphasize intonation differences when you say subordinate clauses, lower your body or head a bit; raise your body or head for main clauses and increase the volume.

⇒ Using Hand Motions for Cohesive Devices, Transitions, and Conjunctions

Especially if you are a science, social studies, or math teacher, give students modeling and practice with the cohesive devices that glue your texts together. These words hold complex ideas together and give the text its shape. One little word that is skipped over or misunderstood can change the entire meaning of a sentence or paragraph. And although it is important to teach students to reread when they are confused, it is better to get it right the first time.

One way to teach these "gluelike" devices is to assign hand motions to them. For opposing thought devices such as *nevertheless, on the other hand, despite*, and *yet*, I move a hand in one direction in front of me, then I lift it in a 180-degree arc and move it in the other direction as I say the word and the rest of the clause or sentence. For cause-and-effect terms such as *therefore, thus, for this reason, as a result*, and *consequently*, I move my hands in a forward rolling motion. For supporting evidence expressions (e.g., *for instance*), I put the fingers of one hand under the palm of the other to make a table. One piece of evidence is one leg—if only one leg is there, the table is rather weak, and I show the table falling.

Look at several texts that you use, identify their commonly used cohesive devices, and try coming up with hand motions for them. See what your students think of your motions and whether they have any better ideas.

⇒ Analyzing Tests

Analyzing tests is a strategy that can improve academic reading. Many of the question stems and answers (distractors) of multiple-choice tests use academic language. Although the testing folks do not directly intend for their products to be used for teaching complex thinking skills, academic language, and communication skills, we can use the tests to our students' advantage. We can "part them out," so to speak. This metaphor comes from taking the useful parts from old cars that are no longer functional. To do this, we look at test questions and pull out the commonly used phrases that we also see in complex texts in our discipline. If an expression occurs frequently on the test (e.g., in released test items) and also in the textbook or other materials that we use, we weave it into our teaching.

For example, tests often use prompts like the ones below. I have boldfaced the more common academic terms that can be taught and woven into everyday teaching. Some of the terms tend to be used a lot, and they tend to confuse many nonmainstream students. (Some argue that their use is even done on purpose to confuse students and test their language skills rather than content.)

EXAMPLES OF COMMONLY USED TEST PROMPTS

- What is the author's **main purpose** for writing this passage?
- The words ___ , ___, and ___ in the passage **suggest a feeling of** . . .
- Which statement **best describes** the author's point of view?
- Which paragraphs **most clearly illustrate information** about . . . ?
- **If** a person travels 12 days in a month, **about what part** of the month do they not travel?
- Then she **randomly removed** another coin. **What is the probability that** the next coin that she removes is a dime?
- Which decade had the **greatest increase in growth**?
- Which **conclusion is most strongly supported** by the table's data?
- **Which expression represents** the volume of the paint that she will need to finish?
- **Given that the water level continues** to decrease at the same rate, what is your **most reasonable estimate** of the level it will reach on Tuesday?

- **Which trait will least likely be observed** in the children of these parents?
- **Which characteristics might allow** a plant species to survive in an area without sufficient soil?
- **Based on** the data chart, **what conclusion can be made** about . . . ?
- The issue of free speech became **increasingly important** because **of opposing views on** . . .
- These ideas **were relevant to the development** of democracy because they **contributed to the notion** that . . .

Tests with prompts such as these use a wide range of academic expressions across and within their many questions. Passive voice is often used (*be observed, is most strongly supported, can be made*). The use of synonyms is also a common practice that can trip up students. For example, there are multiple terms for comparing (*best, least, most, greatest*), describing probability (*probability, likely, might*), and describing cause and effect (*if, given that, contributed to the notion, allow, were relevant to*). As we have seen in these few examples, a host of academic terms and tools can be extracted from tests to build students' reading, writing, and overall communication in school settings.

VOCABULARY INSTRUCTION

One of the main instructional shifts of the Common Core is an increased focus on building academic vocabulary (EngageNY, 2013). The importance of learning content-specific words in each subject area is well documented (Becker, 1977). Vocabulary knowledge highly correlates with such indicators of school success as reading comprehension, writing, test scores, and grades. This is particularly true for English learners (Carlo, August, & Snow, 2005; Nation, 2001). However, because words are small and separate units of information that are easily testable, it is tempting to focus on them as pieces for points rather than as tools for use in constructing meaning. You might give me an adze (a tool for woodworking), for example, but it doesn't do much good if I don't know how or when to use it.

We could spend all day, every day, on teaching new content words in research-based ways, but this would take the place of other necessary instruction (Crawford,

2003; Nagy, 2005). Or we could never teach words at all and let them just sink in—we hope. As usual, we must find the right balance. We achieve this balance when we teach words as tools for understanding and for communicating meaning in our content areas.

It is helpful to use three guidelines offered by Blachowicz, Fisher, and Ogle (2006), who assert that good vocabulary instruction (1) takes place in a language- and word-rich environment, (2) includes intentional teaching of selected words and repeated exposure to them, and (3) includes word-learning strategies that help students learn new words independently.

Teaching Content-Specific Terms

The content terms are generally easy to spot. In textbooks they are often long and in bold. Many are not, though, and we must be able to spot high-yield words that play a key role in the text or the topic of discussion. Words should also be chosen for their usefulness in later units of study or across disciplines, including terms like *technology, resources, culture, density, reaction, revolution, perspective, globalization, reciprocal, tangent, evidence, motivations, diaspora, features,* and *roots.* The words should have a purpose within the unit we are teaching. We shouldn't just teach words because they are on lists: words are tools for building meanings and understandings.

When we have identified several essential terms that are worth the time to teach, research suggests using the following strategies:

- *Use verbal and visual associations.* Give students a quick verbal definition and examples of the word or expression. Then move into visual associations, which include ways to associate the new word with an image (Marzano, Pickering, & Pollock, 2001). For example, draw or use pictures, video, graphic organizers, or real objects. Have students help create symbolic representations of new terms, such as semantic webs, charts, and Venn diagrams.

- *Use "right-away activities"* that help students quickly deal with vocabulary in engaging ways, as opposed to battling the dictionary or making up random sentences. Try a "Have you ever . . ." or an idea completion activity (Beck, McKeown, & Kucan, 2002). With "Have you ever . . . ," you use the target words when you ask students questions about their experience: "Have you ever *critiqued* a movie, *lambasted* a friend, or *chastised* a sibling? Describe what happened." With idea completions, you provide a stem with the target word: "Yesterday I saw the principal chastising a pupil because . . . ," "Because of the density of the black hole . . . ," "She could not calculate the probability because she lacked . . ."

- *Use kinesthetic, auditory, and tactile connections.* These include ways to do, experience, hear, or touch the new word. Students can watch the teacher act it or can act it out themselves in the form of hand motions, role plays, music or chants, or real items (Marzano et al., 2001). Students then create their own verbal and then nonlinguistic representations of the word. This can be done in pairs or groups. Have several students then show that they know the meaning of the word by explaining it or acting it out.

An example of kinesthetic connecting in a statistics unit is having students get up and move around to become mean, median, and mode (Richards, 2003), as shown in table 7.5. Have students grab a small handful of beans from a bag, count them, remember the number, put the beans back in the bag, and then act out measures of central tendency, as described in the left-hand column.

After comparing the mean, median, and mode, students act out the different types of distributions: symmetric, negative, and positive. Students create them as they did for the bean distributions. Then discuss what might cause skewed distributions. Other terms to highlight when they arise include *statistical bias, outliers, differ, on the other hand, then again, contradictory data, frequency distribution, interpret the data,* and *positive and negative distributions.* Thus, this activity builds knowledge of more than just three words.

Building Word-Learning Habits

We have not learned the bulk of our own vocabulary, even the big words, through direct instruction, dictionaries, or glossaries. And even if we do use these resources, they do not cover many of the important general academic terms that confuse diverse students. To acquire a wide range of words, proficient readers have developed several habits over many years and from thousands of pages of reading. These habits are (1) looking at word parts (which I call doing word analysis) and (2) using context (which I call looking at the neighborhood). We must apprentice students into using these habits.

Table 7.5 Visual for Showing What Students Do to Act Out the Measures of Central Tendency

For mode, students line up in ascending order; students with duplicates (the same amount of beans) should stand in front of or behind each other. The most frequent number of beans is the mode.

Mode

For median, students spread out the line but stay in ascending order (duplicates should stand adjacent). Those standing on the outsides of the line leave first. Successively peel off pairs of the largest and smallest until there are only one or two people remaining. If one is remaining, that bean value is the median. If two are remaining, add their bean values together and divide by two.

Median

For the mean, have students find the total number of beans that were grabbed out of the bag and divide by the number of handfuls.

Mean

Analyze the Word

Good readers have the ability to figure out a word by using its roots, suffixes, and prefixes (Blachowicz et al., 2006). The first step is to decide if the unknown word is important for comprehension of the text. If so, students should see if there are other words they know that have similar parts, in any language. For example, I might use the prefix of *anachronism*, *ana-* (not, opposite), along with the root *chron* (time) to decipher its function and possible meanings in context. The other day I used my knowledge of the Spanish word *saltar* (to jump) to help me guess the meaning of the word *desultory*, which means to skip around and not stay on topic. Making such connections can give English learners added advantages for figuring out and remembering difficult vocabulary if we train them to use such strategies.

Use Context

Readers use clues in the sentence and paragraph to trigger background knowledge and make an educated guess about the overall meaning. We do this with words all the time: we use context clues to help us create and sculpt meanings of unknown words (Stahl, 1999). Thus, as we analyze the word, we also scope out the neighborhood around it to guess the meaning that fits best in those surroundings. For example, in the sentence *Geosynchronous satellites appear to hover in one spot above the earth,* a reader might first use word parts *geo, syn,* and *chron,* combined with context of hovering in one spot, to guess the meaning of *geosynchronous.*

Other word skills include the skills of interpreting and expanding the meanings of familiar words in figurative ways to comprehend and express new ideas (Blachowicz et al., 2006). You did this when you read *sculpt meanings* and *trigger background knowledge.* The more that we model these vital word habits with real texts, the more thoroughly students learn how to use words in ways that discipline experts (and textbook authors) use them.

Using Word Walls

An effective visual tool for building academic language is a word wall (see the example in figure 7.4). But to avoid just slapping up words at random over precious wall space, I divide the wall into four sections: (1) content words, (2) general academic words, (3) classroom discussion terms, and (4) terms for writing.

Figure 7.4   Example of a Four-Column Academic Word Wall

Content Words	General Academic Words	Classroom Discussion Terms	Terms for Writing
Reciprocal Complete the square Graph each system Parabola	Define the problem Tell whether the... Write it as a...	I believe that... We don't understand why... But if the number were...	In conclusion The next step is... By using the...

Of course there is overlap, but this format helps because students often get into good discussions about where the words go (sometimes they go on the lines to show overlapping).

Review the word wall terms often and refer to them when they arise in texts and discussion. Sometimes in the last four minutes of a period, I point to word wall terms that pairs of students then discuss for twenty seconds: they tell the meaning or how it would be used in the current unit of study.

CONCLUSION

In this chapter, we discussed ways to fortify students' acquisition of academic language for and by reading. Authors of complex texts often use long sentences, multiple clauses, and big words to pack lots of meaning into a paragraph. The resulting texts are often too dense for linguistically diverse students to read independently. In addition to developing basic content-area reading strategies, we must be aware of how authors construct knowledge and communicate it through writing. We use this awareness to train our apprentices to effectively use the tools and tricks of reading our discipline's texts.

By observing effective modeling of expert thinking while reading and through engaging in scaffolded text discussions, students can absorb the language and thinking processes involved in comprehending complex text. As language develops, comprehension develops. Increased comprehension gives students more to talk, write, and think about. Thus, we create a positive cycle of literacy, language, content, and thinking that grows up and expands.

CHAPTER REFLECTIONS

- How does language proficiency influence reading comprehension? And vice versa?
- What types of language (terms, grammar, organization) make texts in your discipline difficult for students?
- Take a paragraph or two of a difficult text in your discipline and identify the types of thinking required to understand it. Mark up the most difficult sentences and terms. Then reflect on ways you might teach them to your students.

- Why does talking about a text help increase students' comprehension and retention of it?

- Pick several important content-specific terms that you would teach and come up with kinesthetic or visual ways to teach them.

References

Alvermann, D., Dillon, D., & O'Brien, D. (1987). *Using discussion to promote reading comprehension.* Newark, DE: International Reading Association.

Bean, T., Singer, C., & Cowen, S. (1985). Acquisition of a topic schema in high school biology through an analogical study guide. In J. Niles & R. Lalik (Eds.), *Issues in literacy: A research perspective* (pp. 38–41). Rochester, NY: National Reading Conference.

Beck, I., McKeown, M., & Kucan, L. (2002). *Bringing words to life: Robust vocabulary instruction.* New York, NY: Guilford Press.

Becker, W. (1977). Teaching reading and language to the disadvantaged: What we have learned from the field of research. *Harvard Educational Review, 47,* 518–543.

Blachowicz, C., Fisher, P., & Ogle, D. (2006). Vocabulary: Questions from the classroom. *Reading Research Quarterly, 41,* 524–539.

Carlo, M., August, D., & Snow, C. (2005). Sustained vocabulary-learning strategies for English language learners. In E. H. Hiebert & M. Kamil (Eds.), *Teaching and learning vocabulary: Bringing research to practice* (pp. 137–153). Mahwah, NJ: Erlbaum.

Cohen, E. G. (1994). *Designing groupwork: Strategies for heterogeneous classrooms* (2nd ed.). New York, NY: Teachers College Press.

Crawford, A. (2003). Communicative approaches to second language acquisition: The bridge to second language literacy. In G. Garcia (Ed.), *English learners: Reading the highest level of literacy* (pp. 152–181). Newark, DE: International Reading Association.

Daniels, H. (1994). *Literature circles: Voice and choice in the student-centered classroom.* Portland, ME: Stenhouse.

Davey, B. (1983). Think aloud: Modeling the cognitive processes of reading comprehension. *Journal of Reading, 27*(1), 44–47.

Einstein, A. (1920). *Relativity: The special and general theory.* Retrieved from www.bartleby.com/173/5.html

Elley, W. (1991). Acquiring literacy in a second language: The effect of book-based programs. *Language Learning, 41,* 375–411.

EngageNY. (2013). *Common Core toolkit.* Retrieved from http://www.engageny .org/resource/common-core-toolkit

Gallagher, M., & Pearson, P. (1989). *Discussion, comprehension, and knowledge acquisition in content area classrooms* (Technical Report No. 480). Urbana: University of Illinois, Center for the Study of Reading.

Gambrell, L. (1996). What the research reveals about discussion. In L. Gambrell & J. Almasi (Eds.), *Lively discussions! Fostering engaged reading* (pp. 25–38). Newark, DE: International Reading Association.

Haenisch, S. (1998). *Algebra.* Circle Pines, MN: American Guidance Services.

Hafiz, F. M., & Tudor, I. (1989). Extensive reading and the development of language skills. *English Language Teaching Journal, 43,* 4–13.

Harvey, S., & Goudvis, A. (2000). *Strategies that work: Teaching comprehension to enhance understanding.* Portland, ME: Stenhouse.

Herber, H. (1978). *Teaching reading in content areas.* Englewood Cliffs, NJ: Prentice Hall and International Society for Technology in Education.

Holdaway, D. (1979). *The foundations of literacy.* Sydney, Australia: Ashton Scholastic.

Keene, E., & Zimmerman, S. (1997). *Mosaic of thought: Teaching comprehension in a reader's workshop.* Portsmouth, NH: Heinemann.

Krasnow, K. (2004). *Meiosis lesson plan.* Unpublished lesson plan.

Lochhead, J., & Whimbey, A. (1987). Teaching analytical reasoning through thinking aloud pair problem solving. In J. Stice (Ed.), *Developing critical thinking and problem-solving abilities* (pp. 72–93). New Directions for Teaching and Learning, No. 30. San Francisco, CA: Jossey-Bass.

Marzano, R., Pickering, D., & Pollock, J. (2001). *Classroom instruction that works: Research-based strategies for increasing student achievement.* Alexandria, VA: Association for Supervision and Curriculum Development.

McLaughlin, M. (2006). *Comprehending informational text: Strategies to help students understand what they read.* Unpublished workshop materials. Budapest, Hungary: International Reading Association World Congress on Reading.

Nagy, W. (2005). Why vocabulary instruction needs to be comprehensive and long-term. In E. H. Hiebert & M. L. Kamil (Eds.), *Teaching and learning vocabulary: Bringing research to practice* (pp. 27–44). Mahwah, NJ: Erlbaum.

Nation, I. S. (2001). *Learning vocabulary in another language.* Cambridge, UK: Cambridge University Press.

Palinscar, A. S., & Brown, A. L. (1984). Reciprocal teaching of comprehension-fostering and comprehension-monitoring activities. *Cognition and Instruction, 1,* 117–175.

Reinken, B. (2006). *Teaching reading.* Presentation at the International Reading Association World Congress on Reading, Budapest, Hungary.

Richards, S. (2003). *Mean, median, mode.* Unpublished lesson plan. University of San Francisco.

Rose, D. (1997). Science, technology and technical literacies. In F. Christie & J. Martin (Eds.), *Genre and institutions: Social processes in the workplace and school* (pp. 40–72). London, UK: Cassell.

Scarcella, R. (2002). Factors affecting development of literacy. In M. J. Schleppegrell & M. Colombi (Eds.), *Developing advanced literacy in first and second languages: Meaning with power* (pp. 209–226). Mahwah, NJ: Erlbaum.

Schleppegrell, M. J., & de Oliveira, L. C. (2006). An integrated language and content approach for history teachers. *Journal of English for Specific Purposes, 5*(4), 254–268.

Shefelbine, J. (1998). *Academic language and literacy development.* Paper presented at the 1998 Spring Forum on English Language Learners, Sacramento, CA.

Snow, C. E., Burns, S., & Griffin, P. (Eds.). (1998). *Preventing reading difficulties in young children.* Washington, DC: National Academies Press.

Stahl, S. (1999). *Vocabulary development: From reading research to practice.* Cambridge, MA: Brookline Books.

Stegner, W. (1971). *Angle of repose.* New York, NY: Penguin Books.

Taylor, B. (1982). Text structure and children's comprehension and memory for expository material. *Journal of Educational Psychology, 74*(3), 323–340.

Tovani, C. (2000). *I read it, but I don't get it: Comprehension strategies for adolescent readers.* Portland, ME: Stenhouse.

Wallace, C. (1992). *Reading.* Oxford, UK: Oxford University Press.

Weaver, C. (1996). *Teaching grammar in context*. Portsmouth, NH: Boynton/Cook.

Wineberg, S. (2001). *Historical thinking and other unnatural acts: Charting the future of teaching the past*. Philadelphia, PA: Temple University Press.

Wong Fillmore, L. (2004). *The role of language in academic development*. Keynote address given at Closing the Achievement Gap for EL Students conference, Sonoma, CA.

Wong Fillmore, L., & Fillmore, C. (2011). *What does text complexity mean for English learners and language minority students?* Stanford, CA: Understanding Language Initiative.

Zirbel, E. (2004). *Learning, concept formation, and conceptual change*. Retrieved from http://cosmos.phy.tufts.edu/~zirbel/ScienceEd/Learning-and-Concept-Formation.pdf

Chapter 8

Language for Creating Complex Texts

All teachers are writing teachers.

Learning to write academically gives students more than just better scores on writing tests. The thinking that happens during the writing process helps students clarify and refine their thoughts about a complex topic. As Fordham, Wellman, and Sandman (2002) point out, "Considering a topic under study and then writing about it requires deeper processing than reading alone entails" (p. 151). Writing pushes students to use language to organize facts, concepts, and opinions in strategic ways. Such thinking and communication skills are highly valued and required in later grades, higher education, and the majority of professions around the world.

Writing, particularly academic writing, is not just spoken words written down. Many students think this is the case, and such thinking hinders their success. Rather, academic writing in each discipline has its own set of language rules, expectations, and quirks. To write academically, students must often learn new ways to organize and present language in the discipline (Johns, 1997). They must learn to write more like the genres that they read in school, and they must acquire the ability to use academic register features that were described in chapter 2. Furthermore, such writing requires students to expand their vocabulary, vary their sentence structure, and learn how to use dependent clauses (Schleppegrell, 2004). We have the honor of helping our students with all of these skills.

Most teachers have a general sense of the basic differences between oral and written language. Often we simply notice when writing is not academic enough, even though we can't say exactly why. But our students are still at the early stages of developing this sense. They must learn to make vocabulary and grammatical choices in their writing that differ from what might naturally occur when they speak. For this reason, writing depends much more on teaching and school experiences than speaking does.

Academic writing usually requires the thinking skills of analysis, causal reasoning, argumentation, and evaluation (Schleppegrell, 2004). Students must progress from the temporal sequencing of narrative descriptions in younger grades to the logical structures of explaining a concept in upper grades. They must use more technical vocabulary and more varied sentences. In interpretive and argumentative pieces, they must create abstract premises that they then develop and support by evidence that has been evaluated for its effectiveness (see the CCSS writing standards for grades 5 through 12 for more specifics).

One chapter cannot cover the many important aspects of academic writing or the many strategies for teaching it. This chapter therefore focuses on two dimensions: (1) ways to develop language for academic writing and (2) ways in which writing can develop academic language and thinking. After looking briefly at what influences the ability to write academically, I present several ideas for scaffolding writing and teaching academic grammar. Then we look at several techniques for teaching students how to write argument essays and round out the chapter with a few informal writing activities.

THE INFLUENCE OF ORAL LANGUAGE

A fifth-grade advanced-level English learner, responding to a typical literature question, wrote in her journal, "I'm crossing my fingers that you understand why the author wrote the story." This example—like many others that you have likely seen—shows how students typically draw on their oral, informal language when they write (Schleppegrell, 2004). Even our own oral language influences how we teachers write. Yet we are at an advantage because over many years, we have acquired two things: high levels of natural academic language use and heightened senses for what is proper, appropriate, academic, serious, and explicit in writing—heightened enough to edit during and after we write to fit the situation and audience. Many times I have erased—and should have erased—less formal, oral-language-based expressions in my own writings. Oh well.

In the following argument example from an essay, this sixth-grade intermediate-level English learner argues for putting seat belts in buses. This student had had few academic conversations about controversial topics and had read even fewer argument essays that would help him step out of his informal language.

STUDENT EXAMPLE: INFLUENCE OF ORAL LANGUAGE

My issue is the school bus should have seat belts? Have you ever seen a bus whith no seat belts? My issue is about the seat belts. My explanation is the buses don't have seat belts and if a bus has in accident a lot of people wile get heart and will die because buses don't have seat belts. My argument is the all kind of buses should get seat belts to be more safe.

One reason is because buses don't have seat belts and if a bus crashis or something, people wile be hirt because of not havin seat belts on the busses. And one example becau in cause of in accident. Another reason to be more safe on the bus.

In this sample, the colloquial writing style was influenced by the student's oral language patterns. He followed the teacher's suggestion of using a question as a hook, yet he used the more colloquial expressions *My issue is* and *My explanation is,* which are more common in conversations. He also didn't separate his written language from the procedural language of the teacher, who used the terms *issue* and *explanation* frequently to explain how to write the essay and its parts. The student used *or something* at the end of a clause, another common expression in spoken discourse.

The student repeated several points, a phenomenon that occurs frequently in spoken language. I have seen this in the oral samples of many teachers I have observed. Teachers often repeat key points in their oral discourse, yet such repetition is discouraged in presentations and especially in writing. If we don't talk about these differences in class, then we leave it up to the students to puzzle them out.

THE INFLUENCE OF READING

Another powerful influence on writing is reading. The student in the previous example uses the language he has because he doesn't know other possibilities for expression—possibilities that often come from wide reading. Students who haven't read many texts full of academic language tend to default to their oral language patterns. What else can they do?

Reading is especially helpful if students are reading genres similar to the ones they are asked to write about. Such reading can help them acquire the writing techniques, words, and phrases of the discipline (Shaw, 1991). Thus, teaching students to closely read and analyze various texts (see chapter 7) can help them write like accomplished writers. We should work with students to dissect model texts, picking them apart to learn from them and ultimately to create similar and better examples of the writing from one's own pen or computer.

If we want students to write great essays and lab reports, we need to let them read models of great essays and lab reports at their level. Reading the textbook is not enough. One model is not enough. Students, especially diverse students, need to be immersed in the kinds of writing that they will produce. Why? Mainstream speakers have had many more exposures to a wide range of texts, such that they can draw from a much fuller storehouse of phrases and syntax that simply sound right to them. (This is linguistic capital, described in chapter 1.) Nonmainstream students, though, do not have such stores of linguistic knowledge, and they must rely more heavily on the models that we provide.

WRITING EXPOSITORY GENRES

The three broad text types that students need to master for the Common Core are arguments, explanations, and narratives (refer to the CCSS writing standards). Each text type contains various genres. A *genre* is a class of communication events that share common features (Swales, 1990): stories, poems, mathematical proofs, historical accounts, case studies, essays, and letters, for example. Each content-area genre carries with it certain expectations about organization, thinking, grammar, and word use.

The writing of narrative genres, which is emphasized in lower grades, decreases in later grades as the writing of expository genres (nonfiction, informational) increases. Stories and poems give way to nonfiction texts or, as some say, "Students in upper grades need to write to learn rather than learn to write." They still need to do both, of course. Expository genres include biographies, lab reports, responses to literature, essays, articles, and argumentative pieces. Expository writing is challenging for many diverse students because they have not seen a variety of the products they are asked to create, rarely practice it outside the classroom walls, and tend to use their informal language patterns, which often don't line up with school expectations.

Whereas narratives tend to shape the thoughts and language of primary-grade students, older students must quickly acquire expository ways of thinking through reading and school activities. Expository writing, the writing of nonfiction and nonnarrative texts, has complex organizational and cognitive demands that differ from narrative writing, which largely depends on a plot for structure. Students must learn new rules of how information is organized, connected, and categorized in order to write expository pieces. Most expository genres, for example, present a main point and support it with evidence.

Learning these new rules of organizing and writing about knowledge doesn't happen quickly for many diverse students. Just when they start to understand the notion of sequence and story line in narratives, the rules change, and they are asked to write a multiparagraph essay with an abstract thesis that they support with abstract reasons and concrete evidence.

Much of expository writing is based on the ability to analyze and explain. Explanations usually show relationships between ideas and concepts, such as explaining the functions of cell parts, the principles of democracy, the steps for solving a problem, or an author's use of imagery in a novel. Another analytical genre is *exposition,* which involves making a claim or taking a position and supporting it with details and evidence (Martin, 1989). This valued school genre requires the abilities to establish logical ordinate and subordinate categories of information, which are often abstract in nature. Students must move from temporal organization of ideas (as in stories) to logical organization, which tends to use more embedded and subordinate clauses, academic metaphors, and verbs that represent abstractions and generalizations. Such language includes *cause, led to, show, represent, reflects, symbolized, exacerbated, shapes,* and *supports.*

SCAFFOLDING ACADEMIC WRITING

Getting students to think in expository ways when reading is one thing; it is another to get them to communicate their thoughts in an organized way on paper (or on a computer). As we show them plenty of models of what we expect, we also scaffold their abilities to use different features of academic writing, described earlier in this chapter and in chapter 2. The activities that follow will give you ideas for supporting the language of writing in your content area.

⇒ **Using Prewriting Visual Organizers**

Students can generate and organize ideas with a wide range of graphic organizers before they write. Organizers are used to show relationships and the organization of complex and abstract concepts (McKenna & Robinson, 1997). Typical organizers are semantic webs, outlines, Venn diagrams, data charts, time lines, and process charts.

A handy organizer that I have used to get students to prepare for writing is the lens poster, shown in figure 8.1. For this lens, I chose six key dimensions of thinking used in history (Zwiers, 2006), but other dimensions (skills) might be used in other classes. Each day, students generate such questions as *Did the event really happen like that? How do they know all that? Could it happen again? Why didn't he run away?* and *Who started the war?* We categorize the questions into the six dimensions on the poster. During the unit, students can continue to generate questions and add them to the poster. When it is time to write, I help students choose the most interesting questions to prompt their compositions. Other thinking processes that might be used in science, math, and language arts classes include problem solving, hypothesizing, observing, interpreting, identifying life themes, synthesizing, classifying, and describing character traits.

To reinforce their understanding of the six dimensions in the lens, students help me create hand motions to remember each one. When I did this in one class, *bias* was leaning over like a one-sided scale, *causes* was a pushing motion, *effects* was lunging forward as if pushed from behind, *empathy* was pointing to one's heart, *interpret, apply, and connect* was the action of plugging an imaginary cord

Figure 8.1 Historical Thinking Lens for Discussion and Prewriting

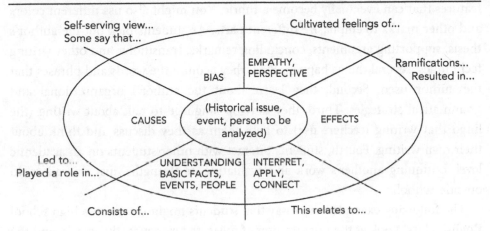

into one's head, and *understanding basic facts, events, and people* was counting fingers on one hand with the index finger of the other hand. These motions make thinking more active, and memorable.

The lens chart can also be used to record academic words. Outside the lens's oval for questions is a space for the terms used in questions and in student answers. Once the language is up on the wall, it conveniently becomes a corpus of terms to use during writing. These terms might include such expressions as *played a role in, this relates to, led to, some people say, one-sided argument,* and *cultivated feelings of.* Of course, this vocabulary is not confined to history, so I encourage students to use their new words in other classes—and even outside classes. For an extensive list of other useful terms, see appendix B.

Dissecting and Analyzing

One of the most important activities for developing academic writing language is the process of dissecting and analyzing other writings. The writings must include good models, but can also include not-so-good models to critique and fix. With your guidance, students analyze model texts (articles, letters, essays) to see what the authors did to make the writing effective. Model texts should be slightly above the level at which the students write. (For this reason, remember to make copies of student work for use as models in future years.)

As you analyze model texts, you and your students can develop a checklist of features that can eventually become a rubric. You might also use different colors and other marks to emphasize different parts. As students pick out the author's thesis, supporting arguments, concluding remarks, transitions, and other writing techniques, several things happen. First, they acquire the words and phrases that the author used. Second, they learn about the author's organizational and grammatical strategies. Third, they develop language to talk about writing (the lingo that writing teachers use) to help them as they discuss and think about their own writing. Fourth, students interact with other students on an academic level, critiquing another's work and evaluating its strengths, just as readers do outside school.

The following example is an essay that students might dissect in a high school English class. Look at the organization of ideas, the evidence, the words, and the grammar.

SAMPLE ESSAY: RESPONSE TO LITERATURE
Do What Is Right

"Do what is right, though the world may perish." The philosopher Kant wrote these words many years ago, but they are timeless. This means being moral even though bad things might happen. An example is Atticus Finch, the father in Harper Lee's novel *To Kill a Mockingbird*. He does what is right, despite the world he might lose.

One part of doing the right thing is being a good parent. Atticus respects his children and talks to them like adults. For example, he lets them call him Atticus instead of dad or father. He also talks to them about serious things like the case he was going take.

Another key part of doing what is right is treating people equally. Atticus obviously did this when he decided to defend Tom Robinson for a crime that he didn't commit. Even though many people in the town were against Atticus because Tom was black, he still took the case. He even risked his life to guard Tom one night when the people might attack the jail. Atticus said courage was "when you know you're licked before you begin but you begin anyway and you see it through no matter what."

> A less obvious part of being moral is respecting people who we don't understand. Atticus knew about Boo Radley's shyness and family problems. Like Tom, Boo Radley was a mockingbird, a symbol in the story for someone who didn't hurt people. Atticus said it was a sin to kill mockingbirds. This meant it is bad to be mean to people even though they are different. Boo was very different and ended up saving the kids in the end.
>
> We may have different problems today, but doing what is right is still important. If more people are like Atticus, who respects and even risks his life for people who are different and powerless, then we will have a better world. We will have more mockingbirds that fill the world with good deeds.

In dissecting this piece, I would have students notice what the author did in the introduction: a catchy quotation as a hook, some explanation of it, and a thesis statement that relates to it. For reinforcement, the author repeated *does what is right, despite the world* . . . in the thesis. The author then broke down the idea of doing right and being moral into three parts that emerged from the novel. In each of the three body paragraphs, the author used transitions (*key part, another part, less obvious part*), concrete examples, and a quotation from the novel to support the points. The author used interpretation and comparison language, such as *This means* . . ., *This meant* . . ., and *Like Tom* . . . In the final paragraph, the author applied the ideas about "doing right" to life today and used an *if-then* structure to challenge readers to think about making the world a better place. The author ended by weaving in a figurative understanding of mockingbirds as those who do only good.

After language arts class, students may have five minutes to get to their science class. In those five minutes, they must shift cognitive gears to think as they think in science. To write a lab report, for example, the student often needs to clearly explain procedures, provide rationale for decisions, provide data, interpret the data, and synthesize the information into a coherent conclusion. Try dissecting the following lab report from a high school physics class (Hammack, 2007) and see what you find.

STUDENT EXAMPLE: SAMPLE LAB REPORT
Spring Lab

Purpose To see if there is a mathematical relationship between the force and the change in length of a spring.

Procedure (1) Obtain three different springs (red, green, and blue), a force meter, and meter stick. (2) Put a pencil in the loop at one side of the spring and place that pencil next to a point on the meter stick so that you can measure the distance traveled. (3) Attach the other end of the spring to the force measurer. (4) Stretch the spring out to a certain distance (do this five different times with five different lengths) and measure from the point on the pencil to where the spring ends and the force sensor begins. (5) Do this for each of the three different springs. (6) Enter this information (the length stretched and the force that you read off the force measurer) into graphical analysis on one graph to make three lines.

Data

Spring A (blue)		Spring B (green)		Spring C (red)	
Force (N)	Change in length (m)	Force (N)	Change in Length (m)	Force (N)	Change in Length (m)
.831	.01	1.108	.01	.806	.01
.907	.02	1.612	.02	1.033	.02
1.511	.03	1.965	.03	1.285	.03
1.562	.04	2.242	.04	1.537	.04
2.418	.05	2.544	.05	1.839	.05

Analysis We used the values from the data table to calculate the average slope (m) of the equation. The y-intercept is the amount of force that keeps the spring together and thus the amount of force that must initially be overcome in order to move the spring.

Calculations

$$Y = m \cdot x + b$$

Variable on the y axis   slope   Variable on the x axis   Y-intercept

Spring A: Force = 38 N/M (Δ in Length) + .3 N
Spring B: Force = 35 N/M (Δ in Length) + .84 N
Spring C: Force = 26 N/M (Δ in Length) + .5 N

Conclusion   The slope represents the tension on the spring, using the units N/m. The mathematical model that we obtained will inform us (providing that we have one of the missing variables) of what to expect from the other variable. So you can predict what the change in the length of the spring will be if you know the amount of force you are going to pull with, and you can predict how much force you will need to pull with if you want to change the length a certain number of meters. For example, if you wanted Spring A to stretch .05 meters, you could use the equation to figure out how much force you would need to pull with (using F = 38 N/m (.05m) + .3 N).

In dissecting this piece, we see different parts of the lab report and note that the student used different types of language in each. The parts, common in most lab reports, are a purpose, procedure, data, analysis, and conclusion. The Purpose section includes a hypothesis or question about a relationship between force and distance. The Procedure section uses numbered steps and very explicit directions for carrying out the steps in the experiment, even though the audience (teacher and other students) knew them well. There is a lot of procedural language, such as *obtain, put, place, attach, stretch, measure,* and *enter.* The Analysis section includes calculations that the student does not fully explain, but there is an attempt to explain the equation. Noteworthy academic terms include *used the values, to calculate, thus the amount of force,* and *that must initially be overcome in order to.*

This report's Conclusion section gave the student a chance to explain what she did and learned. She explained the usefulness of deriving the equation when she wrote *will inform us of what to expect.* She even pointed out the need for knowing one of the missing variables. She provided an explanation of the two different scenarios and an example. Academic language included *represents, you can predict, you will need, if you know, a certain number, if you wanted, you could use.* With respect to grammar, the student effectively used *if* clauses and commas to show her understanding of variables and equations.

As these two samples have shown, a lot of thinking and language goes into the creation of academic texts. Dissecting models of the genres that we will ask students to write offers them a vital window into the thoughts, tactics, and struggles in academic writing. Using these models takes time, but you will find it worthwhile to gather good models and dissect them in class.

Teaching Academic Grammar

Grammar is not that exciting for most students (and for many teachers). Grammar is important, though, because knowing certain rules and patterns can accelerate the growth of academic writing abilities. It is also required by the Common Core writing standards. For example, the "c" standards in each grade level require students to use a variety of transition words, phrases, and clauses to create cohesion; clarify the relationships among ideas, concepts, claims, and evidence; and convey sequences and shifts.

Mainstream students tend to use more academic types of grammar naturally from many years of rich immersion, but they do not know the rules per se. If we directly teach students some of the highly useful rules and patterns, they can apply them in their writing—without waiting many years for them to sink in.

We must choose important grammar and teach it in context (Weaver, 1996). If there is a grammatical insight (structure or rule) that should or shouldn't be used repeatedly, then it might be worth the time to point this out, perhaps with a minilesson. *In context* means to use our curriculum and texts, not separate grammar worksheets or writing assignments. For example, I might want to teach students to vary the length of their sentences in an analytical essay that compares historical accounts. We would see how the authors of several model analytical essays varied their sentences before students practiced on sentence variation in their own drafts.

Understanding Cohesion

A text has *cohesion* when its ideas are logically linked to one another. In expository texts, for example, most paragraphs have a main idea supported by connected sentences that include examples and explanations. Other types of logical relationships in cohesive texts include problems with solutions, questions with answers, causes with effects, and arguments with counterarguments.

Cohesive devices also link ideas together (Halliday & Hasan, 1976). These devices include referents, conjunctions, prepositions, synonyms, pronouns, and verb selection. Referents such as *this* or *that* often refer to a previous concept or action in the text. Such conjunctions as *therefore* or *thus* are often used to signal causal relationships between ideas. Prepositions can signal contrast between two ideas, such as in *The waves grew.* <u>*Instead of*</u> *heading home, they set a course into open water.* Verbs also create cohesion (Schleppegrell, 2004). For example, in *Their resourcefulness allowed them to survive for weeks,* the verb *allowed* expresses a causal relationship. As these examples show, cohesion is often automatic, hard to see, and hard to teach.

Other terms that create cohesion include *such as, but, and, or, while, despite, although, yet, for instance, principal, key,* and *given that.* Many of the cohesive terms can be used to describe cognitive skills such as cause-and-effect, comparison, and supporting points with evidence. I train students to think of common cohesive connectors when they get stuck. They can also look at a list and run through several in their mind to get them going on a thought. For example, they can quickly run through popular sentence starters such as *Because of this, For example, Therefore, This, However,* and *In addition* to see if any help get the ideas flowing again.

Using clauses and commas is another key writing skill. As indicated in chapter 2, subordination shows that a speaker or writer can highlight key points while describing them with a subordinate point, often separated by commas. Subordination is often achieved with embedded clauses that begin with such words as *because, although, since, regardless, given that, despite, even though,* and *while*—for example, *Because he saw moons orbiting Jupiter, Galileo surmised that not everything in the sky revolved around the Earth.* Clauses containing gerunds and infinitives can also be used: *The overzealous ambassador, disregarding the president's obvious warnings, remained in the country.*

A CLOSER LOOK: WRITING ARGUMENT ESSAYS

The Common Core standards require students to write effective arguments. And although the standards do not use the terms *persuasion* or *persuasive,* these are similar types of writing in which students focus on logical reasons and evidence that support and evaluate claims.

This section briefly describes several ways to scaffold the thinking and language of argument writing. Argumentation is a high-yield thinking and language skill because students must see both sides of an issue, come up with evidence, clearly present it, weigh and evaluate arguments, compare, and synthesize—and they need to use a lot of rich language to do these things. Moreover, students often enjoy the tension and challenge of proving they are right (although I hear that parents don't always appreciate their students' newly developed argumentation skills).

The purpose of argument writing is to convince readers to take a certain stance on an issue, take action to change something, or do both (O'Malley & Valdez-Pierce, 1996). The writer must present a logical and developed argument through the use of appropriate clauses, links, words, modals, and organizational features. "Appropriate" means that they must conform to certain teacher and test criteria, which can differ across disciplines and teachers.

Explaining Prompt Language

One of the more rectifiable problems I have encountered is that students don't understand writing prompt language, particularly on schoolwide and statewide assessments. Table 8.1 is a chart I have used to help them understand the prompts and basic elements of argument essays.

Table 8.1 Argument Writing Prompt Language and Its Clarification

Prompt Language	Clarification
State position	Clearly describe your thesis, the side that you are arguing, the main point you are making with your paper.
Address counterclaims	These are the points that people will make to argue against you. Describe their points and how they are weaker than your points.
Recognize or address	Mention and show that you understand whatever you need to "recognize" or "address" with an explanation and perhaps a solution.
Anticipate reader concerns	Predict the arguments that readers will have, mention them, and then explain how they are weak or wrong and how your side is stronger.
Explain	Clarify a process or communicate the significance of the topic. Clarify how your evidence relates to your thesis.

Using a Rubric

It helps to start with an analysis of the features outlined in the Common Core Anchor Standards for Writing and the writing standards for your grade level. In the Anchor Standards, you will notice that argument writing is the first genre of writing listed under the "Text Types and Purposes" category.

As you and your students examine and dissect models of argument-based writing, create a list of the important features that you find. Then, aided by the standards, you can transform the list of features into the rubric or checklist that you use to evaluate and provide feedback to students. Yet a rubric won't help if students don't know what the items of a rubric mean. We need to be very clear about what we expect to be included in the essay or letter. Take time to model how you use the rubric to assess several pieces of writing up front, thinking aloud as you go.

Figure 8.2 is an abridged rubric, a cross between a checklist and a rubric. It tends to be less burdensome and more flexible than a full rubric with descriptions at each level. After analyzing several model essays and discussing the importance and language of each argument element, students have a clearer idea of what "Above Standard" means in each row. Students use the rubric as they write and peer-edit. When I use the rubric in figure 8.2 to assess students' papers, I write specific notes in the boxes. I sometimes put two notes in different boxes of the same row. One piece of evidence may be very weak and another strong, for example.

Using Oral Scaffolds

We must support writing with oral activities, too. Earlier in this chapter we saw how students' social language can influence their writing of academic genres. Yet chapters 5 and 6 also described oral activities that can build the types of language needed for academic writing. For example, I start argument writing with the pro-con activity in chapter 6 to give students an opportunity to hear and use academic transitions before using them in writing. In the last phase of the pro-con, I tell students to use a history issue that I or they pick from the lens organizer like the one in figure 8.1. They ask the question and simply clap to signal the reverse of the argument each time. The take-a-side activity (chapter 5) is also an effective oral scaffold to get students talking about different sides of an issue and using evidence to support their positions.

Figure 8.2 Sample Abridged Rubric for Argument Essays

1 **Below Basic**
2 **Approaching Standard**
3 **At Standard**
4 **Above Standard**

Title	Title gets reader's attention and tells what text is about.				
Introduction	Hook gets reader interested in reading it.				
	Background sentences explain the issue (time, place, misconceptions about the issue).				
	Position (thesis) is clearly stated.				
Reasons and Evidence	Evidence supports the author's position; evidence is specific, strong, and varied.				
	Uses primary sources as evidence; appropriately summarizes or quotes primary sources.				
Opposing Arguments	Respectfully presents main counterarguments and opposing views; describes the weaknesses of opposing evidence.				
Conclusion	Summarizes the argument.				
	Applies and connects ideas to present and future; tells why it is important in history; gives the reader something to think about.				
Organization	Paragraphs are in logical order; appropriate transitions connect ideas.				
Conventions	Minimal mistakes made in spelling, capitalization, paragraphing, punctuation, and grammar usage; sentence lengths varied.				
Word Choice	Words are correct, interesting, varied, academic.				

Oral activities are a chance for us to see if students have enough knowledge and language to begin writing. If not, we fill in the gaps. Gibbons (2002) highlights the importance of the language that emerges in such activities: "This more written-like spoken language serves as a language bridge between the talk associated with experiential activities and the more formal—and often written—registers of the curriculum" (p. 42). Talking gets students to think, and thinking is needed for writing.

⇒ Organizing Ideas with an Argument Scale

During a unit, I encourage students to generate questions and put them up on a lens organizer like the one in figure 8.1. Then I help students choose the most appropriate questions for an argument essay or letter. Students can then use the argument scale in figure 8.3 to stack up reasons and evidence on both sides of their particular issue (adapted from Zwiers, 2004). They put the most influential, or the "heaviest," reasons and evidence in the bigger boxes to show their argument values (i.e., "strength" or "weight").

Figure 8.3   Argument Scale for Organizing Reasons and Evidence before Writing

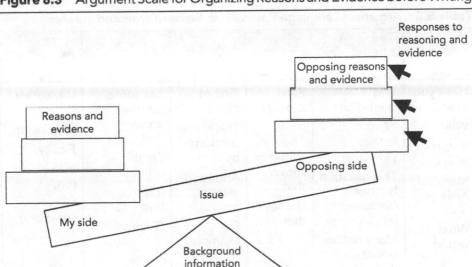

After filling in and discussing the scale, students pull information from their scales to draft their essays. I have students use color codes in their first drafts to show me that they understand different elements of the essay. They can, for example, make hooks yellow, background statements blue, and thesis statements red. Evidence, examples, and explanations can be green, and counterarguments can be orange. This color scheme can also be used on the scale organizer (or any other visual you might use).

As they write, students borrow academic language from the wall posters and the model essays. You can create posters of sample language commonly used in each element of the essays. I have used table 8.2 to create posters for displaying language for academic writing.

Take a moment to analyze the eighth-grade English learner's first draft of a historical argument essay in the box. See how well he created cohesion, supported his argument, used transitions, and met the expectations of the abridged rubric in figure 8.2.

Looking past the many surface-level errors of this draft, we see considerable academic thinking and language here. This student, at the time he wrote this essay in his third year in the United States, used several academic phrases, such as *some people say, I still think, however,* and *putting one's life on the line*. He also included

Table 8.2 Argument Language Posters with Starter Terms and Phrases

Hook	Background	Thesis	Reasons and Evidence	Counter-arguments	Conclusion
Have you ever . . .? Why . . .? It started with . . . Many believe . . . What would . . . ?	This quotation by . . . In the year . . . This question has been discussed by . . . Many history books say that . . .	Even though . . . The evidence shows that . . . I believe that . . .	First of all, . . . This is also supported by . . . Another reason for . . . For example,	Yet some people argue that . . . On the other hand, It is true that . . . Granted,	Ultimately, In conclusion, Finally, In the long run, In summary,

> ## STUDENT EXAMPLE: ARGUMENT
> ### *To Be or Not to Be Fanatic*
>
> Do we need fanatics to change history? Fanatic people have changed history alot. Some people say that we don't need crazy people. However we do need fanatics in history change history.
>
> For example John Brown he was so crazy that he started an uprizes. He gave the slaves wepones and told them to fight there masters. Abraham Lincoln was a fanatic because he was fanatic about keeping the union togther he would go to war.
>
> Some people say we dont need fanatics. like Marten Luther King didn't use vilioenc and he still change history. firefighters change history by puting out fire and dieing and there not fanatics. Hariet tubman wasnt fanatic but still changed history.
>
> I still think that these people are still fanatics because there putting there life on the line. like Luther King was a fanatic he put his life on the line and got shot.
>
> We need fanatics to change the world.

the features of the argument essay genre: hook, background, and thesis, along with supporting examples in the second paragraph, opposing arguments in the third, and a response to opposing arguments in the last paragraph. He had considerable work to do for the next draft, but his thinking was developing, and he was trying out new language to meet the needs of his new thinking. Along these lines, I heard one student say, "Wow—I'm starting to convince myself!"

INFORMAL WRITING ACTIVITIES

In this section, I describe several activities that are effective across disciplines because they get students to think about content material and to become better writers in low-pressure ways. They also require minimal teacher preparation. You are likely to be familiar with them, but take a moment to notice and reflect on how they can be used in more productive ways to build language abilities and writing skills described in the Common Core standards.

⇒ Learning Logs and Journals

Learning logs, journals, and quick-writes are effective ways for students to write about what they are learning (Atwell, 1998). Many variations exist, but most of them require students to reflect on learning over time. Students often write comments on class discussions and responses to teacher prompts. Common thinking prompts include having students explore an issue and choose a side; elaborate on a topic of choice that applies to their lives; visualize, draw, and explain processes; analyze data and organize the information into conclusions; put complex ideas and concepts into their own words; apply learning to life; and compare, evaluate, critique, or interpret.

Informal writing gives students low-stress time to think and organize their thoughts well enough to put them into sentences on paper. They can experiment with new language, increasing the chances that they will retain it for the long term. To help them do this, instead of just giving them a prompt and saying, "Go," I often take a moment to gently encourage students to make some of their sentences sound more like the material they are reading in class. I challenge them to combine sentences and use embedded clauses and transitions. These, of course, need to be modeled in our own learning log samples that we model in front of them.

In their logbooks, students have opportunities to reflect on the various activities and overall learning going on. For example, this seventh-grade student wrote about the class's simulation of the beginnings of the American Civil War (the simulation described in chapter 5).

STUDENT EXAMPLE: LEARNING LOG ENTRY

So then the gray tables were trying to secede from the blue tables because they were lazy and they just wanted to rest and snap their fingers. I thought it was no fair just cuz they had money and they thought they can do what they feel like doing.

Source: Zwiers (2006).

This student adeptly used the new word *secede* without being prompted to do so, and she also used evidence in a *because* clause to support her ideas of why the Gray tables were trying to secede. She began to think about the fairness of the scenario as well. She later wrote in her logbook, "I still want to know why black people were slaves and not white. Every person has freedom rights."

Dialogue journals are written conversations between teacher and student that help students express themselves more academically, even though they might not have mastered academic forms. Students' interest increases because (1) they get to choose topics and guide the direction of what they write, and (2) teacher responses are personal. Language can develop because the teacher's responses connect to and build on students' messages. Teacher comments often contain a variety of comprehensible academic grammar and vocabulary that students indirectly acquire because they are focused on meaning and genuinely want to understand the teacher's message (Peyton, 1990). Students are then more motivated to express themselves clearly on paper, often even borrowing language from teacher remarks.

⇒ Written Recap

This type of learning log entry, similar to an exit ticket, is what I call *written recap*. It is an easy yet powerful way to get students to remember what they are learning while also solidifying language they learned that day. Students use the last three to six minutes of the period by writing down what they learned during the class. It is helpful for them to get into the habit of synthesizing their thoughts on paper at the end of a class. Remind them that sometimes we come to new and exciting insights only through writing. Stipulate that the topic and the writing must show depth of thinking, not just disconnected facts. Model how you take facts, process them, and apply them. Also model how you borrow academic language from the walls and texts to help you build new ideas.

Writing these summary thoughts helps to rein their concentration back in and encourages them (and you can offer further support) to think about the original objectives of the lesson and link to their readings, writings, and activities together. You can also provide an evolving list of sentence starters on a poster, such as these:

- I learned that . . .
- I realized that . . .
- We read about . . . in order to . . .
- An important concept is . . . because . . .
- Someday I would like to . . .

- I do not agree with . . . because . . .

- I would like to learn more about . . .

- This connects to life in that . . .

- What I learned today connects to our big idea about . . . because . . .

- I still wonder . . .

I also encourage students to write questions that they have. Students can write in journals or on note cards if you want to do a quick assessment of current learning. You can have a final one-minute whole-class recap to let them walk away with a clear idea of what they learned (and should have learned). During this time, you can make a culminating chart, tree diagram, or list of class learnings that can stay up for a while to remind students of what they learned.

At times you can have students share ideas in pairs before they write (think-pair-write). They will get ideas from partners and spark their own ideas before jumping into the writing. Knowing that they will write something afterward also improves the quality of their talk. These two minutes of talk, plus the four minutes of writing, can be a high-yield use of the last six minutes of a class. You can even start the next day with reading several excerpts aloud or having pairs read them to each other. Highlight exceptional thinking, word use, and advanced grammar when you can.

⇒ **Written Dialogues**

Tell students to create (in pairs or individually) a written dialogue between two talkers who are academically arguing about a topic. This can also be in the form of a cartoon. Dialogues can make it easier for students to see other perspectives and use the language of the other. In a sense, the more casual or less academic language of the dialogue can provide a foundation for the more academic language of essays. And actually coming up with what an adversary would say, rather than just a list of opposing points, requires more empathy and more organization. Here is a brief example from two sixth graders:

1. *Student A:* I think guns shouldn't be legal.
2. *Student B:* Why not?
3. *Student A:* Because kids die from them every year.

4. *Student B:*   But so do innocent people who don't have guns that could have
had guns to defend themselves.

5. *Student A:*   But more people die from mistakes than being shot on purpose.

6. *Student B:*   What about the Constitution, though? It says . . .

The students who struggle the most with this assignment often lack the ability to recognize conflicting categories in an argument. Thus, we must help them by modeling and scaffolding. For example, in the preceding interaction, some students may not think of such categories as financial costs, future abuses, ethical issues, religion, and opportunity costs. Often these abstract categories will arise, and after plenty of practice and discussion, students begin to generate them on their own.

You can also adapt this idea for other prompts so that it essentially becomes a written think-pair-share. Students write on a paper what they would say and then pass it to a partner. You can put several academic terms on the board for students to use as they respond to the prompt. I have even tried having two ongoing conversations (from two different prompts) so that each partner is writing at the same time (this helps strengthen conceptual multitasking). At the end, you can have students share out summaries of their conversations.

⇒ Try These Terms

This low-prep and quick-write practice activity is what I call "try these terms," where I give a list of academic tools and terms from the text, usually before or after reading, and see if students can use them in coherent paragraphs, not just disconnected sentences. This takes some modeling at first, but after time, students get the hang of putting terms together in this way. Simple sample sets include *friction, force, gravity, motion, law, states that, terminal velocity,* and *prevents; revolt, protest, government, democracy, because of, therefore, dissatisfied,* and *conspiracy; quadratic equation, polynomial, because, like terms, coefficient,* and *radical; plot, literary device, given that, theme, universal, realize, understand, resolution, struggle,* and *characterization.* They can borrow terms from the academic language posters on the walls. When students are finished, they share their paragraphs with other groups or with the whole class. You can give a transparency piece of poster paper to groups so that they can share it in front of the full class.

⇒ **Perspective Papers**

Another quick and effective writing task is perspective papers (adapted from Zwiers, 2004). A student writes from the perspective of a person, place, or thing. This activity supports Common Core standards that focus on establishing point of view and developing characters. In history, for example, students can take on perspectives of different historical characters who were famous, powerful, good, bad, ordinary, oppressed, or misunderstood. In language arts, students can take on perspectives of authors, characters, book critics, and historians. Math is a bit more challenging, but I have heard of students role-playing geometric shapes and describing how people use them for practical applications in the world, along with how their areas and volumes are calculated.

In science, students can "walk in the shoes" of an animal, plant, mineral, process, phenomenon, or scientist. Some ideas are volcano, tectonic plate, electron, whale, bacterium, sloth, astronaut, Louis Pasteur, amoeba, galaxy, gravity, the Earth, and shark. Here are a few sample excerpts.

SAMPLE PERSPECTIVE PAPERS: SCIENCE

- *Water molecule.* "I am H_2O, a water molecule. I am not very complex, but I am very important. The bonds between my oxygen atom and the hydrogen atoms are interesting. They help my precipitate float when I freeze because . . ."
- *Moon.* "No doubt you've seen me up in the sky at night. But I am more than a romantic ball of rock. Without me, life would be very different down there on Earth. I am vital because of the tides and the weather. My gravity makes . . ."
- *Glacier.* "About 60,000 years ago I was born, very slowly. Snow started to fall and build up over many years. It turned to ice. Once I reached about 80 feet tall, I started to move. I guess I was like a teenager, ready to move on. Now I am melting . . ."
- *White blood cell.* "I am a white blood cell. I like to travel and take care of problems, such as bacteria that invade the body. They usually get in through cuts or food. When I find these evil little organisms, I surround them and attack in the following way . . ."

Remind students to include important relationships, purposes, problems, effects, desires, emotions, and any humor that may make it more entertaining to read. Students can also find or draw pictures to include with the text. They can even expand it into a small book for the school or classroom library.

CONCLUSION

In this chapter, we looked at how writing can help students build vocabulary and grammar patterns that seldom occur in their talk. Although the indirect effects of reading academic texts can help writing skills, they are not enough. We need to be explicit about how to write academically in each class. We must apprentice students into making linguistic choices that are well aligned with school-based ways of writing.

Each content area emphasizes certain genres to communicate its concepts in writing. We must show models of these genres and model how to write them. Analysis and dissection of valued models offer a chance for students to identify features of good writing and create rubrics that shape their own writing. Before writing, we provide opportunities to talk about the topic and build ideas; then we show students how to organize their thoughts with visual organizers and outlines. Finally, as they write, we watch, listen, question, support, and encourage. The process is not linear, and with each draft, we work alongside students to give them tools and train them how to use them to effectively construct their expanding ideas.

CHAPTER REFLECTIONS

- What kinds of language, grammar, and organization of ideas does an effective piece of writing need in your discipline?

- What mistakes do students typically make as they write? How do you help them with those mistakes?

- Look at the argument essay about fanatics in the middle of this chapter. What would you suggest to this student? What would you teach him?

- How can you improve the ways in which you model and scaffold writing?

- Pick a genre that you ask your students to write in. Write one good and one poor model of it. Now dissect the good model and list what you find. How well does it align with what you listed in the first reflection here?

References

Atwell, N. (1998). *In the middle: Writing, reading, and learning with adolescents* (2nd ed.). Portsmouth, NH: Heinemann.

Fordham, N., Wellman, D., & Sandman, A. (2002). Taming the text: Engaging and supporting students in social studies readings. *Social Studies, 93*(4), 149–158.

Gibbons, P. (2002). *Scaffolding language, scaffolding learning.* Portsmouth, NH: Heinemann.

Halliday, M., & Hasan, R. (1976). *Cohesion in English.* London, UK: Longman.

Hammack, S. (2007). *Spring lab report.* Unpublished report using the Modeling Instruction Program for Physics.

Johns, A. (1997). *Text, role, and context: Developing academic literacies.* Cambridge, UK: Cambridge University Press.

Martin, J. (1989). *Factual writing.* Oxford, UK: Oxford University Press.

McKenna, M., & Robinson, R. (1997). *Teaching through text: A content literacy approach to content area reading.* New York, NY: Longman.

O'Malley, M., & Valdez-Pierce, L. (1996). *Authentic assessment for English language learners.* Boston, MA: Addison-Wesley.

Peyton, J. (1990). Dialogue journal writing and the acquisition of English grammatical morphology. In J. Peyton (Ed.), *Students and teachers writing together: Perspectives on journal writing* (pp. 67–97). Alexandria, VA: Teachers of English to Speakers of Other Languages.

Schleppegrell, M. J. (2004). *The language of schooling: A functional linguistics approach.* Mahwah, NJ: Erlbaum.

Shaw, P. (1991). Science research students' composing processes. *English for Specific Purposes, 10*(3), 189–206.

Swales, J. (1990). *Genre analysis: English in academic and research settings.* Cambridge, UK: Cambridge University Press.

Weaver, C. (1996). *Teaching grammar in context.* Portsmouth, NH: Boynton/Cook.

Zwiers, J. (2004). *Developing academic thinking skills in grades 6–12: A handbook of multiple intelligence activities.* Newark, DE: International Reading Association.

Zwiers, J. (2006). Integrating academic language, thinking, and content: Learning scaffolds for non-native speakers in the middle grades. *Journal of English for Academic Purposes, 5*(4), 317–332.

Chapter **9**

Building Language Development into Lessons and Assessments

Seriously smudge the line between assessment and instruction.

This chapter synthesizes the previous chapters in a discussion of ways to weave thinking and language into the design of lessons and assessments. There are many points during a lesson where we can build language and thinking and many types of assessment that allow us to see students' thinking and language abilities as they support content learning. But keeping in mind the differences in content areas and the diversity of our students, we must carefully tailor all that we do to fit each unique and challenging setting.

LESSON PLANNING

Lesson plans vary across content areas and individuals, but they tend to have several common elements. First, we establish the learning objectives that are based on standards and student needs. We clarify the objectives during the introduction of a lesson as we build student interest in the topic. An important element early on is to help students access related material in their brains on which to build new learning (Temple, Ogle, Crawford, & Freppon, 2005). Such activities also show us the kinds of background information that we must fill in for students to be successful in subsequent learning activities.

Another key element is modeling the talking, thinking, literacy tasks, products, and performances that students are supposed to be able to do after they learn and practice their new knowledge and skills. Modeling leads into scaffolding, which is the gradually diminishing support that we offer students as they do work just beyond what they can do independently (Bruner, 1986). Toward the end of the lesson or unit, students must apply their new skills and knowledge in novel ways to show their enduring understandings and the key ideas of the discipline that they learned (Wiggins & McTighe, 2005).

Assessment-Driven Instruction

A key principle of lesson planning is using diagnostic, formative, and summative assessments. Diagnostic assessment is the preassessment stage in which we find out what students currently know and can do with language. This gives us a more accurate starting point to avoid overwhelming or underwhelming them. Formative, or ongoing, assessment is finding out what students are doing well and not so well as they learn. These are checkpoints along the way—the real-time, close observations of learning (Díaz-Rico, 2004). Summative assessment is putting it all (content, thinking, skills, language) together in a final performance, product, or test to show their learning. Effective summative assessment motivates and offers direction to students. When students know what is expected of them and it is somewhat interesting and practical to them, they can focus their learning to achieve language and content goals. All three of these assessment phases are important in informing how we plan our school year, semesters, units, lessons, and activities.

Teachers often put the cart of instruction before the horse of assessment. Instead, we must design lessons based on what will help students succeed on ongoing and summative assessments. The ongoing assessments are observations and checkpoints that equip students with the knowledge and skills for summative assessments. Summative assessments are too often tests, mainly due to their statistical advantages, ease of scoring, and habit. But other assessments that are gaining some ground are performances and products that resemble what content experts make and do in the real world.

Table 9.1 lists some condensed examples of the first and second stages of backward-designed curriculum (Wiggins & McTighe, 2005). The summative assessments in the right-hand column (stage 2) are designed to show the learning goals outlined in the middle column (stage 1). The third stage, planning for instruction, takes place after the first two stages. Stage 2 is particularly challenging and time-consuming; it is often easier to simply fall back on using a test. But tests often limit what students get to show us, and they can limit how and what we teach. Preparing students to do well on a more involved performance or product shapes instruction much differently than does preparing them to get 90 percent of the questions right on a test.

An important component of the learning goals in table 9.1 is the *big idea*—the enduring understanding that runs across units and forms a foundational principle that guides expert thinking in that discipline (see Wiggins & McTighe, 2005). It is helpful to post and refer to this big idea because it keeps the learning deep and connected. It keeps the talk academic and gets students to keep thinking about the facts, not just memorizing them. Notice how the teachers in table 9.1 integrated thinking and language goals into the middle column.

Integration of Ongoing Language Goals into Lessons

Most lessons and assessments are focused on content knowledge or reading, writing, and math skills, not on developing academic language. Despite the time and mental energy involved, weaving language and thinking objectives into schools' tasks, products, and performances fortifies the learning of content and builds enduring communication skills.

Like the strands of a cable, academic language skills strengthen content, thinking, and literacy learning. One way to integrate the skills into a lesson is to look back at table 3.1 in chapter 3, from which you can choose three to five target skills from each column to work on over a period of time. Table 9.2 is an example of this. Target skills can also be added over time, based on observations.

Table 9.1 Learning Goals and Performance Assessments for Four Content Areas

	Learning Goals	Performance or Product
History	*Content:* To understand the origins of American involvement in World War II and the constitutional issues raised by events on the US home front, especially the internment of Japanese American citizens.	Students will write an informational article about the Japanese American internment for a news magazine from that time period. Students need to write in an unbiased way, presenting both sides, and they need to expose biases in information from that time period.
	Big idea: We interpret history from the clues that we are given, which can often point in different directions.	
	Thinking: To strengthen students' abilities to persuade, critically analyze events, ask questions, empathize, and infer cause and effect based on evidence.	
	Language: To develop language used for thinking skills (*comes down to, in essence, essentially, resulted in, break it down, weigh evidence, look at motives, given that, while some believe that, biased account, suggests that, evidence, likely, implications*).	
Language arts	*Content:* To learn how to analyze a literary text, specifically, character motivation and traits in the play *A Raisin in the Sun*; to understand how literary themes can be linked to historical events such as the civil rights movement.	Students become experts and discuss whether *A Raisin in the Sun* gets a literary award. As evidence, they write a report that connects the play's scenes and dialogues to universal themes across history and literature. Students also create a then-and-now role play of an important scene from the play that also connects to the present day in the school or community.

	Big idea: To understand how literary characters can portray universal themes of the human experience.	
	Thinking: To develop abilities to predict and infer meaning, compare literary themes, interpret figurative language, and support points with evidence.	
	Language: To understand and use the language of characterization and figurative devices such as metaphors, similes, and symbols (*universal theme, motivation, traits, flaws, subordinate, internal conflict, interaction, evidence, infer, represents, stands for, figurative, literal*).	
Science	*Content:* To understand the process of meiosis and its role in sexual reproduction and how it differs from mitosis.	Students will write a "reproduction instruction manual" to explain to (literate) single cells how to make sperm cells, egg cells, or bacteria. Manuals will include visuals and text to clearly show and tell cells what to do. Students also take a short-answer quiz at the end of the unit.
	Big idea: To understand that cells function as building blocks for organisms.	
	Thinking: To develop abilities to analyze and compare scientific processes and to generate a hypothesis (predict scientific outcomes) based on prior knowledge.	
	Language: To use relevant expressions for thinking about and describing the processes (*exhibit novel traits, each successive generation, resulting*	

(continued)

Table 9.1 *continued*

	Learning Goals	Performance or Product
	cells, components, by which, undergoes, is found in, phase).	
Math	*Content:* To understand measures of central tendency (mean, median, and mode) and their uses. Analyze an article for appropriateness of the data analysis and the validity of conclusions.	Students will create a biased statistical article in which they create their own biased, yet convincing, argument on a topic of their choice (see chapter 8 for a description and a rubric). A quiz will show abilities and knowledge of the measures of central tendency. The quiz will have an article for students to critique.
	Big idea: To understand how people use different forms of numbers to serve different purposes—sometimes to persuade others in biased ways.	
	Thinking: To solve problems, ask critical questions as they read various statistical reports; to persuade and justify using central tendency.	
	Language: To understand and use terms in speech and writing that support thinking about central tendency (*statistical bias, outliers, differ, on the other hand, then again, contradictory data, frequency distribution, interpret data, positive and negative distributions*).	

And when students help in the process, they gain more ownership and understanding of what they need to learn. One teacher, for example, said that in October, she realized that her sixth graders needed to work on being clearer and more explicit to a distant audience. They discussed this target skill and added

Table 9.2 Selected Academic Language Goals to Assess and Teach

Describing Complexity, Abstractness, and Thinking	Academic Vocabulary and Grammar	Audience
Uses language to explore and question complex and abstract ideas (e.g., freedom, justice, truth, science)	Uses qualifiers and hedges to soften message	Makes language explicit for distant audiences
Clearly describes complex relationships	Keeps thoughts ordered, logical, and consistent	Varies pitch, tone, and pace of speech
Supports opinions and assertions with evidence	Uses such connectives as *although, despite, so that,* and *on the other hand*	Reads the audience and self-corrects if there is confusion

it to their list of goals to work on for the rest of the year in both language arts and social studies.

Sample Lesson Plan

This sample lesson plan shows how to fit many ideas from previous chapters into the modeling and scaffolding of content, language, and thinking in a content-area lesson. The activities support the science goals and performance assessment for meiosis in table 9.1. It also highlights the teaching of Common Core Anchor Literacy Standards. This is a science lesson (adapted from a lesson by Kevin Krasnow, 2004), but most of the ideas here can transfer easily to other content areas.

Lesson Introduction

During the lesson introduction, start with an engaging activity that involves every student and piques students' interest in some way. You might act like a character, ask a big idea question, show a strange image, show a video clip, play a song, or run a simulation.

For this biology lesson on meiosis, you can have students trace one hand on a folded piece of paper, with different colors for male and female. They cut out the two hands and write their own traits on them (e.g., tall, brown eyes, dark brown hair). They also write the number 23 on each one. Then they throw them into a large box, pull out one of each color, and read the traits of the resulting combination. The teacher elicits questions about how traits mix and dominate.

This is also the time to go over the content, thinking, and language objectives. Let students know what they will learn and do to become more like content-area experts. In this lesson, they will learn about meiosis well enough to create a manual with illustrated steps and explanations.

Connecting to and Building Background Knowledge

This vital, yet often rushed, stage of a lesson shows us where to begin on several levels. Background knowledge is more than just content and vocabulary; it also consists of motivational factors, thinking skills, and communication abilities. Getting a good read on what students already know, what they are interested in, how they think, and how they communicate can make or break the rest of the lesson. Therefore, begin with activities that help students engage their thinking skills (comparing, inferring cause and effect, perspective taking, persuading, interpreting) and see how they communicate their thoughts. This is a form of diagnostic assessment. If there are content gaps (e.g., they don't know the steps of mitosis), thinking gaps (they struggle to take the point of view of a cell or describe the principles of chemical reactions), or academic vocabulary gaps (*chromosome, chromatid, centromere, spindle fiber, kinetochore, exhibit novel traits, each successive generation, resulting cells*), then you must fill them in.

In this lesson, have students answer the prompt "What is mitosis?" in their journals. Circulate around the room to see how and what students are writing. Then have students quickly check their answers in pairs, filling in gaps and upgrading vocabulary, followed by a shared writing session in which you write a quick class synthesis on the board.

Vocabulary

Choose a few key terms that students will need to use to comprehend the text on meiosis and to show learning. Model different hand motions for the terms. For example, for *centromere*, students might touch the heels of each hand to each other to make an X. Or for *exhibit novel traits*, you can pull on one ear and move your nose to the side. Explain the other terms, perhaps with visuals and in the context of a sentence from the text. You can have students help generate motions for them. Then students briefly practice with one another to test each other, saying the word and waiting for the motion, or vice versa. Some words may need to be illustrated in a drawing. This should not take more than five minutes.

Presentation

A presentation is any type of modeling or explanation that focuses students on the lesson's main ideas. This is a chance to provide needed academic language input (see chapter 3). Presentation may take the form of a minilecture, video, or guided discussion. In any case, it is important to scaffold the language with visuals, movements, intonation, and pauses. This is also a time to connect the lesson to any overarching big ideas, which in this case is: *Cells function as building blocks for organisms.*

Briefly present the problem of doubling chromosomes in mitosis and how it won't work for mixing genes from different people. Pull a paper hand from the box and have students think about how it got twenty-three chromosomes.

Academic Discussion

Discussion in small and large groups allows students to think about, hear, and try out new language. For example, ask students to quickly write down in their logbooks their predictions for how a cell with forty-six chromosomes will divide to get half the number of chromosomes needed in the resulting cells (as compared to the same number in mitosis). After writing, students share their thoughts with partners to build up a theory for how they would solve the problem of doubling chromosomes. Encourage them to use new vocabulary as they share their theories.

One way to monitor participation is to use a checklist or rubric. Students can self- and peer-monitor, and you can notice certain trends that happen during lessons that can be the focus of minilessons and practice activities. You can give one student in the group a checklist like the one in table 9.3 to assess group talk. For example, peer assessors and you might see that students are voicing opinions (arguments) without backing them up with evidence. You then do a minilesson in which you model (remind or reteach) for them what quality argument looks like. Table 9.3 is a sample checklist derived from table 3.1. You can put comments, numbers, or symbols in the columns to the right of each target behavior.

Table 9.3 Sample Checklist for Monitoring Oral Language Behaviors

Productive Behaviors	Notes	Nonproductive Behaviors	Notes
Gives reasons and evidence for opinions		Interrupts others	
Uses academic expressions		Makes fun of others' comments or dismisses them	
Politely disagrees		Distracts others	
Asks helpful and thoughtful questions		Does not listen	
		Takes discussion off topic	
Leads the group toward a goal		Dominates the discussion	

Prereading

Quick prereading activities prepare students for the content, thinking, and language that they will encounter in the text. They may discuss, write, or act out key concepts that they will need. For example, in the take-a-side activity from chapter 5, students must get out of their seats in response to a two-sided prompt (often requiring a yes or no answer). They must then defend their decision with partners next to them and with you if you ask them. Prompts include "All that we need is mitosis"; "Chromosomes disappear during meiosis"; "Mitosis is necessary for meiosis." You can offer them useful terms to help them defend their decisions. This activity serves as a bridge between the oral activity and the text.

During Reading

Read aloud and think aloud to model how you connect to your background knowledge, make predictions, and organize the text information in your mind. Remind students to think about the eventual product (writing a manual) so that they can focus on key processes and language as they read. They will need to put the academic language into their own words and make their descriptions concise. Also ask students to write down additional academic terms and expressions that they might use in their products. They can use sticky notes to mark important parts of the text and any questions they have. You can also have students listen and take notes while you read aloud. This can be done on a periodic basis to build their listening skills and see if their comprehension and note taking are improving over time. Stop at times to ask text-dependent questions and prompt students to "think on paper." Circulate and observe what emerges on their papers.

Then have students read the rest of the text. They can respond to text-dependent questions when they finish, or you can give them a chunk of time to rewrite what they heard (as in a narrative retell) or to write a summary of the most important points of the text.

Postreading

Postreading is a chance to quickly solidify what was read. This can be a pair-share, quick-write, or graphic organizer. For example, have pairs quickly make a Venn diagram of meiosis and mitosis from what they remember from the text. Then share the ideas as a class. Another option, mentioned in chapter 5, is to use yarn and blocks to simulate the cell division process. This can happen in a think-pair-square format.

Another way to get students to remember what they read is an exit slip (Zemelman, Daniels, & Hyde, 1993), also known as an exit ticket, which allows students to synthesize learning in the last few minutes of a class period. The slips are best used on days when students learn new content or have discussed a concept in depth. For this lesson, a good exit slip prompt would be "Write what you learned about meiosis and how it differs from mitosis." Other common prompts are "Write something new that you learned," "Ask questions you still have," "See how this learning connects with previous learnings," "Think about the reasons that we are learning this," and "Name some different viewpoints on this issue." Let students know the types of language you hope to see.

Give the students several minutes to write, and collect the slips as they leave class. Notice students' use of academic language as you look over their slips. Look over several slips after class and comment on the language and thinking exhibited. You can also suggest more academic ways to express certain sentences to the whole class or in comments on the slips when you give them back the following day.

Prewriting

Prewriting is a time to prepare students with content, thinking, and language for their writing task. It involves showing models of the writing they will do and scaffolding students' organization of ideas before they write (e.g., using graphic organizers). For example, show students a sample how-to manual for operating a piece of machinery. Then tell students that they will write a how-to manual for clearly communicating to different cells how to reproduce through meiosis. Have students look at different manuals (books or online) to analyze the important features and text structures. They can make a list of features that you can use to create a rubric, like the one in table 9.4. Have pairs discuss which steps to include, why, and how. Optionally, hold a metadiscussion about important terms that will be helpful in writing the manuals. The terms can go up on the wall in a "language for writing" column.

Table 9.4 shows a few language-oriented rows of a rubric that students use to guide them as they write their manuals. Rows not shown here are "Use of Illustrations" and "Conventions."

Writing

Writing forces students to generate more complex language than they use when they talk. In this lesson, each student creates a draft of the cell reproduction manual, receiving support from partners along the way. They follow the rubric that they generated as a class (table 9.4). At times they trade and analyze each other's manuals to make sure the language is clear and matches the illustrations. Students refer to the classroom walls for the useful writing terms on posters that you have created. You can go around and even be a cell, asking questions to make sure students understand what they are writing. Remember to be a very scholarly cell. After students finish publishing their manuals, spend some time sharing them with the class.

ACADEMIC LANGUAGE IN SUMMATIVE ASSESSMENTS

In the lesson example, a written "performance" was used to summatively assess student learning, but other types of performances and products can also show practical applications of cognitive skill development, language use, and content understanding—all at once.

Another significant advantage of nontest performance assessments is their adaptability to meet the needs of students with different learning styles. We all know that students are different and that one size does not fit all. Through slight modification of the assignment or the rubric, or both, we can give our diverse

Table 9.4 Partial Sample Writing Rubric That Emphasizes Academic Language

Below Standard	At Standard	Exceeding Standard
Organization		
Rare logical sequencing; loosely connected series of events. Some steps repeated or omitted.	Structure developed reasonably well; logical sequencing and use of transitions. Steps are not repeated or omitted.	Structure is clearly logical; transitions between supporting statements are clear and enhanced by appropriate explanations. Logical sequencing of steps and explanations.
Sentence fluency		
Little variation in sentence lengths and use of clauses.	Some varying of clause use and sentence beginnings, endings, length, and structure.	Purposeful and effective use of clauses, varied sentence lengths, and structure that approximates that of a biologist.
Word choice		
Words are sometimes correct, but general, overused, and colloquial.	Words are mostly correct and appropriate for the genre and audience.	Words are specific, accurate, and used how a biologist might use them.
Academic language		
Language is not clear or coherent. Explanations are confusing due to grammar, spelling, and vocabulary choices. Language is not appropriate for audience.	The language is mostly clear, precise, and appropriate for the audience. Properly uses transitions, figurative expressions, and scholarly tone. Adequately uses terms for explaining, comparing, and cause and effect.	The language is clear, precise, and appropriate for the audience. Adeptly uses transitions, figurative expressions, and scholarly tone. Adequately uses expert-like language for explaining, comparing, and describing causes and effects. Uses thinking-skill terms: *exhibit novel traits, each successive generation, resulting cells, components, by which, undergoes, is found in, phase.*

students an appropriate task that challenges without overwhelming, allowing them to build their academic skills and feel successful when they accomplish the tasks. For example, taking into account that I have several second-year English learners in my language arts class, I might adapt a rubric that requires fewer written words but still requires students to use the same thinking skills and learn the same concepts as fluent English speakers in the class.

Building Language with Performance Assessments

All students need chances to use academic language, thinking, and knowledge, not just talk about them. Students might talk about different ways to solve an algebra problem or about various geographical features that influenced a culture, but the quality or lasting value of such talk may be marginal. Such knowledge may be in their heads, but it may not be usable in real-world ways after the test (Bereiter & Scardamalia, 1985). Learning will endure when students work together, think together, and wrestle with content and language together in construction of an authentic performance or product. As they practice with a variety of discourses for different purposes, they acquire them.

As we create effective performance and product assessments, we should design them so that they have these qualities:

- Have high, clear, real-world expectations for quality
- Allow continual feedback from teacher and peers to improve work
- Promote reflection on content and language through discussions
- Require students to work together over a period of time that culminates in a public performance or shared product
- Allow students to tap into their own experiences, languages, and creativity to produce their own texts and interpretations

Most instructional activities can prepare for and even become performance assessments. We can turn graphic organizers, simulations, art-based projects, videos, web page designs, compositions, and role plays into assessments. These forms of assessment tend to be more engaging—and more informative—than question-based tests. This practice smudges the line between teaching and assessment because students learn through the activity that they then do again to show their learning (with some tweaking to show their ability to apply and transform). Rarely does the real world of work give us a list of facts to memorize and questions to answer (multiple-choice questions even more rarely). Instead, we are asked to produce something by analyzing, transforming, synthesizing, interpreting, and communicating. When we create a performance assessment task, we should consider how people in the real world show their proficiency in similar target skills and knowledge. Consider how experts in the topic of study would think and express their learning of the things that our students are to learn.

Table 9.5 contains examples of real-world-based assessments that motivate students and integrate content with thinking and language.

Unlike fixed-answer tests, performance and product tasks tend to show more practical and enduring levels of learning. For example, if the task is to design a new type of chemical additive to fertilizer, students must do the chemistry that goes into it. They must meet real-world expectations for showing their ideas and communicating them to an audience. If students design a new bridge at the lowest cost, they must do the calculations required to meet the safety requirements and the cost limits. If they create a movie scene from a novel, they need to

Table 9.5 Examples of Performance-Based and Product-Based Assessments

Oral	Written	Drama and Movement	Visual
Oral presentation	Essay	Role play	Poster
Song or chant	Historical fiction	Monologue	Web page
Debate	Editorial letter	Readers' theater	Video commercial
Court case	Business plan	Movie script	Computer game
Speech	Book review	Dance	Design a building or park or school
Panel discussion	Children's book	Design a video	Magazine
Talk show	Collection of poems or stories or art	Lab experiment	A mural
Teach a lesson	How-to manual	Write a play	Slide show
Conduct interview		Puppet show	

interpret what is needed in the scene, the dialogue, and the action and why it takes place. And if they design a museum exhibit, they must know the facts and controversies, synthesize the importance of artifacts, and organize them in a logical way.

These assessment ideas, as you can imagine, are quite complex—and that's the point. Lots of thinking and language development happens as students work with one another (and ponder on their own) to accomplish the tasks. Throughout the lessons, we nudge and build the types of thinking and communication skills that experts in our discipline would use in similar situations (see chapters 3 through 8). We also come up with ways to formatively assess the developing knowledge, skills, and language that students will need to succeed on the performance. This formative assessment is described in more detail at the end of this chapter.

Performance Assessment Examples

This section contains three ideas for performance assessment from different content areas that are fleshed out a bit more to show their propensities for developing thinking skills and language. Performance assessments like these can become part of a student's evidence-of-learning portfolio, a way to keep track of content, language, and thinking growth in a variety of ways over time. When I use portfolios, I add a rubric for language and thinking evidence that I glue to the inside of a folder. This shows the importance of language and gives some helpful goals to guide students as they work on their communication skills.

History: Debate a Historical Issue or Question

Students prepare for a debate on whether scientific developments in the twentieth century made the world a better place. They choose a side and then prepare their arguments and counterarguments. They need to use evidence and citations. They develop a working rubric with the teacher in the initial stages as they analyze descriptions and transcriptions of debates. You can help students notice and post helpful language from these examples. Students work in pairs to prepare their notes, but for individual accountability, each prepares written summaries of his or her position after the debate and takes a short quiz. Notice how this type of assessment allows you to use multiple checklists and rubrics for the same project: a checklist for pair work, a rubric for the performance (the debate), and a rubric for the final written summary.

Students need plenty of argument language tools for supporting points with evidence, addressing opposing arguments, and synthesizing. They also need abstract terms to describe such ideas as cause and effect, the quality of life, perspectives from different groups of people, and the weighing of positives and negatives. You can see a few of these terms in the debate excerpt here:

Student A: It is clear that the technological advances in the early part of the twentieth century made the world a better place to live. The airplane allowed people to visit faraway places and do business with one another. They learned from one another and learned about other cultures and ways of doing things. The radio and television got more popular and allowed people to learn about the world without wires or even without reading.

Student B: True, we had more toys and could go farther and faster, but was life better? Even though airplanes made travel easier, they were also used for war. Just think about all the bombs that were dropped by planes in World War II. And television. A study done by a famous psychologist, Albert Bandura, showed that children learned new ways to be violent after watching TV. And many people in other countries were exploited for their raw materials. Perhaps a few people gained a better life, but it was at the expense of the quality of living for many others.

Math: Prepare a Proposal for a Construction Project

Students write a proposal for a new school and show the costs of each component. Students are given parameters, such as minimum number of classrooms, area of floor space for all rooms, ceiling heights, and land needed. Some rooms and walls have circular and triangular shapes. The students design the school and estimate the costs. Costs per square meter are given to them for land, floor tiles, and paint. Provide two separate forms with differing costs, so that students need to compare costs resulting from different supply chains. Finally, they must consider different hourly labor costs. One contractor estimates more hours than the other contractor but costs less per hour. Students will need to use different types of language for geometry calculations, cost estimates, comparing costs and quality, and persuading readers in order to win the bid. After pairs present their proposals and designs, they take a short quiz to show their learning.

Language Arts: Write a Children's Book and a Teacher's Guide

Students write a children's book based on a theme from a novel they are reading (e.g., "cunning is more powerful than strength" in *The Odyssey* or "challenging the system" in *The Chocolate War*). They write a picture book story for younger readers. This allows students to become authors and think about how to write from an author's viewpoint. Use popular children's books as models to design your rubric. Have students use a story map to create the plot. They illustrate their books; perhaps an art teacher can train students to use watercolors and make basic drawings. Students edit and critique each other's stories and guides. They then share them with elementary school students if possible.

A key component of this task is a "teacher's guide" that students write to explain the meaning of their book, its connection to the currently studied work of literature in the class, and how to connect the themes to young readers' lives. There is also a checklist for this component. For the guide, students need to be given literary language tools, such as terms for interpretation, figurative expression, symbolism, comparison of themes, and character development.

Designing Rubrics

As we design performance or product assessments, we design their rubrics—the scoring guides that describe different types of criteria for success for a performance or product (Díaz-Rico, 2004). Levels for each criterion or component are described in a table format. In designing rubrics, we must keep in mind what rubrics should do:

- Score independent traits, habits, and language separately
- Describe the quality of a student's use of language
- Be explained by using a variety of work samples that show performance differences
- Use precise descriptors and indicators that enable speakers and readers to verify their scores and accurately self-assess

Once a rubric is developed, we can go through the following stages: (1) show examples to clarify the rubric's criteria to students, (2) have students use rubrics to modify and self-assess their work before turning it in, (3) offer feedback on various criteria before the work is turned in, (4) ask students to turn work in to us, (5) use the rubric to assess the work, and (6) discuss strengths and weaknesses for future work.

Proper use of a rubric to self- and peer-assess takes a hefty amount of modeling with both good and intentionally flawed samples. Students need a clear idea of what they are to do and not do, what the product looks and sounds like, and how to evaluate each feature that goes into the rubric. For example, in the rubric in table 9.6, we must show students what it means to be "clear" and "not assume that

Table 9.6 Sample Oral Presentation Rubric That Emphasizes Academic Language

Feature	Below	Approaching	Standard	Above
Uses academic transitions	Few or no transitions	Simple transitions, such as *so*, *and*, and *but*	Uses additional transitions, such as *however*, *in addition*, and *therefore*	Varied transitions in appropriate places
Stays on topic	Multiple ideas or topics that don't relate	A few deviations from the topic; slight confusion with evidence	Mostly on topic, with slight deviations	No deviations; messages are connected and support main idea
Does not assume that the audience shares our background knowledge	Assumes much shared knowledge; uses *this, that, he* without referencing; much confusion	Some background knowledge assumed, which creates some confusion	Few or no assumptions of background knowledge and unexplained pronouns	Appropriately fills in background knowledge; very explicit
Uses examples and evidence	No or few examples	Some examples and evidence	Most points have convincing evidence or examples	Uses strong evidence and examples for all points made

the audience shares our background knowledge." We must be diligent in explaining and providing clear examples of what it means to have a well-organized presentation, present a strong point of view, include logical arguments, justify opinions, and properly address the audience. Many of these school tasks have never been sufficiently shown to students. And all along the way we must continuously model, scaffold, and highlight the academic language used to successfully accomplish these tasks.

We should spend time teaching the language of the rubrics that we use. I have discovered in many classrooms, including my own, that many students have only vague ideas of what the different categories mean in many rubrics. Have students verbally explain rubrics and tasks to other students, either in groups or to the whole class. This helps students listen and organize the parts of the task while it solidifies in their minds the overall purpose of the task. Have students explain how the task relates to the big ideas and essential knowledge or skills being learned. This also builds students' procedural language, which is especially helpful for diverse learners who did not grow up speaking English and hearing such language at home or in earlier grades.

Oral Presentations

Oral presentations are often used as performance assessments in secondary schools. Yet oral presentations and speeches can be a waste of time. I often see students reading from note cards copied from some source, mispronouncing words they don't know, taking up valuable class time, and providing the audience with information they already know. Students are often nervous and unmotivated to be in front of a large class and think that the less they say, the sooner they can sit down. English learners in particular get nervous about making grammatical and pronunciation mistakes and being laughed at. The audience often fidgets, whispers, laughs, passes notes, or does homework.

Nevertheless, with some modification, presentations can be effective learning tools and assessments for several reasons. First, the preparation of the presentation can teach hefty amounts of content and language as a student becomes an expert on his or her topic. As students read multiple sources, they see redundant language. They are exposed to academic grammar and new words in texts. Second, as they work with others, they build collaboration skills. Bouncing ideas off other students and the teacher can foster deeper learning. Third, students can actually learn content from others' presentations. Fourth, students who don't like to write are given a chance to show what they know through speaking or through the visuals they prepare. Fifth, students can feel empowered as they use complex language to creatively teach others and pass on knowledge and skills.

Students can also benefit by learning to communicate to large groups in more formal ways, using presentational language. Presentational language is required by the Common Core standards: "Present claims and findings, emphasizing salient points in a focused, coherent manner . . . Include multimedia components and visual displays . . . Adapt speech to a variety of contexts and tasks, demonstrating command of formal English" (CCSS.ELA-Literacy.SL.7.4–6). This type of language is used to communicate to a distant audience (one that is unfamiliar with the topic) that listens to longer stretches of talk.

Developing Oral Presentation Skills

Presentational language involves finding the best way to reach the audience with a message, including oral, written, and visual methods for communicating. Oral communication in particular requires a wide range of skills in order to be effective. Figure 9.1 is a helpful matrix for working on speaking skills in large groups, small groups, or in pairs (National Governors Association Center for Best Practices, 2010; National Standards in Foreign Language Project, 1999). Most of the skills are helpful for all types of talking.

Here are a few other ideas to improve oral presentations:

- Make sure the information is new to the audience; that is, there should be different topics for presenters.

- Have a minidebate in which two students argue two sides of an issue in front of the class.

- Add a slice of drama, in which the presenter offers a monologue on the topic or students act out a scene. Drama can augment the presentation without taking its place.

- Rather than having students present to the whole class, have them present to small groups to practice their skills. Groups can offer feedback afterward.

Figure 9.1 Assessment Matrix for Oral Presentations

Body Language	Act the Words	Pause
Straight posture Legs not crossed Hands not in pockets	Use expressions and gestures to show words and emphasize them.	Pause before and after words or phrases to emphasize them.
Pronunciation	**Emotion**	**Visuals**
Clearly articulate words.	Appropriately show emotional content; enjoy sharing.	Use pictures or diagrams to highlight evidence.
Inappropriate Slang	**Eye Contact**	**Authenticity**
"You know" "Ummm" "He was all, like, . . ."	Maintain eye contact with others in pair, group, or room. Do not read from cards.	Show passion and some emotion. Use some drama elements.
Pitch and Volume	**Pace**	**Audience Link and Think**
Vary the tones and volume to avoid monotone and to emphasize points or words.	Vary the pace to keep the listeners interested. Try to keep to 140–160 words per minute.	Have listeners think about a question or issue that touches them.

Teacher Modeling of Presentation Skills

One of the biggest hindrances to oral presentation quality is that students haven't seen many good oral presentations and therefore need us to model full presentations. Come to think of it, I have never seen a teacher model a full-length sample presentation, and I have modeled them rarely in my own classes. When I did model a presentation about explorers, it helped to have students "assess" me using the sample rubric with which they would be assessed. I also modeled and highlighted common presentational language in several minilessons.

We should also model the process of creating the presentation. These are the thoughts (think-alouds) that we have while we research texts and web pages and transfer the information into an outline or to note cards:

- Model how to synthesize chunks of information and discard less important pieces.

- Model the logic of creating conclusions and formulating reasons to support your thesis.

- Model the thinking behind the creation of visual aids to be used.

- Emphasize the importance of understanding concepts and their meanings, not merely presenting a string of facts.

- Model the various options for communicating your thoughts and reaching decisions on how to present.

What the Audience Does

In most real-world academic presentation settings, the audience is there for a reason: to learn something. Thus, we must create a context where student audiences need to (and want to) listen, beyond just evaluating and tolerating their peers' presentations. First, this implies the need for some kind of information gap. The student who is up front should have information that others need—and ideally have more than just the need to fill in a worksheet or chart. For example, in the real world, the notes we teachers take at presentations and workshops are used for something tangible—often to improve our teaching practices or enrich discussions with other teachers later.

Presenters can have the audience do quick-writes, share with a partner, vote, stand up when they hear certain words, do hand motions, participate with drama, or fill in a graphic organizer.

I observed one teacher who had students present their research on different authors and how their lives influenced their written works. Each pair shared the poignant parts of an author's life, along with summaries and excerpts from key works. They used visuals and some drama to teach us and involve us rather than just lecture at us.

⇒ When Students Teach

Students often learn more about a topic by teaching it to others. In this version of oral presentations, students become temporary teachers. Prepare students by explaining (in a nutshell) what teaching entails. Explain how you prepare a lesson and what you need to think about as you teach. Discuss the importance of clear communication in teaching. Then brainstorm as a class various ways to teach a concept. You can remind them of the interactive ideas that you have already used in previous classes. Go over the theories of multiple learning styles and generate possible activities that they might choose from. Remind them to think about how to get their students (peers) to participate and be active. Discuss the importance of modeling thinking and academic language as they teach.

Students then choose a topic of interest from the current unit, clarify learning objectives for it (concepts, thinking, language, skills), design a performance assessment, and prepare a teaching activity. When they do this in pairs or groups, some great discussion happens about the content and about how to teach the thinking processes needed to understand the content. Finally, as a bonus, they even come up with great ideas that we can use in our own future teaching.

⇒ Professional Conference

A related idea is to have pairs design and give workshops on a topic to other pairs or groups, much like a scaled-down version of the conference workshops that we teachers attend. In pairs, students create handouts and interactive activities to give a miniworkshop to six other students. This can work for history, science, math, literature, and other courses. Similar to jigsaw groups, described in chapter 6, students become experts on a topic of interest and then share it with others, noting its significance. The beauty is that students get to be creative in coming up with ways to teach others. When students teach other students, this activity allows them to engage in speaking behaviors and use language that is usually reserved for the teacher. The teacher benefits as well by seeing students play more active roles and express their thinking in different ways.

Provide language commonly found in conferences as you help students create their workshops: *according to, address, approach, argument, assert, assume, category, characteristic, claim, consist of, tends to, procedure, strategy, objectives, support, perspective, emphasize, highlight,* and so on.

FORMATIVE ASSESSMENT OF ACADEMIC LANGUAGE

In the sample lesson described earlier, we saw several ways to assess students as they learn, as opposed to solely after they learn. As we observe students, we try to see into their heads. We concurrently interpret their words, infer their thoughts, and provide helpful feedback. This is ongoing, or formative, assessment. It includes the "looking, listening, and commenting" that we do during class, such as checking student answers to questions, taking anecdotal notes, marking checklists, and providing helpful feedback and modeling while learning is happening. These are the "before it's too late" types of assessments that help us to help students sculpt their learning into something that guarantees success on the bigger, summative assessments at the end of a unit. It is during formative assessment that the most smudging occurs of the line between assessing and teaching.

The many different features of academic language are hard to see, and even more so if we are not looking for them. But they are important for success on the summative assessments and in life. Formative assessment therefore is a vital bridge between teaching and final assessments.

Atkin, Black, and Coffey (2001) offer three helpful questions of ongoing assessment to reflect on with students: Where are you trying to go? Where are you now? How can you get there? To these I add a language dimension and ask, "What types of language do you need to get there?" For example, I might check in with a group of students who are writing up a lab report on combustion. I check to see if they have terms they might need, such as *activation energy, exothermic, maintain, affect, conditions, reaction, evaporation,* and *gases.*

Academic Feedback

High-quality feedback is a key element of formative assessment. John Hattie (1992), after analyzing close to eight thousand studies, writes, "The most powerful single modification that enhances achievement is feedback. The simplest prescription for improving education must be 'dollops of feedback'" (p. 9). Yet we seldom work on or reflect on our feedback. What is it?

The first part of feedback is showing students what resulted from their actions. Often this has to do with clarity of their messages. For example, I might tell a student that her use of transitions in an essay helped me organize my thoughts as I read it. The second part of feedback is information about what to keep doing or what to change (Marzano, Pickering, & Pollock, 2001). It is the guidance from a more proficient speaker or writer or thinker of the discipline that helps apprentices properly use the language of the discipline. For example, a teacher might say, "Here you wrote that you thought Lincoln was bad. That is quite general. It would help your argument to put some examples of why you think that." Or, "You said 'you know' twelve times and used 'like' too much for an academic presentation. It was a bit distracting. Try practicing it again to reduce these." Or, "I like the way you draw little pictures to remember new vocabulary. Perhaps you can teach others in the group your strategy." Feedback should be customized, based on observations, and student specific. It should clearly describe student progress (Marzano et al., 2001). Feedback should also:

- Be immediate
- Be specific to student utterances
- Be focused, not overloaded with information or things to think about
- Not be evaluative
- Assume students will have other opportunities to use revised language
- Model target language

If the feedback is in the form of encouragement, it needs to be academically specific. This means that we must not only be specific about what we like, such as a student's use of imagery in a certain paragraph, but also use the chance to model appropriate language. I might say, "I appreciated your use of imagery to show the character's underlying intentions." If the student doesn't understand, I can then explain what I mean. The student will reflect on the comment and perhaps even acquire some of its language. Academic encouragement offers a chance for students to hear, one-to-one, academic responses to their own work. The language will stick better because it is more personalized.

Here are some sample academic encouragement starters:

"I liked the way that you added supporting details to your . . ."

"Wow, I didn't know that . . ."

"You really synthesized the information from different places very well."

"Excellent interpretation of the antagonist's actions."

"I liked the way you systematically solved this problem."

As most of the examples show, throughout our interactions with students we need to show warmth, patience, and genuine interest in what students say.

We can't be simply right-answer hunters; rather, we must be supportive coaches in the learning process, advocates who listen to all answers, questions, and issues and then provide tools and skills to enable students to reach their goals. An environment with helpful feedback emphasizes that students don't have to learn everything the first time. They should get second, third, and fourth chances (even fifth and sixth chances) to generate the best work they can do. Each time, we can scaffold their academic patterns of thinking and model the discipline's conventions for communicating ideas.

Diagnostic Observations

During the early diagnostic stages of assessment, we gather evidence to get a picture of students' initial language and thinking skills. We talk with their previous years' teachers and look at evidence from before. We can look at pretests, chat with students in pairs or individually, and gather writing samples (e.g., a persuasive quick-write, a science description, or a written explanation of how to solve a math problem). We can create a checklist, like the one in table 9.3, to hand out to students. Then we describe and model for students what we will look for in their writing and oral language. We can choose one or two items from each column to work on at different times of the year.

The following is an example of a quick-write that I gathered during the first days of a geometry unit. The prompt was "Explain the usefulness of pi to an engineer":

> Pi is very important because it allows you to figure out the area of a circle. It is a constant that equals 3.1415. It keeps going but that is enough. Every circle has a radius and a long time ago someone got the area of a circle to equal 3.14 times the radius squared. Maybe you gotta figure out the area of a circular room that you are designing. If the radius is 8 meters, then you square it and get 64 times 3.1415. You get 201 meters squared.

A quick analysis of this text reveals that this student appropriately used the academic cause-and-effect term *allows you* and the problem-solving term *figure out*. The example supported his argument, and the order of the sentences was logical. Some nonmath expressions were used (*keeps going, got the area to equal, let's say you gotta*). This sample showed me that this student has a good grasp of logical organization of ideas and explicit description for distant audiences. Perhaps some work could be done to make the nonmath expressions more mathematical. For instance, he could have used *For example, let's say you need to* instead of *Maybe you gotta* to introduce his example.

Recording the Language of Thinking

You can also use a chart like the one in table 9.7 (you might make it smaller) to gather language data and also provide specific feedback to students about their thinking. For example, you might respond to a student with "Well done, Lorena. When you talked about leaving your town, you connected to your background knowledge to help you understand this concept in history!" Or you might say, "Interesting interpretation of the fable! You said that the author used the story to show that's how a literary critic would say it." Granted, we do not have the time to respond like this to every student, but these feedback moments are precious to the ears of many students, and such communication builds an academic ambience that is precious to us.

The information in table 9.7 can remind us what to keep in mind and notice when it comes to reading strategies and cognitive skills. Feel free to adapt it to meet your needs. I have even put charts like this on a transparency and gathered language during group discussions to share with the class on the overhead projector afterward.

You can use smaller versions of this chart to record the language used to describe complex concepts and abstract relationships within a discipline. For example, in language arts I might chart the use of new figurative terms that students create to describe feelings and relationships. Or in math I might chart the use of problem-solving expressions and language that describes abstract mathematical relationships. A helpful way to generate chart categories is to consider what you want students to think about.

Minute-by-Minute Assessment of Learning

Here are several popular formative assessment techniques that allow us to get a better sense of student learning beyond just asking for raised hands or whether there are any questions as the bell is about to ring. The main goal of these

Table 9.7 Reading Strategies and Thinking Skills with Student Language Samples

Reading Strategy	Student Comments	Thinking Skill	Student Comments
Using background knowledge	That reminds me of when I had to move from my home village to a new country.	Arguing	Some argue that it is natural, but I think humans have caused . . .
Monitoring comprehension	"The man was flagged for his crimes?" That couldn't be right. I need to reread it.	Interpreting	We believe that the author used the ant story to show us how humans behave.
Summarizing	This section tells about the different parts of the government and their checks and balances.	Cause and effect	Mixing the two chemicals created an endothermic reaction because . . .
Inferring	I think that King Arthur was based on a real person but the magic stuff was made up.	Problem solving	We need to figure out exactly what they are asking us to do here.
Predicting	I predict that the next part will tell me what happens to the army and their nation.	Comparing	Plant cells have chloroplasts, while animal cells do not.
Questioning	How did humans figure out how to split an atom?	Evaluating	This case was important because it changed our ideas of immigrant rights.
Visualizing	I am picturing a really wide bell curve based on this data.	Empathizing	If I were in her shoes, I would have escaped the first week.
Figuring out word meanings	*Their specious arguments were shot down. Specious* must be something like *weak* or *empty*.	Categorizing and classifying	This earthquake would be considered a . . . I would put them in a group called . . .

techniques is to quickly build a clear sense of students' understanding and their abilities to describe it:

- *Thumbs.* Students put thumbs up for good understanding, thumbs sideways for some understanding, and thumbs down for little understanding.

- *Four fingers.* Students put four fingers up or against their chest to show understanding, three for less understanding, down to one finger for little understanding.

- *Cards.* Students put different-colored cards up on their desks, depending on their grasp of the material. Green can mean "Let's move on"; red, "Let's go over it again."

- *Quick-write.* Have students quickly write a response to a prompt. You then walk around to see how well they understand. You can even have them use some terms in their responses to see if they comprehend the language. They can also write responses on individual whiteboards and hold them up for you to see.

- *Draw and describe.* Many students are much better at drawing their understandings than writing or talking about them. Go around as students are drawing, and have students explain their drawing to you. Other students can be drawing or writing about their drawings.

- *Analogy prompts.* Have students quickly think about and write about how a target concept or process is like something common and unrelated. You can provide the analogy (*How is a cell like a factory?*) or have students come up with their own. You can speed things up by giving them a sentence starter, such as *Synapses are like a . . . because they . . .*

Individualized Assessment

Closely analyze student work. Looking at student work samples is a powerful way for us to see thinking and language abilities. Many students need this extra watching and attention; if they don't get it, they simply get moved on from grade to grade and struggle in high school because their language differences weren't addressed earlier. I suggest picking three or four focal students per quarter. Spend a little extra time analyzing their work and discussing it with them afterward. You can comment on the length of each piece, the organization, the use of new academic text features, and new vocabulary (Temple et al., 2005). Also notice any significant patterns or errors to highlight.

Helpful Questions to Guide Analysis of Student Work

What can this student do and not do with language?

How have home language and culture influenced this work?

What are strong and weak patterns of language use?

What extra type of scaffolding does this student (or the whole class) need?

What future work will better show me this student's abilities and knowledge?

⇒ Journals

A popular assessment and learning strategy is to have students write in journals or learning logs. These give students a chance to organize their thoughts and write them down with less pressure and scrutiny than other types of assessment. It gives students a chance to take risks with new words and grammar structures. For example, I often encourage them to create longer sentences with multiple clauses and the use of commas. You can decide how often you will look at them and how to assess them. In addition to content understanding, a primary aim is to encourage students to improve the academic nature of their responses over time. They can do this by using an ongoing journal rubric that emphasizes language.

⇒ Read-Alouds

School literacy experiences are key factors in developing academic language, especially in linguistically and culturally diverse students (Wong Fillmore, 2004). Student read-alouds can provide a window into student language proficiency. By listening to students read, think aloud, and answer questions, we can make preliminary inferences about language needs and strengths. Granted, this takes time, and it is probably most time-efficient with a handful of low-performing students. But this time can provide priceless information.

Have the student read a passage to you. Listen for intonation and pauses that indicate confusion about content and general academic terms. Listen to how the student handles embedded clauses and how the student reads it differently than you might. Make notes of these differences on the text (you need to have a copy as well). Notice the use of punctuation and where students pause and do not pause. Then have the student stop at times to think aloud (see chapter 7). You can prompt the student to generate questions, summaries, opinions, definitions of words, main ideas, and so on. Students can even take notes, fill in a visual organizer, or highlight the text as they read to show what they focus on and how they are organizing the information.

⇒ **Academic Oral Proficiency Interviews**

This one-on-one procedure, developed by Stanford University researchers Bunch, Abram, Lotan, and Valdés (2001), gradually nudges a student into sharing increasingly academic talk. You record the conversation and then use a checklist or rubric to analyze the student's language and thinking. For example, you might first prompt the student to tell about a favorite holiday in a narrative form. Then you would tell the student that visitors from another country are coming who know very little about that holiday. The student needs to explain (to a "distant" audience) the features of the holiday. The last stage is getting the student to pick a side of a controversial aspect of the holiday and persuade you to take the same side. For example, some say that Halloween should not be celebrated or that people spend too much money on gifts for Christmas. Students need to support their points with evidence or examples. Any topic that can progress from narrative to explanation to persuasion will work.

Here is an abridged example from eighth-grade history. Notice how the teacher keeps gently nudging and digging to get the student to share academic thinking:

1. *Teacher:*   Okay, can you tell me about an important person in your life?
2. *Student E:*   Well, my grandma is . . . I dunno how old she is. She's old, she got white hair and smiles a lot. She makes us cake and stuff.
3. *Teacher:*   She sounds nice. Why is she important to you?
4. *Student E:*   She tells stories about our family. She listens to me complain about school and stuff. I don't know.
5. *Teacher:*   Okay, how about telling me a little about an interesting person from history you have studied.
6. *Student E:*   Like, ummm, Harriet Tubman?
7. *Teacher:*   Yes, tell me who she was and what she did.
8. *Student E:*   Well, she helped slaves escape the south. They called it the Underground Train or something like that. They hid 'em and they, like, walked at night.

9. *Teacher:*   She sounds important. Can you convince me that she is important enough to teach about her next year? Persuade me that she was important.

10. *Student E:*   Well, she started it was like the first organized protest against slavery—that's important. And she only helped a few hundred out of millions, but it showed more people it was important to be free. Like one time she pointed a gun at a man and told him she'd kill him if he turned back. Like in a movie or something. And she, like, also risked getting killed to help those people that she didn't know. So, students should study her.

This student successfully communicated at all three levels. And in the argument part, she even presented a counterargument ("she only helped a few hundred [people]") and used a poignant example about the gun. She described abstract concepts, such as showing the importance of being free and sacrificing life to help others.

Telling students the types of thinking and language you are looking for during the interview, describing the types of questions they will be asked, and allowing students to practice such conversations can give them a better understanding of how academic conversation works. They can even use the whole year to work toward a final academic interview.

CONCLUSION

In this chapter, we looked at various ways to integrate the development of academic language into lesson plans and assessment of Common Core and other standards. This assessment of content, thinking, and language needs to inform our instruction. Formative assessment is the hourly and daily observation of students' language and thinking that we do as they learn. Yet observation without feedback is of little value; we must be active advocates who support, correct, encourage, and suggest new ways of describing learning. Summative assessment is the performance or product that students then use to show their integrated learning of the important facts, concepts, big ideas, skills, and language of experts in a discipline. More than just tests, though, summative assessments also foster a lot of learning along the way.

Assessment can and should provide an effective way to teach language, not just test it. As students become engaged in a project or the pursuit of an interesting and relevant goal, they will seek the tools—which are the features of academic language—that best serve their needs. We must be ready to provide them with these tools, similar to an assistant who hands instruments to surgeons during a complicated surgery. The assessments that we create should allow students to step into real communication practices for a moment and permanently borrow useful language. As students work on the various stages and lessons that help them be successful on the assessment tasks, we model and scaffold the language and thinking.

We and our students must continue to think of assessments as both destinations and avenues for learning the language and content of the new standards. All the while, we make the language and thinking that we are desiring to see in student assessments as visible and explicit as we can. With good assessments that are based on performance, both the outcome and the journey are fun, motivating, and powerful for learning. Finally, if we are to train students in the language of any discourse community (e.g., biologists, historians, lawyers, software engineers), we must continue to interweave modeling, scaffolding, and assessing in every lesson. When this happens over multiple years, the cumulative effect can be significant, especially for diverse students.

CHAPTER REFLECTIONS

- What should students in your courses know and be able to do? Why?

- What kinds of assessments best show student learning of content, thinking, and language in your discipline?

- How do real-world experts in your discipline show what they know and what they can do?

- Design a performance assessment for what you teach, and then create a rubric for it. Include thinking and language criteria.

- Design several instructional activities that would help build the language and thinking skills needed for success on the assessment you just designed.

- What are some general principles that guide your philosophy of how students learn? How do these principles shape your lesson planning? Where does language fit in?

- Hold a quick academic oral proficiency interview with a teacher, friend, or student. Write down some of the language used at each level.

References

Atkin, J., Black, P., & Coffey, J. (Eds.). (2001). *Classroom assessment and the National Science Education standards*. Washington, DC: National Research Council, National Academies Press.

Bereiter, C., & Scardamalia, M. (1985). Cognitive coping strategies and the problem of "inert knowledge." In S. Chipman, J. Segal, & R. Glaser (Eds.), *Thinking and learning skills: Current research and open questions* (Vol. 2, pp. 65–80). Hillsdale, NJ: Erlbaum.

Bruner, J. (1986). *Actual minds: Possible worlds*. Cambridge, MA: Harvard University Press.

Bunch, G., Abram, P., Lotan, R., & Valdés, G. (2001). Beyond sheltered instruction: Rethinking conditions for academic language development. *TESOL Journal, 10*(2/3), 28–33.

Díaz-Rico, L. (2004). *Teaching English language learners: Strategies and methods*. Boston, MA: Allyn & Bacon.

Hattie, J. (1992). Measuring the effects of schooling. *Australian Journal of Education, 36*(1), 5–13.

Krasnow, K. (2004). Meiosis lesson plan. Unpublished lesson plan.

Marzano, R., Pickering, D., & Pollock, J. (2001). *Classroom instruction that works: Research-based strategies for increasing student achievement*. Alexandria, VA: Association for Supervision and Curriculum Development.

National Governors Association Center for Best Practices. (2010). *Common Core State Standards*. Washington, DC: Council of Chief State School Officers.

National Standards in Foreign Language Education Project. (1999). *Standards for foreign language learning: Preparing for the 21st century*. Yonkers, NY: American Council on the Teaching of Foreign Languages.

Temple, C., Ogle, D., Crawford, A., & Freppon, P. (2005). *All children read: Teaching for literacy in today's diverse classrooms*. Boston, MA: Allyn & Bacon.

Wiggins, G., & McTighe, J. (2005). *Understanding by design* (2nd ed.). Alexandria, VA: Association for Supervision and Curriculum Development.

Wong Fillmore, L. (2004). The role of language in academic development. Keynote address given at Closing the Achievement Gap for EL Students conference, Sonoma, CA.

Zemelman, S., Daniels, H., & Hyde, A. (1993). *Best practice: New standards for teaching and learning in America's schools*. Portsmouth, NH: Reed Publishing.

Chapter 10

Concluding Thoughts

A builder has learned to use basic tools to build houses over the years. The builder then gets a contract to build a large office building. The construction process is complex, involving many new tools and materials. The builder finds a more experienced contractor to provide the tools and show how they are used with the materials to properly construct the big building.

Over time, with the support of the experienced contractor, the builder gets accustomed to using the new tools, and more skilled behaviors become automatic to him. Yesterday the builder signed a contract to construct a large research laboratory. The builder can use the tools and skills acquired from previous jobs but will need even more specialized materials, procedures, and tools for this project.

As students learn to use language in school settings more skillfully, we must keep working alongside them, helping them construct and communicate complex meanings. We must use our expertise in the discipline to train students when and how to use different academic language tools, such as general academic terms, content-specific vocabulary, grammar, and organizational conventions. If we teach these things well, students will be able to build whatever types of meaning they are asked to build in later years of school and beyond.

This chapter offers a few final thoughts that sum up the previous chapters.

BUILDING FRAMEWORKS AND FILLING IN GAPS

As we saw in chapter 1, the deepest layers of academic language are the social and cultural foundations. These are ways of thinking, communicating, and learning that students grow up in and bring with them to school. Students with diverse linguistic and cultural backgrounds often enter schools that have different frameworks of how to learn and talk. When their ways of building and describing meaning do not merge with schools' expectations, the students tend to perform poorly on typical measures of school achievement.

Academic language is a set of tools that we can train our low-performing students to use in order to close the achievement gap between them and their higher-performing peers. But this gap, which tends to be measured with test scores that compare different students, is not the only one. An important yet much less visible gap is the one that exists between the current and potential abilities in the same student. It is the difference that schools could have made—and still can make—in the academic development of each student each year. In other words, regardless of test percentile rankings and grades, we need to continually ask if we are creating learning experiences that maximize each student's overall potential.

TEACHING THE TOOLS OF THE TRADE

One way to close gaps and accelerate students' acquisition of academic abilities is to directly teach students how the system works. Each discipline has specialized ways of constructing meaning with certain linguistic and cognitive tools. These tools are used to fit the ideas of each discipline together in valued ways. When we teach students how to use these new tools, such as how to interpret symbolism in a novel or organize a lab report, we accelerate the acquisition and expansion of their communication skills for any situation.

Conversely, if we teach just the content, we drastically shortchange our students. They may end up with a few more facts and skills but miss out on the cultivation of rich dialogue and thinking that will serve them their entire lives. Academic language is not just for academic purposes. Whatever students do in the future, they will need to use their academic language tools for a variety of purposes, such as reading contracts, debating issues, arguing for rights, identifying deception and persuasion, solving complex problems, interpreting religious texts, and communicating their ideas in written and oral formats.

For many diverse students, school is the only place where they can gain access to academic tools and thinking skills that they need for the future. For this reason, we must use the time wisely. Here are several suggestions.

Dig

Just as we need to have a depth of knowledge about the content we are teaching, so must we have an advanced awareness of the language and thinking of our discipline if we are to train our apprentices in the ways of our craft. We need to overcome our expert blind spots and see the discipline through the eyes of students, many of whom have very different backgrounds and interests.

We must dig into our discipline and become aware of its complex ideas, abstract concepts, and higher-order thinking skills. At the same time we need to become aware of the language used to describe these things. We must uncover the less obvious and more general academic terms that clarify the content-specific terms of our discipline. Academic language must be visible: we must highlight the unique ways that experts in our discipline organize words and larger chunks of text to communicate. We must lay the blueprints out in front of students so they can have a more meta- and macro-view of language use in each content area.

Connect

The classroom tends to be one big abstract experience. School essentially uses a variety of symbols and manipulates them to approximate real experience. These symbols are words, images, actions, and objects. We read, write, and watch to learn, rather than actually learning from being there at, let's say, the Fall of Rome, in a research lab, at an engineering office, or in a novel. To make all this abstraction more understandable, we must connect the learning to students' lives. As we find and create tangible connections to what students know and what they think is important, they become better at building academic meanings and more motivated to use higher levels of language in the process.

Mix

Diversity is often seen as a weakness when it should be seen as a strength. Differences in any setting provide new ideas and energy to the mix. There are new perspectives, new ways of creating, and new ways of solving problems that come from having diverse students in our classrooms. Therefore, we must learn to weave the knowledge and practices of all our students into instruction and assessment. Just as students must adapt to new ways of knowing and talking, so must we adapt our ways of knowing and teaching.

Do

We must model for students the skills and language that we expect from them. To get students to engage in meaningful and purposeful discussion, we must model ways in which experts organize the abstract and complex ideas of the discipline. We need to write essays, perform labs, solve problems, make posters, and give sample presentations. We must share our thinking processes and highlight language along the way. And as students practice with the language, we must provide dollops of feedback about language, thinking, and content.

We then design performance assessments so that students can show what they know and can do with what they are learning. Summative assessment is a chance for students to show off their content knowledge and next levels of thinking about the discipline. It is also a chance for us to see how well students are weaving together the strands of literacy, thinking, and language as discipline experts might do. If there are weaknesses in the learning, we can use this information to shape future instruction.

Reinforce

Teaching something once is not enough. This is especially true for thinking skills and abstract language. A student might learn what sound waves are, but the skills of comparing these waves to other types of waves or applying the knowledge in practical ways take longer to build. A student might quickly learn the meanings of *communism, proletariat,* and *bourgeoisie,* but will take longer to learn more broad-reaching and abstract mortar terms, such as *distribution, production, class, struggle, society, establish, revolution,* and *state.*

In math a student might quickly learn the terms *transversal, supplementary,* and *complementary* but take longer to understand how to write proofs and use such terms as *corresponding, by previous theorem,* and *relationships exist in the figure.* In order to reinforce these terms, skills, and language abilities, students need to use them over and over with different topics throughout the year.

Add On

What we do in class should help students add new ways of understanding and new language for describing them. This is the opposite of "subtracting," which happens when schools expect diverse students to replace their ways of knowing and talking with mainstream ways. We must show that we value the tools and skills that students already have as we train them in the new and specialized practices of school. Our students then become multilingual in a broad sense—proficient at the languages of home, hallway, language arts, math, science, history, and so on.

CONCLUSION

I realize that this book has likely added yet another set of important things for you to think about as a teacher. Such is the nature of teaching, the most complex and important profession on the planet. Teachers have the task of preparing students for the future in a variety of fundamental ways. We prepare them to know, think, create, and communicate so that they reach their potentials in different dimensions of life and play a role in making the world a better place. This huge task takes many hours—over ten thousand, if I remember correctly. Each hour in class is one more hour that builds up the language, thinking, content, and character of each student. Let's make the most of each minute.

Recommended Resources on Academic Language

THEORY AND RESEARCH

Anstrom, K., DiCerbo, P., Butler, F., Katz, A., Millet, J., & Rivera, C. (2010). *A review of the literature on academic language: Implications for K–12 English language learners*. Arlington, VA: George Washington University Center for Equity and Excellence in Education.

Bunch, G. (2013). Pedagogical language knowledge: Preparing mainstream teachers for English learners in the new standards era. *Review of Research in Education, 37*, 298–341.

Cazden, C. (2001). *Classroom discourse: The language of teaching and learning*. Portsmouth, NH: Heinemann.

Halliday, M. (1978). *Language as social semiotic*. Baltimore, MD: University Park Press.

Johns, A. (1997). *Text, role, and context: Developing academic literacies.* Cambridge, UK: Cambridge University Press.

Mercer, N. (2000). *The guided construction of knowledge: Talk amongst teachers and learners.* Clevedon, UK: Multilingual Matters.

Scarcella, R. (2003). *Academic English: A conceptual framework* (Technical Report No. 2003–1). University of California Linguistic Minority Research Institute.

Schleppegrell, M. J. (2004). *The language of schooling: A functional linguistics approach.* Mahwah, NJ: Erlbaum.

Schleppegrell, M. J., & Colombi, M. (2002). *Developing advanced literacy in first and second languages: Meaning with power.* Mahwah, NJ: Erlbaum.

Vygotsky, L. (1978). *Mind in society: The development of higher psychological processes.* Cambridge, MA: Harvard University Press.

Wong Fillmore, L., & Snow, C. (2000). *What teachers need to know about language.* Washington, DC: ERIC Clearinghouse on Languages and Linguistics.

SOCIOCULTURAL DIMENSIONS

Delpit, L. (2006). *Other people's children: Cultural conflict in the classroom.* New York, NY: New Press.

Delpit, L., & Dowdy, J. (2008). *The skin that we speak: Thoughts on language and culture in the classroom.* New York, NY: New Press.

Gee, J. (1996). *Social linguistics and literacies: Ideology in discourses.* London, UK: Routledge Falmer.

Heath, S. (1983). *Ways with words: Language, life, and work in communities and classrooms.* Cambridge, UK: Cambridge University Press.

ORAL LANGUAGE AND DISCUSSION

Chapin, S., O'Connor, C., & Anderson, N. (2009). *Classroom discussions: Using math talk to help students learn, grades K–6* (2nd ed.). Sausalito, CA: Math Solutions.

Fisher, D., Frey, N. and Rothenberg, C. (2008). *Content-area conversations: How to plan discussion-based lessons for diverse language learners.* Alexandria, VA: Association for Supervision and Curriculum and Development.

Johnston, P. (2004). *Choice words: How our language affects children's learning.* Portland, ME: Stenhouse.

Johnston, P. (2012). *Opening minds: How classroom talk shapes children's minds and their lives.* Portland, ME: Stenhouse.

Juzwik, M. M., Borsheim-Black, C., Caughlan, S., & Heintz, A. (2013). *Inspiring dialogue: Talking to learn in the English classroom.* New York, NY: Teachers College Press.

Nichols, M. (2006). *Comprehension through conversation: The power of purposeful talk in the reading workshop.* Portsmouth, NH: Heinemann.

Opitz, M., & Zbaracki, M. (2004). *Listen hear! 25 effective listening comprehension strategies.* Portsmouth, NH: Heinemann.

Spiegel, D. (2005). *Classroom discussion: Strategies for engaging all students, building higher-level thinking skills, and strengthening reading and writing across the curriculum.* New York, NY: Scholastic.

READING AND WRITING

Atwell, N. (1998). *In the middle: Writing, reading, and learning with adolescents* (2nd ed.). Portsmouth, NH: Heinemann.

Fang, Z., & Schleppegrell, M. (2010). Disciplinary literacies across content areas: Supporting secondary reading through functional language analysis. *Journal of Adolescent and Adult Literacy, 53*(7), 587–597.

Harvey, S., & Goudvis, A. (2000). *Strategies that work: Teaching comprehension to enhance understanding.* Portland, ME: Stenhouse.

Robb, L. (2003). *Teaching reading in social studies, science, and math: Practical ways to weave comprehension strategies into your content area teaching.* New York, NY: Scholastic.

Schleppegrell, M., & O'Hallaron, C. (2011). Teaching academic language in L2 secondary settings. *Annual Review of Applied Linguistics, 31,* 3–18.

Tovani, C. (2000). *I read it, but I don't get it: Comprehension strategies for adolescent readers.* Portland, ME: Stenhouse.

Wong Fillmore, L., & Fillmore, C. (2011). *What does text complexity mean for English learners and language minority students?* Paper presented at Understanding Language conference, Stanford University.

Zwiers, J. (2010). *Building reading comprehension habits in grades 6–12: A toolkit of classroom activities* (2nd ed.). Newark, DE: International Reading Association

VOCABULARY DEVELOPMENT

Allen, J. (1999). *Words, words, words: Teaching vocabulary in grades 4–12.* York, ME: Stenhouse.

Bear, D., Invernizzi, M., Templeton, S., & Johnston, F. (2000). *Words their way: Word study for phonics, vocabulary, and spelling instruction* (2nd ed.). Englewood Cliffs, NJ: Prentice Hall.

Beck, I., McKeown, M., & Kucan, L. (2013). *Bringing words to life: Robust vocabulary instruction* (2nd ed.). New York, NY: Guilford Press.

Blachowicz, C., Fisher, P., & Ogle, D. (2006). Vocabulary: Questions from the classroom. *Reading Research Quarterly, 41*(4), 524–539.

Yu, R. D. (2011). *Unlocking the power of academic vocabulary with secondary English language learners.* Gainesville, FL: Maupin House.

ENGLISH LEARNERS

Coelho, E. (2004). *Adding English: A guide to teaching multilingual classrooms.* Toronto, Canada: Pippin Publishing.

Díaz-Rico, L. (2004). *Teaching English language learners: Strategies and methods.* Boston, MA: Allyn & Bacon.

Echevarria, J., Vogt, M., & Short, D. (2010). *Making content comprehensible for secondary English learners: The SIOP model.* Boston, MA: Allyn & Bacon.

Garcia, G. (2003). *English learners: Reaching the highest level of English literacy.* Newark, DE: International Reading Association.

Gibbons, P. (2002). *Scaffolding language, scaffolding learning.* Portsmouth, NH: Heinemann.

Oxford, R. (2011). *Teaching and researching language learning strategies.* New York, NY: Routledge

Valdés, G. (2001). *Learning and not learning English: Latino students in American schools.* New York, NY: Teachers College Press.

World Class Instructional Design and Assessment. (2012). *WIDA 2012 Amplified ELD Standards.* Retrieved from http://wida.us/standards/eld.aspx

Frequently Used Academic Words

The first list is a selection of words from the sublists of the *Academic Word List in the Academic Corpus* (Coxhead, 2000). The main purpose of this list is to heighten awareness of the many less obvious terms that describe complex and abstract concepts across disciplines. The second list contains terms that are often used to describe five academic communication skills. The third list shows how terms and grammatical tactics are used to build academic sentences. All of these lists can and should be adapted and expanded to fit each classroom context. Additional words and information can be found at www.vuw.ac.nz/lals/research/awl/awlinfo.html.

Partial Academic Word List

access
achieve
acquisition
adequate
administration
affect
alternative
analysis
apparent
approach
appropriate
approximated
area
aspects
assessment
assistance
assume
attitudes
attribute
authority
available
benefit
categories
chapter
circumstances
civil
code
commission
commitment
communication
community
compensation
complex
components
concentration
concept
conclusion
conduct
conference
consent
consequences
considerable
consistent
constant
constraints
construction

consumer
context
contract
contrast
contribution
convention
coordination
core
corporate
corresponding
create
credit
criteria
cultural
cycle
data
debate
deduction
definition
demonstrate
derived
design
despite
dimensions
distinction
distribution
document
domestic
dominant
economic
elements
emerged
emphasis
ensure
environment
equation
error
established
estimate
ethnic
evaluation
evidence
excluded
export
factors
features

final
financial
focus
formula
framework
function
goals
granted
hence
hypothesis
identified
illustrated
immigration
impact
implementation
implications
implies
imposed
indicate
individual
initial
instance
institute
integration
interaction
internal
interpretation
investigation
investment
involved
issues
items
journal
justification
label
labor
layer
legal
legislation
link
location
maintenance
major
maximum
mechanism
method

minorities
negative
normal
obtained
obvious
occupational
occur
option
outcomes
output
overall
parallel
parameters
participation
partnership
perceived
percent
phase
philosophy
physical
policy
positive
potential
predicted
previous
primary
principal
principle
prior
procedure
process
professional
project
promote
proportion
published
purchase
range
reaction
regime
region
registered
regulations
relevant
reliance
removed

required
research
resident
resolution
resources
response
restricted
retained
role
scheme
section
security
select
sequence
series
shift
significant
similar
site
sought
source
specific
specified
statistics
status
strategies
stress
structure
subsequent
sufficient
summary
survey
task
technical
techniques
technology
text
theory
traditional
transfer
undertaken
validity
variable
volume

Frequently Used Terms and Tactics for Building Academic Sentences

To Describe Sequence	To Give an Example	To Soften a Statement	To Compare and Contrast	To Show Results or Conclude
first, second	for example	sometimes	whereas	this led to
at this time	for instance	many	nevertheless	hence
at this point	consider the time	few	however	brought
meanwhile	in this case	seldom	on the other	about by
finally	on this occasion	rarely	hand	in conclusion
concurrently	in this situation	can	on the	as we have
consequently	to demonstrate	might	contrary	shown
previously	to illustrate	most	by comparison	therefore
simultaneously	in fact	occasionally	ironically	accordingly
subsequently	indeed	apparently	yet	thus
concurrently	. . . in practice	theoretically	compared to	as a result
while	such as	probably	although	consequently
following this		likely	even though	ultimately
			in contrast	in view of this
			just as so	due to

Frequently Used Terms and Tactics for Building Academic Sentences

Words

For dependent clauses: *after, even though, as, because, before, even if, in spite of, if, rather than, given that, since, because, unless, until, once, when, where, whereas, whether, which, while*

Sentence Samples

Given that the sum of the two angles must equal 180°, we can figure out the unknown angle by subtracting.

As you analyze the structural formulas above, you will see that every carbon atom forms four bonds.

When Constantinople fell to the Ottoman Turks in 1453, the overland spice trade to Europe was cut off.

The author is showing that if each person cannot overcome the temptation to choose what is wrong rather than right, evil will prevail in a human society.

For relative clauses: *which, who, whom, that, whose, those, whoever, whomever*

An exothermic reaction, which releases energy in the form of heat, has many practical applications.

A triangle's angles and sides have relationships that can be proven.

José María Morelos, whose rebel army had some success, was captured and executed in 1815.

And then the old man, who talked only when absolutely necessary, faced the window and cleared his throat.

For prepositional phrases: *above, across, after, against, along, among, around, as, behind, below, besides, by, except, for, from, in, inside, near, next to, of, off, on, out, over, regardless, to, under, until, with*

Regardless of the data they had gathered, they proceeded with the next phase of the project.

Except for a handful of rebels concealed in the surrounding hills, all hope was lost.

They wound their way through the forest, with some trepidation, for they had heard many stories of its dangers.

Words	Sentence Samples
For participial clauses: (verb + ing) or past participle of verb	By comparing densities, a person can explain why some objects float in water and why some objects sink.

Despite the many dangers of the Silk Road, traders risked their lives for the profits they could earn.

Dantès remained tenuously bound together by threads of human love until the death of Abbé Faria.

The nation's powerful landowning class, wanting to protect their wealth and retain control, resisted all land reform programs.

The planet Mercury, lacking atmospheric gases to retain the sun's energy, measures 430°C during the day and −170°C at night.

The high and low points, indicated on the graph by the letters A and B, can be used to derive an equation.

Torn between his strict commitment to enforce the law and his debt to Valjean for sparing his life, Javert becomes deeply perplexed. |

Reference

Coxhead, A. (2000). A new academic word list. *TESOL Quarterly, 34*(2), 213–238.

Suggestions for Before, During, and After Minilectures

Minilectures can help students develop academic language and thinking. Here are a few ways to make the content and language more comprehensible and enduring.

PRELECTURE IDEAS

Just as we employ many prereading activities, we can use prelecturing activities to prepare students for lectures and build their listening and note-taking skills. No matter what activity you use, plan ahead, even if you have taught the topic before. Sketch an outline or semantic map as your notes. Then follow your plan and try not to stray far from it. Too often, we cut out the most important ideas and understandings because we go off-plan with tangents that take up too much time.

Here are more suggestions:

- Use a write-pair-share with an object, photo, or visual to get thinking started.

- Show something; then have students quickly write their thoughts and predictions. Have them share with partners.

- Make a chart listing the content vocabulary and academic terms that typically arise in lectures and oral presentations (see table 5.2).

- Create a partially filled-in outline or graphic organizer that students can use for note taking.

- Organize the minilecture around a story, analogy, or big question or problem.

Model Note Taking

- Give a lecture and stop periodically to think aloud and take notes on your lecture, giving reasons that you chose to write what you did. Use a system such as two- or three-column notes or semantic maps (see chapter 5).

- Use an anticipation guide that gets students to think about questionable topics before hearing about them (examples: *Genetic engineering is good; Life would not exist without the moon; TV is bad; Statistics never lie*).

DURING-LECTURE IDEAS

- Use visuals, video, and graphic organizers to show concepts and capture the main ideas (a poster that stays up and accumulates ideas rather than just fleeting slides that never return).

- Have students fill in a graphic organizer or partially filled-in outline as they listen and interact.

- Check comprehension with thumbs-up, fingers, pair-shares, and quick-write responses.

- Be purposefully redundant. Create redundancy by repeating words (and associated gestures) and paraphrasing.

- Use multiple examples, and then ask what the examples show. Sometimes examples, anecdotes, and analogies get so long that students forget what the abstract concept was that is being "clarified."

- Connect back to the minilecture focus: *And this relates back to our purpose [focus] because it . . .* Pairs can also do this.

- Have students, some or all, get up and act out a word or part of the lecture in an improvisational way. For example, they can pair-share to come up with an idea for one minute and use the next minute to act it out. (That's only two minutes.)

- Use appropriate and clear academic transitions between such ideas as *first, second, in addition, nevertheless, despite*. Emphasize academic language with gestures, voice, and pauses. Use consistent language throughout and across lectures.

- Walk around the room to give all students a chance to be near you, and you can check their attention and notes.

- Keep blocks of teacher talk short—about a minute per year of students' age.

- Give a thirty-second pause for students to catch up and look over their notes to write in reflections and questions. Give students time to think.

- Ask few and key questions to the whole class. Give them extra time (four to ten seconds) to think before they raise their hands. The room should be silent while students think. Use think-pair-shares every five to seven minutes or so.

- Have students pause and ask questions from their notes. Train them to ask critical thinking questions that relate to the topic.

- Modify your speech to speak more slowly than you think you should. Enunciate clearly, and emphasize important terms with exaggerated intonation, gestures, and expressions.

- Use choral response at times for words, terms, and quotations.

- Use kinesthetic responses, such as hand motions, to remember key ideas.

POSTLECTURE IDEAS

- Leave time for questioning, summarizing, and processing. Most students will not share their questions with the entire class, so use a pair-share.

- Have students immediately do something with the important information, sharing how it relates to their lives, perhaps with a visual or movement.

- Give some quick-write time at the end to have students write two things: what they think they were supposed to learn and what they did learn.

- Have students in groups or pairs compare and share notes, fill in gaps, and generate a final summary of key points of the lecture.

- Let students reteach important points to partners.

About the Author

Jeff Zwiers, EdD, is a senior researcher at Stanford University. He has taught elementary, middle, and high school students in Latin America, Asia, Africa, and the United States. He has taught graduate courses on language development, bilingual education, and content literacy at Stanford University and the University of San Francisco. He works closely with teachers and schools to promote academic language development, critical thinking, disciplinary literacy, and formative assessment practices.

About the International
Reading Association

The International Reading Association (IRA) is a nonprofit, global network of individuals and institutions committed to worldwide literacy. More than 53,000 members strong, IRA supports literacy professionals through a wide range of resources, advocacy efforts, volunteerism, and professional development activities. Find out more at www.reading.org.

Index

and, 59–63; for historical thinking, 90; importance of making connections to, 283; organization of, 15; planning discussions and, 127–128; in sample lesson plan, 252. *See also* Shared knowledge

Backward-designed curricula, 246–247

Bakhtin, M., 115

Banking education, 131

Barrera, R., 31

Bartolomé, L. I., 9–10, 11, 22, 32

Basic interpersonal communication skills (BICS), 22

Bean, T., 198

Beck, I., 24–25, 209

Becker, W., 208

Beers, K., 139

Behaviorist theories, 48

Bereiter, C., 258

Bever, T., 49

Bias, 94

Biology, 98, 143

Blachowicz, C., 209, 211, 212

Black, P., 269

Blind spots, of experts, 80

Bloom, B. S., 27

Bolton, G., 167–168

Book talks, 154

Bourdieu, P., 7

Bower, B., 140

Brain folders, 201, 203

Brenner, D., 86, 87

Brinkley, A., 90

Brinton, D., 28, 40

Broussard, A., 90

Brown, A. L., 195

Bruner, J., 246

Bunch, G., xi, 80, 129, 276

Burns, S., 203

C

Capital. *See* Academic capital

Card matching, 137–138

Carlo, M., 25, 208

Carroll, M., 49

Cause-and-effect thinking: in history, 89–91; in language arts, 87–88; modals in, 34–35; in science, 98, 99*t*

Cazden, C., xii, 14, 15, 70

CCSS. *See* Common Core State Standards

Celce-Murcia, M., 35

Character development, 87

Chemistry, 98, 100

Children's book writing, 262

Chinn, P. C., 2

Chomsky, N., 48

Chunking: for effective reading, 186; as listening strategy, 133

Clarification: checks for, 50; questions for, 121–122

Clarity: description of, 41; of elaboration questions, 122; negotiating meaning and, 50; students' challenges with, 42; use of examples for, 61

Classroom talk. *See* Discussions

Clauses: in academic writing, 231; analysis of, while reading, 186–187; in condensed messages, 41; definition of, 37–38; in long sentences, 37–38

Clichés, 30

Closed questions. *See* Explicit questions

Coaches, 55

Coelho, E., 34, 35, 39, 169

Coffin, C., 89

Cognitive academic language proficiency (CALP), 22

Cognitive level, of group work, 155

Cohen, E. G., 151, 156–157, 195

Cohesive devices, 206, 230–231

Collaboration. *See* Groups

Collaborative reasoning, 159–160

Collectivist cultures, 86–87

Collier, V., 1

Colloquial expressions, 129

Color coding, 201, 204

Commas, 231

Comment habits, 50

EngageNY, 25, 183
Engelhar, M. D., 27
Enriched conversations, 69–70
Ethics, 70
Evaluation language, 168
Evidence: in academic writing, 232–237; description of, 33–34; in group work, 159; to support claims in arguments, 85, 138
Examples, connecting through, 60–61
Exit slips, 255
Expert panels, 167–169
Explanations, 223
Explicit language: in academic texts, 31–32; description of, 32–33; importance of, 32; lack of, in home life, 32
Explicit questions. *See* Display questions
Exposition, 223
Expository writing: genres of, 222–224; versus narratives, 223; scaffolding for, 224–231. *See also specific genres*

F

Facial expressions: example of, 55–56; importance of, 55, 56; wall chart of, 56
Facione, P., 26–27
Faltis, C., 152
Farr, R., 52
Federalist Papers (Hamilton), 38
Feedback: about language of thinking, 272, 273t; elements of, 269–270; as encouragement, 270; in formative assessment, 268–271; rephrasing with, 67; strategies for improving, 269; in traditionally structured discussions, 123
Ferree, A. M., 165
Ferris Bueller's Day Off (movie), 119
Figurative expressions: activities for interpreting, 198, 199t; description of, 30; in discussions, 129; examples of, 30; as feature of academic language, 29–31; importance of instruction in, 31. *See also specific types*
Fillmore, C., 48, 184

Fillmore, L., xi
Fisher, P., 209, 211, 212
Fitzgerald, J., 31
Fordham, N., 219
Formative assessments: in backward-designed curricula, 246–247; definition of, 246; description of, 246–247
Freire, P., 11–12, 131
Freppon, P., 246, 274
Furst, E. J., 27

G

Gallagher, M., 194
Gallimore, R., 126
Gambrell, L., 193
Gamoran, A., 114
Garcia, G., 31
Gee, J., xii, 3, 8, 9, 11, 35, 145–146
Generalizations, 93
Genres: of academic writing, 222–224; definition, 222
Gerunds, 231
Gestures: example of, 55–56; importance of, 55, 56; in prewriting activity, 224–225; for quick assessments, 272, 274; to teach academic grammar, 206; wall chart of, 56
Gibbons, P., 136, 137, 156–157, 235
Gilles, C., 114, 152
Glachan, M., 157
Goals, for learning, 247–251
Goldenberg, C., 126
Gollnik, D. M., 2
Gordon, D., 158
Goudvis, A., 184
Grammar: definition of, 37; importance of, 37; listening versus speaking and, 49; skills required for, 53t. *See also* Academic grammar
Graphic organizers: for deep discussions, 73f; for prewriting, 224–225, 235
Graphs, 103
Grieve, R., 70
Griffin, P., 114, 203

Groups: academic language for, 159–160; activities for, 161–178; in CCSS, 156; designing and supporting, 156–158; higher-order thinking in, 154–155, 157; language for, 159–160; metadiscussions about, 158; modeling how to work in, 157–158; reporting-out techniques for, 160–161; rubrics for assessing, 158, 160. *See also* Discussions, small group

Group-work ability levels, 154–155

H

Haenisch, S., 205

Hafiz, F. M., 184

Halliday, M., 8, 231

Hamilton, A., 38

Hammack, S., 227

Hammond, J., 71

Hand motions. *See* Gestures

Harvey, N., 39

Harvey, S., 184

Hasan, R., 231

Hatchet (Paulsen), 87–88

Hattie, J., 269

Headings, 139, 200

Heath, S., xii, 3, 8

Heathcote, D., 166, 167–168

Hedges. *See* Qualifiers

Herber, H., 194

Hernandez, A., 49–50

Hierarchical thinking: description of, 15; requirements of, 16

Higher-order thinking/skills: Bloom's levels of, 27; in CCSS, 27; comments to deepen, 69; function of academic language in, 26–27; in group work, 154–155, 157; list of, 53*t*; metadiscussions of, 71; vocabulary associated with, 25

Hill, W. H., 27

Historical thinking: background knowledge and, 90; in CCSS, 89, 92; description of, 89

History textbooks, 89–90; making generalizations in, 93; source analysis of, 201, 202*t*

History/social studies language: cause and effect in, 89–91; description of, 89; development of, 23–24; interpreting meaning in, 91–93; performance assessment of, 260–261; perspective taking in, 94–95; purpose of, 89

Holdaway, D., 191

Holt, T., 92

Home life: knowledge organization and, 16; lack of explicit language in, 32; role of, 3–4; teachers' rewarding of, 9–10; transfer of academic capital in, 8

Huckin, T. N., 140

Hyde, A., 255

Hypotheses, 97*t*

I

If-then clauses: description of, 34; examples of, 34–35; in personifying, 62

Immersion, failure of, 2

Imperatives, math, 105*t*

Improv read-alouds, 191–192

Individualistic cultures, 86–87

Individualized assessments, 274–277

Inferences, 139, 185

Infinitives, 231

Informal writing activities, 237–242

Information gap activities, 176–177

Input processing, 48

Instructional time, 114

Instructions, students' confusion about, 11

International students, xi

Interpreting meaning: academic language of, 84*t*, 93*t*; in history, 91–93; in language arts, 81–84; in math, 103–105; in science, 99–100

Interview grids and mixers activity, 136–138

Intonation, 36, 37

J

Jigsaw activities, 139; description of, 169; for small-group discussion activities, 169–171

Jimenez, R., 31

Johns, A., 220

Johns, K., 151

Nonmainstream students: academic capital of, 6–8; adding on proficiencies for, 285; challenging of, by teachers, 12–13; confusing nonverbal strategies for, 56–57; confusion of, about instructions, 11; connecting to background knowledge of, 59; content area language difficulties of, 80; coshaping conversations of, 64–65; definition of, 2–3; diversity of, 4–6; getting to know, 16–17; home and community life of, 3; importance of school to, 283; invisible criteria and, 9–11; knowledge organization of, 15–16; lack of shared knowledge by, 13–14; modeling academic language for, 51–52; principles for working with, 284; registers of, 8–9; teachers' valuing of, 12–13; topics of importance to, 14–15. *See also specific types of students*

Nonverbal strategies: in discussions, 128; example of, 55–56; importance of, 55, 56; negotiating meaning and, 49–50; wall chart of, 56

Note taking. *See* Taking notes

Noun phrases, 39–40

Nudges, 114, 128

Nystrand, M., 114, 153

O

Objectives, 246

Objectivity, 96

O'Brien, D., 193

O'Conner, M., 68

Ogle, D., 209, 211, 212, 246, 274

Olshtain, E., 35

O'Malley, J. M., 27

O'Malley, M., 232

Open-ended questions: description of, 119; examples of, 119, 120; prompts for, 120

Oral communication: importance of prosody in, 35–37; influence of, on academic writing, 220–222; proficiency interviews, 276–277; resources for, 288–289

Oral presentations, 264–267

Oral scaffolds, 233, 235

Organizing knowledge. *See* Knowledge organization

Output production: benefits of, 49; description of, 48–49

Ovando, C., 1

P

Pace and emphasis, 52

Padilla, M., 40

Pair activities: areas of improvement in, 171; benefits of, 171; speaker/listener behaviors needed in, 172*t*

Palinscar, A. S., 195

Panel discussions. *See* Expert panels

Paraphrasing, by students, 68

Parents: influence of students' registers by, 8–9; passing along of academic capital by, 8; reading aloud by, 4

Parker, W., 154

Parks, S., 86, 87

Partners: problem solving by, 197–198; workshops presented by, 268; written dialogues by, 240–241; written recaps by, 240

Passive voice: description of, 39; in science language, 96; in test questions, 208

Pauk, W., 134

Paulsen, G., 87–88

Pearson, P., 194

Pedagogical language knowledge (PLK), 80

Pedagogy of entrapment, 11

Performance assessments, 258–262

Perkins, D., 146

Personalized questions, 119

Personifying, 61–62

Perspective papers, 242–243

Perspective taking: bias and, 94; in CCSS, 242; in history/social studies, 94–95; informal writing activities for, 240–241, 242–243; modeling of, 94; non-English-speaking students and, 95; personifying and, 62

Persuasion, versus argumentation, 85

Petrosino, A. J., 80

Peyton, J., 239

Themes: definition of, 16; list of, used in schools, 82*t*

Theories, 287–288

Thier, M., 98

Think-alouds: description of, 52; modeling with, 52–54; for reading comprehension, 189–191; in sample lesson plan, 254

Thinking time, 134–135

Think-pair-share: challenges of, 173; description of, 172–173; in discussions, 128; procedure for, 173, 174–175; prompts for, 173–174*t*; variations of, 175; written form of, 241

Think-pair-square, 175–176

Thomas, D., 102

Thornbury, S., 138, 162

Three-column notes, 134

Thumbs up/down, 274

Tier 2 words, 25

Tovani, C., 184

Transitions, 206

Tudor, I., 184

U

Underperforming students: backgrounds of, x, xi, 5–6; challenges of, 1–2; linguistic enabling of, 57–59; needs of, x

Ur, P., 176

V

Vague referents, 33

Valdés, G., xi, xii, 22, 33, 276

Valdez-Pierce, L., 27, 232

van Lier, L., 24

Venn diagrams, 255

Verbal associations, 209

Verbal strategies, 49–50

Verbs: in academic writing, 231; for cause and effect, 90; in history textbooks, 90; in long sentences, 204; in science language, 95

Verbs, modal: description of, 34; importance of, 34–35

Visuals: for prewriting, 224–225; to teach academic vocabulary, 209

Vocabulary. *See* Academic vocabulary

Voting, 139–140

Vygotsky, L., xii, 54, 57, 115

W

Wajnryb, R., 133

Wallace, C., 184

Walqui, A., 24

Weaver, C., 203, 230

Weed, K., 22

Wellman, D., 219

Wells, G., xii, 3

Whimbey, A., 197

White, C., 25

Wiggins, G., 27, 246, 247

Wilhelm, J., 138, 143, 165, 169

Williams, G., 4

Wineberg, S., 89, 94, 185

Wong Fillmore, L., x, xii, 14, 48, 183, 184, 275

Wood, D., 117

Word analysis, 211–212

Word lists, 293–297

Word networks, 164, 165*f*

Word walls, 212–213

Working world, 26

Worksheets, 203

Workshops, 268

Writing. *See* Academic writing

Writing development, 220

Written dialogues, 240–241

Written recaps, 239–240

Z

Zamel, V., 12–13

Zemelman, S., 255

Zimmerman, S., 184

Zirbel, E., 200

Zone of proximal development (ZPD), 54

Zwiers, J., xi, 15, 59, 61, 80, 95, 116, 117, 119, 153, 224, 235, 238, 242